THE TIMES TOP 100 GRADUATE EMPLOYERS

The definitive guide to the leading employers
recruiting graduates during 2016-2017.

HIGH FLIERS

HIGH FLIERS PUBLICATIONS LTD
IN ASSOCIATION WITH THE TIMES

Published by High Fliers Publications Limited
King's Gate, 1 Bravingtons Walk, London N1 9AE
Telephone: 020 7428 9100   *Web:* www.Top100GraduateEmployers.com

Editor Martin Birchall
Publisher Gill Thomas
Production Director Robin Burrows
Production Manager Nathalie Abbott
Portrait Photography Sarah Merson

Printed and bound in Italy by L.E.G.O. S.p.A.

A CIP catalogue record for this book
is available from the British Library.
ISBN 978-0-9559257-7-1

Contents

Foreword

By **Martin Birchall**
Editor, *The Times Top 100 Graduate Employers*

Welcome to the eighteenth edition of *The Times Top 100 Graduate Employers*, your guide to the most prestigious and sought-after employers that are recruiting graduates in 2016-2017.

The UK's decision to leave the European Union has turned 2016 into a year of almost unmatched political chaos and economic turmoil. In the dramatic aftermath of the 'leave' vote, Theresa May replaced David Cameron as Prime Minister, the pound dropped to a 31-year low on the world's currency markets, stock markets fluctuated wildly, George Osborne lost his job as Chancellor of the Exchequer and the Bank of England reduced interest rates to their lowest level in its 322-year history.

It's too early to know what the immediate impact of the Brexit vote will have on the graduate job market but recruitment was certainly hit hard by the global financial crisis of 2008 and 2009. Many of the best-known employers scaled back their graduate recruitment while they assessed what the UK recession meant for their organisations and, in just two recruiting seasons, a quarter of entry-level vacancies for new graduates were cut.

It has been a long, slow recovery since then, despite graduate recruitment increasing in six out of the last seven years, but the good news for those graduating in the summer of 2016 was that the number of graduate vacancies available at the country's top employers rose again, taking graduate recruitment beyond the pre-recession peak recorded in 2007.

This latest surge in graduate vacancies echoed the bouyant economic outlook for the country in general. According to the Office for National Statistics, the UK's economy grew by almost 5 per cent in the two years leading up to the Brexit vote, unemployment fell to its lowest level for a decade and inflation remained consistently below 1 per cent.

On university campuses, the mood was determinedly optimistic too. Research featuring student job hunters from the 'Class of 2016', compiled for *The Times Top 100 Graduate Employers*, showed that 28 per cent of final year students expected to start a full-time graduate job straight after university, the highest proportion for fifteen years. A record number of finalists received job offers as a result of completing successful work placements with employers and fewer students than ever had 'no definite plans' or were expecting to take time off or travel after university.

If you're one of almost 400,000 finalists due to graduate in 2017, the initial signs are encouraging too. At least two-thirds of the graduate employers

“ This year's rankings have been compiled from the results of interviews with more than 18,000 final year students. ”

featured within this edition of *The Times Top 100 Graduate Employers* plan to either maintain their recruitment at 2016 levels or increase their graduate intake in 2017.

Since the first edition was published in 1999, more than a million copies of *The Times Top 100 Graduate Employers* have been produced to help students and recent graduates from the UK's top universities research their career options and find their first job. Seventeen years on, the *Top 100* continues to provide an unrivalled, independent annual assessment of the graduate employers that university-leavers rate most highly.

This year's rankings have been compiled from the results of face-to-face interviews with more than 18,000 final year students who graduated from universities across the UK in the summer of 2016. Students were asked to name the employer that they thought offered the best opportunities for new graduates.

Between them, the 'Class of 2016' named organisations in every major employment sector – from top City investment banks, management consultants and the Big Four accounting & professional services firms, to high street retailers,

charities, public sector organisations, media groups and the country's leading manufacturers. The one hundred employers that were mentioned most often during the research form *The Times Top 100 Graduate Employers* for 2016-2017.

This book is therefore a celebration of the employers who are judged to offer the brightest prospects for graduates. Whether through the perceived quality of their training programmes, the business success that they enjoy, the scale of their graduate recruitment, or by the impression that their on-campus promotions have made – these are the employers that were most attractive to graduate job hunters in 2016.

The Times Top 100 Graduate Employers won't necessarily identify which organisation you should join after graduation – only you can decide that. But it is an invaluable reference if you want to discover what Britain's leading employers are offering for new graduates in 2017.

Leaving university and finding your first graduate job is one of the most important steps you'll ever take. Having a thorough understanding of the range of opportunities available must be a good way to start.

THE TIMES TOP 100 GRADUATE EMPLOYERS — Finding Out about the Top 100 Graduate Employers

IN PRINT

Each employer featured in this edition of the *Top 100* has their own **Employer Entry**, providing details of graduate vacancies for 2017, minimum academic requirements, starting salaries, and the universities employers will be visiting in 2016-2017.

ONLINE

Register now with the official *Top 100* website for full access to the very latest information about the UK's most sought-after graduate employers.

This includes details of employers' internships & work experience programmes, local campus recruitment events and application deadlines.

And get ready for your applications, interviews and assessment centres with up-to-the-minute business news about each of the organisations featured in this year's *Top 100*.

www.Top100GraduateEmployers.com

BY EMAIL

Once you've registered with the *Top 100* website, you'll receive **weekly email bulletins** with news of the employers you're interested in, their careers events at your university, and their forthcoming application deadlines.

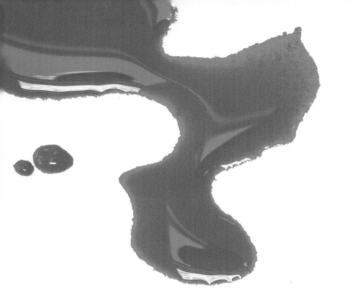

SHOW YOUR

We're BDO.
Welcome to our world.

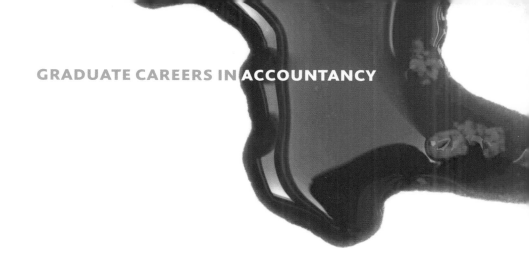

GRADUATE CAREERS IN ACCOUNTANCY

TRUE COLOURS

WHAT CAN YOU ADD TO OUR MIX? ▶

COLOURFUL CAREERS | COLOURFUL CHARACTERS

FIND OUT A SHADE MORE ABOUT BDO

f BDO-TraineesUK   t @BDO_TraineesUK
www: bdo.co.uk/careers | e: student.recruitment@bdo.co.uk

TIMES

TOP 100 GRADUATE EMPLOYERS

TOP 100 GRADUATE EMPLOYERS 2005-2006

THE TIMES TOP 100 GRADUATE EMPLOYERS

TIMES TOP 100 GRADUATE EMPLOYERS 2004-2005

E TIMES TOP 100 GRADUATE EMPLOYERS

THE TIMES TOP 100 GRADUATE EMPLOYERS

E TIMES TOP 100 GRADUATE EMPLOYERS

TIMES TOP 100 GRADUATE EMPLOYERS 2001-200

TIMES TOP 100 GRADUATE EMPLOYERS 20

TIMES TOP 100 GRADUATE EMPLOYERS

TOP 100 GRADUATE EMPLOYERS 2003-2004

TOP 100 GRADUATE EMPLOYERS 2015-2016

THE TIMES TOP 100 GRADUATE EMPLOYERS

TIMES TOP 100 GRADUATE EMPLOYERS

TOP 100 GRADUATE EMPLOYERS 2010-2011

TOP 100 GRADUATE EMPLOYERS 20 2012

Researching The Times Top 100 Graduate Employers

By **Gill Thomas**
Publisher, High Fliers Publications

Every year up to ten thousand employers, large and small, recruit graduates from the UK's top universities. Many provide formal development programmes for university-leavers, others are simply recruiting for vacancies which require a particular degree or qualification, but together they provide an estimated 200,000 entry level jobs for new graduates each recruitment season.

Such a promising range of potential employment opportunities can present quite a challenge. How can you assess so many different opportunities and decide which employers offer the best career paths? What basis can you use to compare organisations and their graduate vacancies?

It's clear there are few simple answers to these questions and that no individual employer will ever be the preferred choice for every graduate – everyone makes their own judgement about the organisations they want to work for and the type of job they find the most attractive.

How then can anyone produce a meaningful league table of the UK's leading graduate employers? What criteria can define whether one individual organisation is 'better' than another? To compile the new edition of *The Times Top 100 Graduate Employers*, the independent market research company, High Fliers Research, interviewed 18,353 final year students who left UK universities in the summer of 2016.

These finalists from the 'Class of 2016' who took part in the study were selected at random to represent the full cross-section of students at their universities, not just those who had already secured graduate employment.

The research examined students' experiences during their search for a graduate job and asked them about their attitudes to employers. The key question used to produce the *Top 100* was "Which employer do you think offers the best opportunities for graduates?". The question was deliberately open-ended and students were not shown a list of employers to choose from or prompted in any way.

Within the full survey sample, finalists named more than 1,500 different organisations – from the smallest local or regional employers, to some of the world's best-known companies. The responses were analysed and the one hundred organisations that were mentioned most often make up the *The Times Top 100 Graduate Employers* for 2016.

Looking at the considerable selection of answers given by finalists from the 'Class of 2016', it is evident that students used several different criteria

> **❝** *PwC's reign as the UK's leading graduate employer represents a real renaissance for the entire accounting & professional services sector.* **❞**

THE TIMES
TOP 100
GRADUATE EMPLOYERS
The Times Top 100 Graduate Employers 2016

	2015				2015	
1.	1	PWC		51.	64	EXXONMOBIL
2.	2	ALDI		52.	81	AMAZON
3.	4	TEACH FIRST		53.	55	NEWTON EUROPE
4.	5	CIVIL SERVICE		54.	34	M&S
5.	3	GOOGLE		55.	83	MI5 – THE SECURITY SERVICE
6.	9	KPMG		56.	50	SLAUGHTER AND MAY
7.	6	DELOITTE		57.	63	BAKER & MCKENZIE
8.	7	NHS		58.	78	NESTLÉ
9.	8	EY		59.	48	CITI
10.	10	BBC		60.	66	DANONE
11.	13	UNILEVER		61.	85	PENGUIN RANDOM HOUSE
12.	14	J.P. MORGAN		62.	58	POLICE
13.	12	GSK		63.	NEW	SANTANDER
14.	25	LIDL		64.	NEW	VIRGIN MEDIA
15.	15	GOLDMAN SACHS		65.	59	DEUTSCHE BANK
16.	18	HSBC		66.	100	BANK OF ENGLAND
17.	17	ACCENTURE		67.	47	ROYAL NAVY
18.	11	JOHN LEWIS PARTNERSHIP		68.	62	AIRBUS
19.	19	JAGUAR LAND ROVER		69.	96	HERBERT SMITH FREEHILLS
20.	16	BARCLAYS		70.	97	AECOM
21.	22	MCKINSEY & COMPANY		71.	70	BOOTS
22.	28	L'ORÉAL		72.	95	WELLCOME
23.	23	ROLLS-ROYCE		73.	NEW	ROYAL AIR FORCE
24.	21	IBM		74.	60	DLA PIPER
25.	30	LLOYDS BANKING GROUP		75.	71	MOTT MACDONALD
26.	20	BP		76.	76	NETWORK RAIL
27.	26	SHELL		77.	84	BANK OF AMERICA MERRILL LYNCH
28.	35	BRITISH ARMY		78.	87	NORTON ROSE FULBRIGHT
29.	29	MICROSOFT		79.	93	LLOYD'S
30.	33	CLIFFORD CHANCE		80.	54	DIAGEO
31.	36	MORGAN STANLEY		81.	90	GRANT THORNTON
32.	24	TESCO		82.	61	HOGAN LOVELLS
33.	31	ARUP		83.	73	SIEMENS
34.	27	P&G		84.	86	OXFAM
35.	51	RBS		85.	NEW	IRWIN MITCHELL
36.	39	ALLEN & OVERY		86.	45	EUROPEAN COMMISSION (EU CAREERS)
37.	53	BOSTON CONSULTING GROUP		87.	52	BRITISH AIRWAYS
38.	32	FRESHFIELDS BRUCKHAUS DERINGER		88.	67	LOCAL GOVERNMENT
39.	41	LINKLATERS		89.	79	BLACKROCK
40.	42	ATKINS		90.	89	FACEBOOK
41.	43	SKY		91.	46	CANCER RESEARCH UK
42.	40	FRONTLINE		92.	92	UBS
43.	49	BAE SYSTEMS		93.	99	CREDIT SUISSE
44.	37	APPLE		94.	NEW	SAVILLS
45.	38	MARS		95.	NEW	STANDARD LIFE
46.	75	ASTRAZENECA		96.	65	BLOOMBERG
47.	44	BT		97.	80	MONDELĒZ INTERNATIONAL
48.	69	TRANSPORT FOR LONDON		98.	68	MCDONALD'S
49.	72	WPP		99.	NEW	BMW GROUP
50.	56	BAIN & COMPANY		100.	94	BDO

Source **High Fliers Research** 18,353 final year students leaving UK universities in the summer of 2016 were asked the open-ended question 'Which employer do you think offers the best opportunities for graduates?' during interviews for *The UK Graduate Careers Survey 2016* to determine which employer they considered offered the best opportunities for graduates. Many evaluated employers based on the information they had seen during their job search – the quality of recruitment promotions, the impression formed from meeting employers' representatives, or their experiences during the application and selection process.

Some focused on employers' general reputations and their public image, their business profile or their commercial success. Finalists also considered the level of graduate vacancies that organisations were recruiting for as an indicator of possible employment prospects, or were influenced by employers' profiles at their university.

Other final year students, however, used the 'employment proposition' as their main guide – the quality of graduate training and development an employer offers, the starting salary and remuneration package available, and the practical aspects of a first graduate job, such as location or working hours.

Irrespective of the criteria that students used to arrive at their answer, the hardest part for many was just selecting a single organisation. To some extent, choosing two or three, or even half a dozen employers would have been much easier. But the whole purpose of the exercise was to replicate the reality that everyone faces – you can only work for one organisation. And at each stage of the graduate job search there are choices to be made as to which direction to take and which employers to pursue.

The resulting *Top 100* is a dynamic league table of the UK's most exciting and well-respected graduate recruiters in 2016. For an unprecedented thirteenth consecutive year, the accounting and professional services firm PwC has been voted the UK's leading graduate employer, with a total of 8 per cent of finalists' votes. The firm has a convincing lead of nearly five hundred votes ahead of retailer Aldi and its popular trainee area manager programme which remains in second place once again.

Despite slipping back in the rankings in last year's *Top 100*, the widely-acclaimed Teach First scheme that has grown to become the UK's largest individual recruiter of graduates since its launch in 2003 has moved back up to third place, just ahead of the Civil Service which has climbed to fourth place, its highest ranking since 2010. In a surprise

move, after rising up the rankings in nine of the previous ten years and reaching number three in last year's *Top 100*, internet giant Google has slipped back to fifth place.

All four of the Big Four accounting & professional services firms are ranked within this year's top ten and KPMG has climbed to sixth place, overtaking rivals Deloitte who despite spending eight years in second place in the *Top 100* until 2013, has dropped back in the rankings three years running and is now in seventh place. EY has also moved down, slipping one place to ninth.

The NHS is ranked lower too this year but the BBC is unchanged in tenth place. Consumer goods company Unilever has moved up to 11th position, its best ranking since 2002 and J.P. Morgan has climbed another two places to its highest-ever rating in the *Top 100*. Having only joined as a new entry in 89th place in 2009, retailer Lidl has climbed the rankings in six of the seven years since and has jumped an impressive eleven places this year, to reach 14th place. Banking group HSBC has moved up for the second year running, to 16th place but the John Lewis Partnership drops back seven places to 18th place.

It has been an excellent year for the leading strategy consulting firms – McKinsey & Company has moved up for the third consecutive year, taking it to just outside the top twenty employers, the Boston Consulting Group has jumped sixteen places to 37th, its best ranking so far in the *Top 100*, and Bain & Company has moved into the top fifty.

The highest climbers in this year's *Top 100* are led by the Bank of England which has jumped an impressive thirty-four places to 66th place and pharmaceuticals company AstraZeneca and online retailer Amazon which have both climbed twenty-nine places, to 46th and 52nd places respectively. A further eight organisations have moved up at least twenty places in the new rankings, including MI5 - The Security Service, law firm Herbert Smith Freehills and technical consultants AECOM. But Cancer Research UK, the European Commission, British Airways, Bloomberg and McDonald's have each dropped at least thirty places this year.

There are a total of seven new entries or re-entries in this year's *Top 100*, the highest being for banking group Santander, which has had a convincing return to the rankings in 63rd place, just ahead of telecoms company Virgin Media, which makes its *Top 100* debut in 64th place.

WHAT WⓄULD HAPPEN TⓄ A WⓄRLD WITH NⓄ XYGEN?

Whether an O in your eyes means oxygen, omicron, or the number zero, you can inspire the next generation with your passion and knowledge. Become a teacher and you could start on a salary of £28k, after receiving a tax-free bursary while you train.* See the difference you can make every day. Teaching is a great way to make your degree, skills, and knowledge really count.

Start planning your future today at
education.gov.uk/teachtimes

TEACHING
YOUR FUTURE | THEIR FUTURE

The Royal Air Force and property firm Savills are back in the league table in 73rd and 94th places respectively. Law firm Irwin Mitchell and motor manufacturer BMW are both ranked in the *Top 100* for the first time and Edinburgh-based finance company Standard Life is a re-entry in 95th place this year, its first time back in the league table since 2004.

Organisations leaving the *Top 100* in 2016 include retailer Sainsbury's – which had appeared in the rankings every year since 1998 – Dyson, Asda, Centrica and GE, as well as two graduate employers that were new or re-entries in last year's rankings – the Northern Ireland-based technology and consulting company First Derivatives and National Grid.

It's now seventeen years since the original edition of *The Times Top 100 Graduate Employers* was produced in 1999 and in that time there have been just three organisations at number one. Andersen Consulting (now Accenture) held onto the top spot for the first four years and its success heralded a huge surge in popularity for careers in consulting – at its peak in 2001, almost one in six graduates applied for jobs in the sector.

In the year before the firm changed its name from Andersen Consulting to Accenture, it astutely introduced a new graduate package that included a £28,500 starting salary (a sky-high figure for graduates in 2000) and a much talked-about £10,000 bonus, helping to assure the firm's popularity, irrespective of its corporate branding.

In 2003, after two dismal years in graduate recruitment when vacancies for university-leavers dropped by more than a fifth following the terrorist attacks of 11th September 2001, the Civil Service was named Britain's leading graduate employer. Just a year later it was displaced by PricewaterhouseCoopers, the accounting and professional services firm formed from the merger of Price Waterhouse and Coopers & Lybrand in 1998. At the time, the firm was the largest private-sector recruiter of graduates, with an intake in 2004 of more than a thousand trainees.

Now known simply as PwC, the firm has remained at number one ever since, increasing its share of the student vote from five per cent in 2004 to more than 10 per cent in 2007 and fighting off the stiffest of competition from rivals Deloitte in 2008 when just seven votes separated the two employers.

PwC's reign as the UK's leading graduate employer represents a real renaissance for the entire accounting & professional services sector. Whereas fifteen years ago, a career in accountancy was regarded as a safe, traditional employment choice, today's profession is viewed in a very different light. The training required to become a chartered accountant is now seen as a prized business qualification and the sector's leading

THE TIMES TOP 100 GRADUATE EMPLOYERS — Number Ones, Movers & Shakers in the Top 100

NUMBER ONES		HIGHEST CLIMBING EMPLOYERS		HIGHEST NEW ENTRIES	
1999	ANDERSEN CONSULTING	1999	SCHLUMBERGER (UP 13 PLACES)	1999	PFIZER (31st)
2000	ANDERSEN CONSULTING	2000	CAPITAL ONE (UP 32 PLACES)	2000	MORGAN STANLEY (34th)
2001	ACCENTURE	2001	EUROPEAN COMMISSION (UP 36 PLACES)	2001	MARCONI (36th)
2002	ACCENTURE	2002	WPP (UP 36 PLACES)	2002	GUINNESS UDV (44th)
2003	CIVIL SERVICE	2003	ROLLS-ROYCE (UP 37 PLACES)	2003	ASDA (40th)
2004	PRICEWATERHOUSECOOPERS	2004	J.P. MORGAN (UP 29 PLACES)	2004	BAKER & MCKENZIE (61st)
2005	PRICEWATERHOUSECOOPERS	2005	TEACH FIRST (UP 22 PLACES)	2005	PENGUIN (70th)
2006	PRICEWATERHOUSECOOPERS	2006	GOOGLE (UP 32 PLACES)	2006	FUJITSU (81st)
2007	PRICEWATERHOUSECOOPERS	2007	PFIZER (UP 30 PLACES)	2007	BDO STOY HAYWARD (74th)
2008	PRICEWATERHOUSECOOPERS	2008	CO-OPERATIVE GROUP (UP 39 PLACES)	2008	SKY (76th)
2009	PRICEWATERHOUSECOOPERS	2009	CADBURY (UP 48 PLACES)	2009	BDO STOY HAYWARD (68th)
2010	PRICEWATERHOUSECOOPERS	2010	ASDA (UP 41 PLACES)	2010	SAATCHI & SAATCHI (49th)
2011	PWC	2011	CENTRICA (UP 41 PLACES)	2011	APPLE (53rd)
2012	PWC	2012	NESTLÉ (UP 44 PLACES)	2012	EUROPEAN COMMISSION (56th)
2013	PWC	2013	DFID (UP 40 PLACES)	2013	SIEMENS (70th)
2014	PWC	2014	TRANSPORT FOR LONDON (UP 36 PLACES)	2014	FRONTLINE (76th)
2015	PWC	2015	DIAGEO, NEWTON EUROPE (UP 43 PLACES)	2015	DANONE (66th)
2016	PWC	2016	BANK OF ENGLAND (UP 34 PLACES)	2016	SANTANDER (63rd)

Source **High Fliers Research**

> Every week brings new challenges, and every day I know I'm making a difference to people's lives

Simon
Mental health social worker

Most people know someone who's had mental health problems.
But not everyone knows someone who can make a difference.
Apply your mind to mental health.

- Paid two-year fast-track scheme
- Master's degree in social work
- Leadership training

thinkahead.org

firms are regularly described as 'dynamic' and 'international' by undergraduates looking for their first job after university.

A total of 211 different organisations have now appeared within *The Times Top 100 Graduate Employers* since its inception and over forty of these have made it into the rankings every year since 1999. The most consistent performers have been PwC, KPMG and the Civil Service each of which have never been lower than 9th place in the league table. The NHS has also had a formidable record, appearing in every top ten since 2003, and the BBC, Goldman Sachs and EY (formerly Ernst & Young) have all remained within the top twenty throughout the last decade.

Google is the highest-climbing employer within the *Top 100*, having risen over eighty places during the last decade, to reach the top three for the first time this year. But car manufacturer Jaguar Land Rover holds the record for the fastest-moving employer, after jumping more than seventy places in just five years, between 2009 and 2014.

Other employers haven't been so successful though. British Airways, ranked in 6th place in 1999, dropped out of the *Top 100* altogether a decade later and Ford, which was once rated as high as 14th, disappeared out of the list in 2006 after cancelling its graduate recruitment programme two years previously. The latest high-ranking casualty is retailer Sainsbury's, which having reached 18th place in 2003, tumbled out of the *Top 100* this year.

Thirty four graduate employers – including Nokia, Maersk, the Home Office, Cable & Wireless, United Biscuits, Nationwide, Capgemini and the Met Office – have the dubious record of having

THE TIMES TOP 100 GRADUATE EMPLOYERS — Winners & Losers in the Top 100

MOST CONSISTENT EMPLOYERS	HIGHEST RANKING	LOWEST RANKING
ANDERSEN (FORMERLY ARTHUR ANDERSEN)	2nd (1999-2001)	3rd (2002)
PWC	1st (FROM 2004)	3rd (1999-2001, 2003)
KPMG	3rd (2006-2008, 2011-2012)	9th (2015)
CIVIL SERVICE	1st (2003)	8th (2011)
BBC	5th (2005-2007)	14th (1999)
GLAXOSMITHKLINE	11th (2000)	22nd (2002-2003)
IBM	13th (2000)	24th (2012)
EY (FORMERLY ERNST & YOUNG)	7th (2013)	20th (2001)
BP	14th (2013-2014)	32nd (2004)
ACCENTURE (FORMERLY ANDERSEN CONSULTING)	1st (1999-2002)	20th (2014)

EMPLOYERS CLIMBING HIGHEST	NEW ENTRY RANKING	HIGHEST RANKING
GOOGLE	85th (2005)	3rd (2015)
LIDL	89th (2009)	14th (2016)
JAGUAR LAND ROVER	87th (2009)	16th (2014)
ALDI	65th (2002)	2nd (2015-2016)
MI5 – THE SECURITY SERVICE	96th (2007)	33rd (2010)
TEACH FIRST	63rd (2004)	2nd (2014)
APPLE	87th (2009)	27th (2012)
ATKINS	94th (2004)	37th (2009)
BOSTON CONSULTING GROUP	90th (1999)	37th (2016)
ARCADIA GROUP	99th (2001)	47th (2007)

EMPLOYERS FALLING FURTHEST	HIGHEST RANKING	LOWEST RANKING
BRITISH AIRWAYS	6th (1999)	Not ranked (2010, 2011)
FORD	11th (1999)	Not ranked (FROM 2006)
SAINSBURY'S	18th (2003)	Not ranked (2016)
THOMSON REUTERS	22nd (2001)	Not ranked (2009-2012, FROM 2014)
ASTRAZENECA	24th (2003)	Not ranked (2012-2014)
ASDA	27th (2004)	Not ranked (2016)
ROYAL AIR FORCE	32nd (2005)	Not ranked (2015)
MINISTRY OF DEFENCE	35th (2003)	Not ranked (2007, FROM 2012)
MARCONI	36th (2001)	Not ranked (FROM 2002)
DIAGEO	37th (2004)	Not ranked (2008-2009)

Source High Fliers Research

only been ranked in the *Top 100* once during the last fifteen years. And Marconi had the unusual distinction of being one of the highest-ever new entries in 36th place in 2001, only to vanish from the list entirely the following year.

One of the most spectacular ascendancies within the *Top 100* has been the rise of Aldi which joined the list in 65th place in 2002, rose to 3rd place in 2009, helped in part by its memorable remuneration package for new recruits (currently £42,000 plus an Audi A4 car), and has now been in 2nd place for the last two years running. And Teach First, which appeared as a new entry in 63rd place in 2003, climbed the rankings in each of years following and achieved 2nd place in the *Top 100* in 2014.

This year's edition of *The Times Top 100 Graduate Employers* has produced a number of significant changes within the rankings and the results provide a unique insight into how graduates from the 'Class of 2016' rated the UK's leading employers. Almost all of these organisations are featured in the 'Employer Entry' section of this book – from page 61 onwards, you can see a two-page profile for each employer, listed alphabetically for easy reference.

The editorial part of the entry includes a short description of what the organisation does, its opportunities for graduates and its recruitment programme for 2016-2017. A fact file for each employer gives details of the business functions that graduates are recruited for, the number of graduate vacancies on offer, likely starting salaries for 2017, their minimum academic requirements, application deadlines, the universities that the employer is intending to visit during the year, plus details of their graduate recruitment website and how to follow the employer on social media.

If you would like to find out more about any of the employers featured in *The Times Top 100 Graduate Employers*, then simply register with **www.Top100GraduateEmployers.com** – the official website showcasing the latest news and information about *Top 100* organisations.

Registration is entirely free and as well as being able to access the website, you'll receive regular email updates about the employers you are most interested in – this includes details of the careers events they're holding at your university during the year, up-and-coming job application deadlines, and the very latest business news about the organisations.

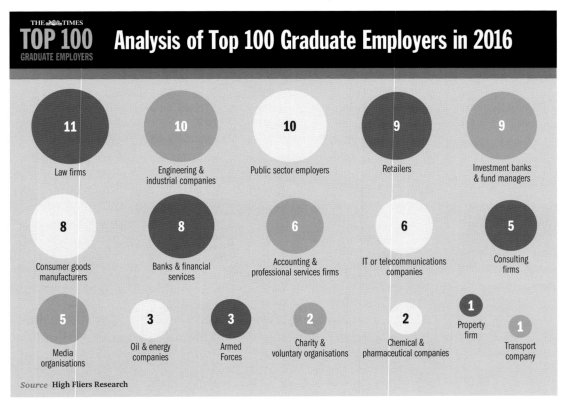

THE TIMES
TOP 100
GRADUATE EMPLOYERS
Analysis of Top 100 Graduate Employers in 2016

11	10	10	9	9
Law firms	Engineering & industrial companies	Public sector employers	Retailers	Investment banks & fund managers

8	8	6	6	5
Consumer goods manufacturers	Banks & financial services	Accounting & professional services firms	IT or telecommunications companies	Consulting firms

5	3	3	2	2	1	1
Media organisations	Oil & energy companies	Armed Forces	Charity & voluntary organisations	Chemical & pharmaceutical companies	Property firm	Transport company

Source **High Fliers Research**

Sometimes it pays to get in early.

Early birds are often rewarded and it's the same with Launch Pad, our streamlined approach to graduate recruitment. It's a one day event at the final stage of our graduate recruitment process, and if you're successful you could be offered a role within two working days. An interactive experience, where you'll get to demonstrate your talent through assessment activities and interview with a senior member of the team. Plus you'll gain some new skills, meet lots of people and find out more about the many opportunities at KPMG in the UK. Apply now.

kpmgcareers.co.uk/graduates

Anticipate tomorrow. Deliver today.

THE TIMES TOP 100 GRADUATE EMPLOYERS — The Top 10 Graduate Employers 2001-2015

2001
1. ACCENTURE
2. ANDERSEN
3. PRICEWATERHOUSECOOPERS
4. PROCTER & GAMBLE
5. GOLDMAN SACHS
6. CIVIL SERVICE
7. KPMG
8. UNILEVER
9. BRITISH ARMY
10. MARS

2002
1. ACCENTURE
2. PRICEWATERHOUSECOOPERS
3. ANDERSEN
4. CIVIL SERVICE
5. BRITISH ARMY
6. KPMG
7. UNILEVER
8. PROCTER & GAMBLE
9. GOLDMAN SACHS
10. MARS

2003
1. CIVIL SERVICE
2. ACCENTURE
3. PRICEWATERHOUSECOOPERS
4. BRITISH ARMY
5. KPMG
6. HSBC
7. BBC
8. PROCTER & GAMBLE
9. NHS
10. DELOITTE & TOUCHE

2004
1. PRICEWATERHOUSECOOPERS
2. CIVIL SERVICE
3. ACCENTURE
4. KPMG
5. NHS
6. BBC
7. BRITISH ARMY
8. PROCTER & GAMBLE
9. HSBC
10. DELOITTE (FORMERLY DELOITTE & TOUCHE)

2005
1. PRICEWATERHOUSECOOPERS
2. CIVIL SERVICE
3. ACCENTURE
4. KPMG
5. BBC
6. DELOITTE
7. NHS
8. HSBC
9. GOLDMAN SACHS
10. PROCTER & GAMBLE

2006
1. PRICEWATERHOUSECOOPERS
2. DELOITTE
3. KPMG
4. CIVIL SERVICE
5. BBC
6. NHS
7. HSBC
8. ACCENTURE
9. PROCTER & GAMBLE
10. GOLDMAN SACHS

2007
1. PRICEWATERHOUSECOOPERS
2. DELOITTE
3. KPMG
4. CIVIL SERVICE
5. BBC
6. NHS
7. ACCENTURE
8. HSBC
9. ALDI
10. GOLDMAN SACHS

2008
1. PRICEWATERHOUSECOOPERS
2. DELOITTE
3. KPMG
4. ACCENTURE
5. NHS
6. CIVIL SERVICE
7. BBC
8. ALDI
9. TEACH FIRST
10. GOLDMAN SACHS

2009
1. PRICEWATERHOUSECOOPERS
2. DELOITTE
3. ALDI
4. CIVIL SERVICE
5. KPMG
6. NHS
7. ACCENTURE
8. TEACH FIRST
9. BBC
10. ERNST & YOUNG

2010
1. PRICEWATERHOUSECOOPERS
2. DELOITTE
3. CIVIL SERVICE
4. KPMG
5. ALDI
6. NHS
7. TEACH FIRST
8. ACCENTURE
9. BBC
10. ERNST & YOUNG

2011
1. PWC (FORMERLY PRICEWATERHOUSECOOPERS)
2. DELOITTE
3. KPMG
4. ALDI
5. NHS
6. BBC
7. TEACH FIRST
8. CIVIL SERVICE
9. ACCENTURE
10. ERNST & YOUNG

2012
1. PWC
2. DELOITTE
3. KPMG
4. TEACH FIRST
5. ALDI
6. NHS
7. CIVIL SERVICE
8. ERNST & YOUNG
9. BBC
10. JOHN LEWIS PARTNERSHIP

2013
1. PWC
2. DELOITTE
3. TEACH FIRST
4. KPMG
5. CIVIL SERVICE
6. ALDI
7. EY (FORMERLY ERNST & YOUNG)
8. NHS
9. JOHN LEWIS PARTNERSHIP
10. GOOGLE

2014
1. PWC
2. TEACH FIRST
3. DELOITTE
4. ALDI
5. NHS
6. CIVIL SERVICE
7. KPMG
8. BBC
9. GOOGLE
10. JOHN LEWIS PARTNERSHIP

2015
1. PWC
2. ALDI
3. GOOGLE
4. TEACH FIRST
5. CIVIL SERVICE
6. DELOITTE
7. NHS
8. EY
9. KPMG
10. BBC

Source High Fliers Research

DRIVERS WANTED

To take us in new directions. To steer our future. To help drive new ideas forward.

At HSBC, we're looking for forward-thinking, perceptive and motivated people to join our Global Graduate Programmes, to help fulfil our customers' hopes, dreams and ambitions. Along the road, we'll help guide and encourage you to explore new paths and support you on your own journey.

Are you ready to take the wheel?

PROGRESSIVE MINDS APPLY

hsbc.com/careers

HSBC

GRADUATE MANAGEMENT DEVELOPMENT PROGRAMME

Two years. One intensive, extensive, comprehensive training programme. And you. If that's not a recipe for retail success, we don't know what is. This newly created scheme has been especially designed to equip you with everything you need to be a stand-out, be-the-best, know-your-stuff retail manager. As well as leadership, team working, communication and organisational skills, we'll see to it that you get all the early responsibility, breadth of exposure and in-depth training you need to excel.

We're creating our future leaders. So we'll immerse you in every aspect of our core operations. This means you'll spend your first year across Sales, Logistics, Property and Supply Chain. After your end-of-year appraisal, you'll kick off your second year with a week in Administration and 18 weeks' worth of Head Office experience. Next up is one week's centralised training, development and assessment, followed by 24 weeks in a specialised area of development. Do well, impress us consistently and give everything you do your all and you should finish the programme with your perfect job. Not to mention the confidence, expertise and judgement to make your mark.

Find out more at www.lidlgraduatecareers.co.uk

Letters to The Times
From Karl Marx to Mussolini, Queen Victoria to Florence Nightingale, from Charles Dickens to Oscar Wilde and Ian Fleming, letters to The Times made compelling reading - and still do - and sometimes changed the course of history.
24TH
26TH
28TH

Finding the Right Graduate Job

By **Greg Hurst**
Education Editor, The Times

Choosing the right graduate job for after university may seem a daunting prospect. The careers services at each of the UK's leading universities advertise graduate vacancies from several thousand employers each year, ranging from global and national companies to regional and local employers, in both the private and public sectors.

So where should you start? The good news is that, such is the demand for able, well-motivated graduates, recruiters are likely to come to you.

Many employers have expanded their graduate programmes in recent years as Britain's economy has grown, and stepped up their activities on university campuses as competition intensifies to hire the best students.

Last year a record 59 per cent of final year students attended recruitment presentations by employers and over half went to careers fairs to meet employers, talk to recent graduates working for them and find out more about their business and working culture.

Undergraduates in the second or even first year at university are increasingly going along to such events as, conscious of the need for a future return on tuition fees of £9,000 a year plus substantial living costs, students take planning their future careers more seriously than ever.

THE TIMES
TOP 100
GRADUATE EMPLOYERS

❝ The 'Class of 2016' stand out as being some of the most organised, motivated and careers-minded graduates of their generation. ❞

Both before and after meeting employers' representatives at careers events, it is important to do some careful homework. Most organisations publish detailed information about their graduate programmes online and it should pay dividends later to explore employers in sectors that interest you, understand how they differ and study the types of roles they offer.

Savvy students take this a step further by using online discussion forums. One of the most popular is *Glassdoor*, although *RateMyPlacement* and *The Student Room* host similar conversations. Current students and recent graduates use these to review and share impressions of work experience, internships or other placements with employers, what the application process was like and so on. Some university careers websites host their own forums and students often value them as a source of authentic testimonies of what it's really like to work within organisations.

For graduates leaving university in 2016, the most popular career destinations are consulting, marketing and the media, although there are sharp differences by gender. According to *The UK Graduate Careers Survey 2016*, the survey of 18,353 final year students at Britain's top thirty universities that provides the data for *The Times*

BRAVE ENOUGH TO DO SOMETHING DIFFERENT?

MAKE REAL CHANGE FOR CHILDREN AND FAMILIES.

FRONTLINE

CHANGING LIVES

Frontline is an initiative designed to recruit outstanding individuals to be leaders in social work and broader society. Successful applicants will take part in an intensive and innovative two year leadership programme and gain a master's degree. But most importantly, they'll be working to transform the lives of vulnerable children and young people.

www.thefrontline.org.uk

Top 100 Graduate Employers, the top career sectors for male undergraduates were consulting, investment banking, engineering, finance, and research and development. The sectors attracting the highest number of applications from women students were marketing, charity or voluntary work, the media, teaching and consulting.

What students are looking for in a graduate job has, however, shifted. The 'Class of 2016' stand out as being some of the most organised, motivated and careers-minded graduates of their generation. Almost half began researching their career options in the first year of their degree, and 63 per cent had applied for graduate jobs by February of their final year, well up from 47 per cent a decade ago.

They want fulfilling jobs in which they can develop their employability skills further. When asked about their first graduate job, the most common feature cited by the graduates of 2016 was 'being challenged and stretched on a daily basis', followed by having 'genuine responsibility from day one', structured training & development,

and working towards a professional qualification.

They were altruistic, too. More than a third said it was very important to them to do a job which enabled them to give something back to the community.

Leading graduate employers have noticed that students are becoming more demanding. "What we have seen over the last couple of years is more questions about 'what do I get from joining you?' and 'what can you give me?', which probably indicates quite a candidate-centric market place," says Georgina Greer, head of student recruitment at Deloitte, the professional services network which hires more than 1,100 graduates a year.

"We try to give them a lot of information, not just about the work we do but what they would get from a career – development opportunities, how their career might progress, the breadth of opportunities that joining us might give them, things like working abroad or indeed what kind of professional qualifications we could offer."

Rob Gill, in charge of student recruitment

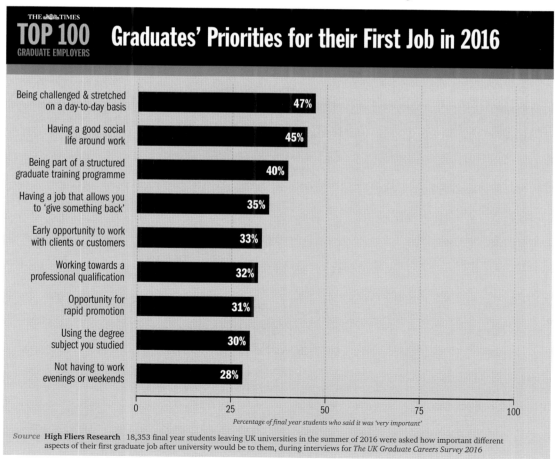

THE TIMES
TOP 100 Graduates' Priorities for their First Job in 2016
GRADUATE EMPLOYERS

Priority	Percentage
Being challenged & stretched on a day-to-day basis	47%
Having a good social life around work	45%
Being part of a structured graduate training programme	40%
Having a job that allows you to 'give something back'	35%
Early opportunity to work with clients or customers	33%
Working towards a professional qualification	32%
Opportunity for rapid promotion	31%
Using the degree subject you studied	30%
Not having to work evenings or weekends	28%

Percentage of final year students who said it was 'very important'

Source **High Fliers Research** 18,353 final year students leaving UK universities in the summer of 2016 were asked how important different aspects of their first graduate job after university would be to them, during interviews for *The UK Graduate Careers Survey 2016* at Jaguar Land Rover, which hires around 250 graduates annually, reports similar experiences, coupled with more candidates at interview or assessment days asking about promotions and pay progression. He cautions that this can give an unhelpful impression.

"I would probably say, just hold back on that," he advises. "The workplace is a crowded place, especially if you are joining a large complex organisation where there are people you'll be working with who may not be as well qualified or educated but they have lots of experience and have been doing the job for a number of years.

"Don't get preoccupied with being on this fast progression tread mill. You need to come into an organisation and learn, contribute and deliver and then hopefully that will get noted."

So how do students choose a sector or industry, and narrow down which employers to apply to? Some degree courses, such as engineering, medicine, pharmacy, accountancy, marketing, may steer undergraduates naturally towards a certain path. Others, notably in the humanities and social sciences, can lead in many different directions..

Some graduates are attracted to companies with a strong reputation in their sector or for particular graduate roles, which Alex Burnett, graduate talent manager at L'Oréal, the cosmetics company, says is

the case with its marketing jobs. "We are very well known for marketing and students who come to us specifically for marketing have a very clear idea of what they want to do," she says. L'Oréal hires 30 graduates a year, some in marketing but others in roles such as finance, supply chain, IT and human resources.

Around one in seven graduates from the 'Class of 2016' applied for graduate positions with organisations in the public sector, such as Teach First, MI5, local government, the Civil Service and National Health Service. Rob Farace, who is responsible for the NHS graduate recruitment scheme, is looking for applicants who understand public service, and stresses the need for prior research by applicants.

"We are very keen that people who apply to us share our values and they are really motivated to come and work for us as an organisation," he says. "If you have been tracking us for a while you can tend to answer that much better, you can talk about how you started off at this point and as you got to know us better your expectation grew, changed and developed, so in that respect it can tend to be an advantage."

Graduates from the 'Class of 2016' who had done an internship or work placement whilst at university were three times more likely to have secured a

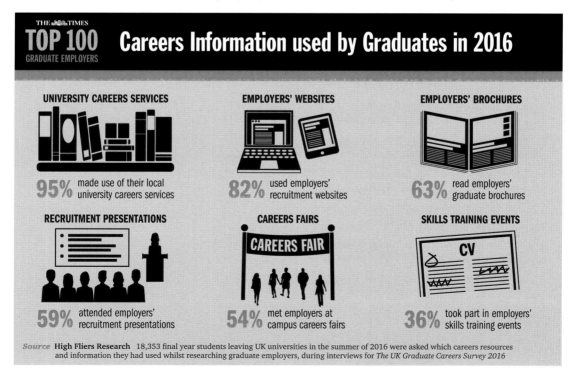

TOP 100 GRADUATE EMPLOYERS — THE TIMES

Careers Information used by Graduates in 2016

UNIVERSITY CAREERS SERVICES
95% made use of their local university careers services

EMPLOYERS' WEBSITES
82% used employers' recruitment websites

EMPLOYERS' BROCHURES
63% read employers' graduate brochures

RECRUITMENT PRESENTATIONS
59% attended employers' recruitment presentations

CAREERS FAIRS
54% met employers at campus careers fairs

SKILLS TRAINING EVENTS
36% took part in employers' skills training events

Source **High Fliers Research** 18,353 final year students leaving UK universities in the summer of 2016 were asked which careers resources and information they had used whilst researching graduate employers, during interviews for *The UK Graduate Careers Survey 2016*

'Where will you **lead**?

Education. Health. Justice. Commercial. Human Resources. Defence. Transport. Climate change. International development. Foreign affairs. If the government has a policy on something, it is guaranteed that Fast Streamers are working at the heart of it, putting their brains and their skills at the disposal of the whole of society.

The Civil Service Fast Stream offers the kind of variety of roles and leadership training you simply can't have anywhere else. Choose from an exciting range of generalist and specialist streams with a programme that's ranked among the top five of The Times Top 100 Graduate Employers.

Learn more: www.gov.uk/faststream

Civil Service
Fast Stream

definite job offer before graduation, compared with those who had no experience of work at all. Work experience has advantages on both sides of the equation because employers can watch an applicant's performance, while students can make an informed view over whether that industry or employer is right for them.

"We do look for someone that has had previous work experience," says Alex Bennett at L'Oréal. "It doesn't have to be in a big corporate. Personally when I am looking I just like to see that element of proactivity and whilst I absolutely value the experience you get from backpacking and reading poetry, it is good to be able to see some transferrable skills from a work environment."

So is it too late for students who return for their final year at university without much employment history to show on their CV? Not necessarily, says Rob Gill at Jaguar Land Rover.

"No matter what you do, whether it's travelling or charity work or something not related to the profession you want to go into, reflect on it and understand it, and be able to convey the competency skills and positive attributes that it has given you,"

he says. "Although they might not be direct work-based examples you can use them to answer a question in the same way as someone who has done an internship could do."

Another recent trend offers hope, too. In 2015, the country's best-known employers were unable to fill more than a thousand of their graduate positions, because the most-confident students accepted more than one job offer and left it until the last minute to decide which to take up. Recruiters call this 'reneging' and it has extended the graduate recruitment cycle later into the calendar year.

Georgia Greer at Deloitte believes this can suit the more academically-focused students who want to concentrate on their studies before applying for jobs. "We do see a number of very high quality applications coming through in what classically wouldn't be a period where we would expect to see applications, so that's exciting for us," she says.

"Any time from the Easter period, when maybe students have completed a dissertation. Or if they are doing final examinations, it tends to be after those in late May or early June, and all the way through the summer."

THE TIMES TOP 100 GRADUATE EMPLOYERS — Job Applications made by Graduates in 2016

2016	2015	Sector	% OF FINALISTS APPLYING TO SECTOR	APPLICANTS RATIO MEN:WOMEN	GRADUATE EMPLOYER OF CHOICE 2016
1.	1	CONSULTING	16.2%	56:44	PWC
2.	2	MARKETING	14.6%	33:67	UNILEVER
3.	3	MEDIA	12.2%	35:65	BBC
4.	5	RESEARCH & DEVELOPMENT	12.0%	50:50	GLAXOSMITHKLINE
5.	7	INVESTMENT BANKING	11.4%	64:36	GOLDMAN SACHS
6.	8	FINANCE	11.4%	57:43	HSBC
7.	6	TEACHING	11.0%	34:66	-
8.	4	CHARITY OR VOLUNTARY WORK	10.7%	24:76	OXFAM
9.	10	ACCOUNTANCY	10.0%	53:47	PWC
10.	9	LAW	9.9%	38:62	ALLEN & OVERY
11.	11	ENGINEERING	8.9%	78:22	ROLLS-ROYCE
12.	13	HUMAN RESOURCES	8.5%	25:75	UNILEVER
13.	12	SALES	7.9%	42:58	UNILEVER
14.	14	GENERAL MANAGEMENT	6.3%	41:59	ALDI
15.	16	IT	4.7%	72:28	GOOGLE
16.	15	RETAILING	4.7%	33:67	JOHN LEWIS PARTNERSHIP
17.	17	BUYING OR PURCHASING	4.0%	35:65	-
18.	18	TRANSPORT OR LOGISTICS	3.2%	54:46	TRANSPORT FOR LONDON
19.	19	ARMED FORCES	2.3%	68:32	-
20.	20	PROPERTY	2.1%	54:46	SAVILLS

Source **High Fliers Research** 18,353 final year students leaving UK universities in the summer of 2016 were asked which sectors they had applied to for graduate jobs and which employers they would most like to work for, during interviews for *The UK Graduate Careers Survey 2016*

Children growing up in social housing are 37% more likely to become victims of crime.

Join us.
Change the story.

National Graduate Leadership Programme

This is big. This is where life chances hang in the balance. This is where you can make a difference. Police Now is a **two-year programme** that offers the top graduates the opportunity to become Police Officers and transform communities. Not just for people today but for generations to come. The challenge is unique. The environment is high paced. And you can lead the change here **policenow.org.uk**

POLICE:NOW
INFLUENCE FOR GENERATIONS

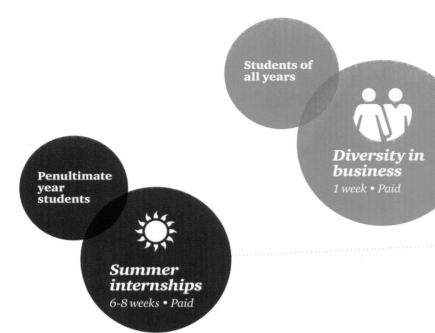

Students of all years

Diversity in business
1 week • Paid

Penultimate year students

Summer internships
6-8 weeks • Paid

Work placement
11 months • Paid

Sandwich or placement students

Talent academies
2-5 days

First to final year students

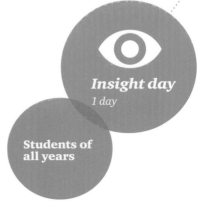

Insight day
1 day

Students of all years

pwc

Boost your employability

The experience stays with you

We've got lots of different work experience programmes for every year of study, so you can learn more about our business and boost your employability. They'll help you make an informed decision about which of our career opportunities is best for you. Some could even lead to a job.

Join us. We're focused on helping you reach your full potential.

Take the opportunity of a lifetime
pwc.com/uk/work-experience

 **/pwccareersuk**   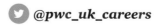 **@pwc_uk_careers**

Work experience is key to success

Graduate recruitment on rise, survey finds

SARAH O'CONNOR
EMPLOYMENT CORRESPONDENT

Britain's graduates are finding it easier
to secure ... the outlook for this year's gra...
of univer... "as good as it has been since...
that your... recession: most graduates...
improving...

An offic...
who grad...
76.6 per...
within s...

Work experience on a CV h...
applicants score highly. "If you...

'Picky' university graduates tur... down record number of top job.

'Gazumping' graduates leave jobs unfilled

Greg Hurst

Leading employers were left with more
than 1,000 vacancies last year as they

years when employers scaled back recruitment and students were likely to
be glad of any graduate job offer.

In recent years, fierce competition

to fill the posts because most had accepted positions elsewhere.

A survey by High Fliers Research, a
specialist market research company,

...tes as
...the top
...oming

...top
...ng to
...ever
...adu-

accounting & professi...
services firms has incre...
this year.

The most generous sal...
in 2016 are those offere...
investment banks (me...
of £47,000), law fi...

Record number of job vacancies up for grabs

Graduates getting choosier about the jobs they take

A total of 22,300 positions are being

research with more than 18,000
graduates from the Class of 2015 who
left UK universities this summer. The
results confirm ... PwC, the global...

12th position, its strongest
performance for 15 years. JP Morgan
has climbed another four places to its
high...

UNIVERSITY leavers are ge...
"choosier" about jobs, with more
...cancies left un...

Graduate gazumping on job offers increases

Graduate jobs going begging

MORE than 1,000 graduate vacancies

You're hired!

Jobs are back – as long as you're one of the new
...f ...ious digital natives ruthlessl...

Why Class of 2015 is smiling

'Choosy' graduates turn down a record number of job offers

By Sarah Cassidy
EDUCATION CORRESPONDENT

High-flying "choos" ...aduates

fers they had accepted before graduation, according to the analysis by
High Fliers Research.

"Last year record num...
turned down employers' j...
fers or ch... ...ir mind ab...
...ted dur...
...vers

Jobs bonanz... promised for country's top graduates

It's never too early to start job hunting

Make good use of every opportunity and remember to

portfolio presentation and freelancing
are particularly popular. The
university also holds events where
groups of students can meet
professionals from a range of
industries.

Most universities will invite
recruiters from industry-specific

By CHRIS MARSHALL

Employers are preparing
to recruit their biggest-ever
intake of university graduates
in 2016, according to a new
report.

The Graduate Market in
2016, a trusted annual survey of the UK's biggest firms,

Freehills and Linklate...
also £42,000) and the...
pean Commission (£41...

Martin Birchall, n...
ing director of High...
Research, said: "For s...
leaving university th...
mer, it's very welcom...
that Britain's top em...
are recruiting their...

Understanding the Graduate Job Market

By **Martin Birchall**
Managing Director, High Fliers Research

For those leaving university in the summer of 2016, the news about the graduate job market and the employment opportunities for university-leavers has been upbeat and encouraging. The 2016 graduate recruitment season proved to be one of the busiest ever for the UK's leading employers, with many reporting record numbers of entry-level vacancies and a greater variety of graduate jobs than ever before.

These reassuring headlines about better career prospects for graduates certainly came at the right time. The 'Class of 2016' were the first full cohort of university students to have paid £9,000-a-year for their tuition fees, in addition to ever-increasing living costs, leaving new graduates with average debts of £36,100 at the end of their studies.

Vacancies for graduates at the country's top employers increased by a convincing 8.4 per cent in 2016, the biggest annual rise in new jobs for six years, taking graduate recruitment in the UK to its highest level ever.

This marked a significant milestone for the graduate job market. The global financial crisis and the recession that followed in the UK in 2008 and 2009 had a profound effect on graduate vacancies and recruitment at the country's top

THE TIMES
TOP 100
GRADUATE EMPLOYERS

" *The UK's vote to leave the European Union means there is considerable uncertainty about how the economy will fare in the months ahead.* "

employers dropped by an unprecedented 23 per cent in less than eighteen months.

Although the graduate job market bounced back in 2010 with an annual increase in vacancies of more than 12 per cent, it has taken a further six years for graduate recruitment to overtake the pre-recession peak recorded in 2007.

Graduate vacancies in 2016 were almost 43 per cent higher than in 2009, the low point in the graduate job market during the economic crisis, and 9 per cent ahead of graduate recruitment in 2007.

For employers, this lengthy recovery has not been uniform or straightforward and graduate vacancies in six key employment sectors – oil & energy, the City's investment banks, law firms, media organisations and the Armed Forces – remain lower than they were a decade ago.

And over the last two years, a new phenomenon has emerged. The buoyant employment market has seen more final year university students getting multiple job offers from employers, with increasing numbers leaving their decision about which organisation to join until just a few weeks before starting work.

For many employers this has meant that graduates who had accepted a job offer during their last few months at university have reneged

THE TIMES

PRESENTS

THE ⚖ BRIEF

The free daily bulletin legal people swear by.

Drawing on decades of experience and the unique access The Times has to the UK's legal profession, The Brief will bring you comprehensive news, comment and analysis from experts and insiders.

⚖ All the latest news and in-depth analysis

⚖ Exclusive comment and all the big debates

⚖ Professional moves and court updates

⚖ The gossip that has the industry buzzing

Sign up free at
thetimes.co.uk/thebriefemail

on their employment contract and joined another employer instead. In 2015 alone, the impact of these last-minute changes was that more than 1,100 well-paid graduate vacancies were left unfilled by employers who were unable to recruit additional graduates at short notice. This was equivalent to more than 5 per cent of the total number of graduate vacancies available that year.

So what is the outlook for final year students due to graduate from university in 2017? Inevitably the UK's vote to leave the European Union means that there is considerable uncertainty about how the economy will fare in the months ahead, but the initial recruitment targets published by the employers featured in this edition of *The Times Top 100 Graduate Employers* suggest that graduate vacancies are set to increase again in 2017.

Almost a third of employers plan to hire more graduates than they did in 2016 and two-fifths believe they will take on a similar number of new recruits in the next 12 months. Together, the employers appearing in this year's *Top 100* are advertising 22,009 vacancies for 2017, compared to the 21,328 graduates hired in 2016, equating to an annual rise of 3.2 per cent.

The UK's leading accountancy and professional services firms are set to dominate the graduate job market again this year, with an intake of more than 5,000 new trainees in 2017, almost a quarter of the total number of graduate vacancies available at the *Top 100* employers.

Whilst recruitment remains limited in many parts of the public sector, the ten Government departments and agencies that appear in the latest *Top 100* rankings are planning to step up their graduate intake again in 2017 – making this the eighth time in nine years that recruitment of graduates has increased in the public sector.

The City's investment banks & fund managers and banking & financial services employers are intending to take on almost 400 additional graduates in 2017 and for the eighth year running, the number of graduate roles at the top engineering & industrial firms is expected to increase.

In all, employers in eleven of the fifteen industries and business sectors represented within the Top 100 expect to either maintain or step up their graduate recruitment in 2017 but there are likely to be fewer opportunities at media organisations, IT & telecommunications companies, accounting

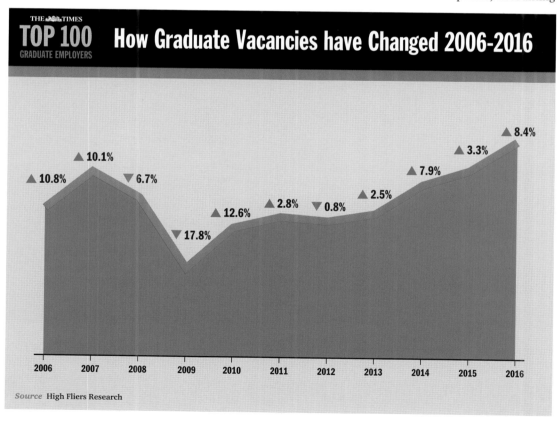

THE TIMES
TOP 100 **How Graduate Vacancies have Changed 2006-2016**
GRADUATE EMPLOYERS

▲ 10.8%   ▲ 10.1%   ▼ 6.7%   ▼ 17.8%   ▲ 12.6%   ▲ 2.8%   ▼ 0.8%   ▲ 2.5%   ▲ 7.9%   ▲ 3.3%   ▲ 8.4%

2006   2007   2008   2009   2010   2011   2012   2013   2014   2015   2016

Source High Fliers Research

WORLD CHANGERS WANTED

VOLUNTARY INTERNSHIPS UK-WIDE

Take on a voluntary internship with Oxfam, and you'll change lives around the world. Alongside thousands of passionate staff and volunteers, you'll help tackle the injustice of poverty, and save and rebuild lives. If you won't live with poverty, join us.

Apply now at
www.oxfam.org.uk/interns

WE WON'T LIVE WITH POVERTY

OXFAM

& professional services firms and chemical & pharmaceuticals companies in the year ahead.

The rapid recent expansion of the popular Teach First programme means that for the fifth year running, its graduate recruitment targets are the largest of any organisation featured in *The Times Top 100 Graduate Employers*, with 1,750 places available in 2017.

Other substantial individual recruiters include the 'Big Four' professional services firms – PwC (1,500 vacancies), Deloitte (1,200 vacancies), KPMG (1,000 vacancies) and EY (900 vacancies).

Three-fifths of the employers featured in this year's *Top 100* have vacancies for graduates in IT, over half have opportunities in finance, a third

are recruiting for human resources positions, marketing jobs, general management roles, sales or engineering graduates. A quarter of employers are looking for recruits to work in research & development or consulting, but fewer than a sixth want retail staff or have vacancies in property or the media.

More than eighty *Top 100* employers have graduate vacancies in London in 2017 and over half have posts available elsewhere in the south east of England. Up to half also have graduate roles in the north west of England, the Midlands and the north west. Northern Ireland, Wales, East Anglia and the north east of England have the fewest graduate vacancies.

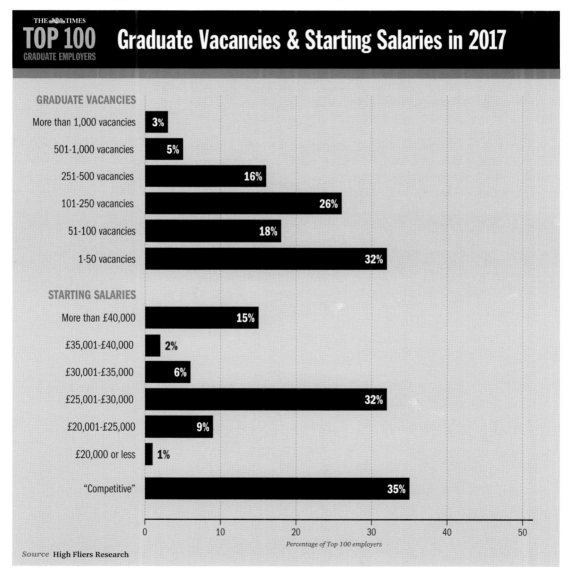

THE TIMES TOP 100 GRADUATE EMPLOYERS

Graduate Vacancies & Starting Salaries in 2017

GRADUATE VACANCIES

Category	Percentage
More than 1,000 vacancies	3%
501-1,000 vacancies	5%
251-500 vacancies	16%
101-250 vacancies	26%
51-100 vacancies	18%
1-50 vacancies	32%

STARTING SALARIES

Category	Percentage
More than £40,000	15%
£35,001-£40,000	2%
£30,001-£35,000	6%
£25,001-£30,000	32%
£20,001-£25,000	9%
£20,000 or less	1%
"Competitive"	35%

Percentage of Top 100 employers

Source **High Fliers Research**

Graduate starting salaries at the UK's leading employers have changed little over the last seven years. After annual increases every year until 2008, the average salary on offer from the country's top employers remained at £29,000 for four consecutive years, before increasing again in 2014 and 2015. The average starting salary in 2016 was £30,000.

Half of the organisations featured in this year's edition of *The Times Top 100 Graduate Employers* have opted to leave their graduate starting salaries unchanged for 2017 but a number of major employers, including several top law firms, banks and consulting firms, have announced increases to their graduate pay packages – typically of between £1,000 and £2,500 each.

Over a third of the *Top 100* graduate employers simply describe their salary packages for next year as "competitive" but one in six organisations, mainly investment banks, strategic consulting firms, City law firms, the leading oil & energy companies and two well-known retailers, are planning to pay starting salaries in excess of £35,000.

The most generous graduate package publicised within this edition of the *Top 100* is at Newton, the consulting firm, which is offering graduate salaries of between £45,000 and £50,000, with a starting-work bonus of £3,000. Leading law firms Baker & McKenzie and Herbert Smith Freehills are offering new trainees salaries of £45,000 and £44,000 respectively. The retailer Aldi continues to pay its recruits a sector-leading graduate starting salary of £42,000 plus an Audi A4 company car, and the European Commission offers new graduates a salary of at least £41,500.

Up to half of the UK's leading employers now recruit graduates year-round, or in different phases during the year, and will accept applications throughout the 2016-2017 recruitment season, until all their vacancies are filled. For employers with a single application deadline, most are in either October, November or December, although a limited number of organisations have post-Christmas or early summer deadlines for their graduate programmes.

Three-fifths of *Top 100* employers insist that applicants for their graduate schemes should have a 2.1 degree or better and a fifth now specify a minimum UCAS tariff too, most in the range of 300 to 340 – the equivalent of 'BBB' to 'AAB' grades at A-level.

So for those who make the grade, there continues to be a wide range of career opportunities and some excellent starting salaries on offer from *The Times Top 100 Graduate Employers* in 2017.

THE TIMES TOP 100 GRADUATE EMPLOYERS — Graduate Vacancies at Top 100 Employers in 2017

	2015		NUMBER OF VACANCIES IN 2017	CHANGE SINCE 2016	MEDIAN STARTING SALARY IN 2016
1.	1	ACCOUNTANCY & PROFESSIONAL SERVICES FIRMS	5,050	▼ 1.4%	£30,000
2.	2	PUBLIC SECTOR EMPLOYERS	4,020	▲ 5.1%	£23,000
3.	3	ENGINEERING & INDUSTRIAL COMPANIES	2,230	▲ 2.5%	£26,000
4.	4	INVESTMENT BANKS & FUND MANAGERS	2,120	▲ 8.6%	£47,000
5.	5	BANKING & FINANCIAL SERVICES	1,685	▲ 15.2%	£32,500
6.	7	ARMED FORCES	1,600	NO CHANGE	£30,000
7.	6	RETAILERS	1,460	▲ 32.4%	£28,000
8.	9	IT & TELECOMMUNICATIONS COMPANIES	915	▼ 11.5%	£30,000
9.	10	LAW FIRMS	797	▲ 2.2%	£42,000
10.	8	CONSULTING FIRMS	750	▲ 7.9%	£31,500
11.	11	MEDIA ORGANISATIONS	437	▼ 23.1%	£28,500
12.	12	CONSUMER GOODS MANUFACTURERS	386	▲ 4.3%	£30,000
13.	13	OIL & ENERGY COMPANIES	195	▲ 15.4%	£32,500
14.	-	PROPERTY FIRMS	170	NO CHANGE	£24,000
15.	14	CHEMICAL & PHARMACEUTICAL COMPANIES	130	▼ 10.3%	£28,000

Source High Fliers Research

CAN WE INSPIRE THE LEADER IN YOU?

worldwide in fresh **DAIRY PRODUCTS**

in Western Europe in **MEDICAL NUTRITION**

worldwide in **WATERS** (packaged & by volume)

worldwide in **EARLY LIFE NUTRITION**

Discover how our pioneering spirit and passion for innovation keep us at the forefront of industry

Find out more on our profile on page 118

Contribute to a healthier world

DANONE

TAKE YOUR CAREER

At Newton, we bring together talented people to work with organisations that set global agendas and change the way the world works.

Whilst our commitment to hiring top talent is unrivalled, it's our innovative and award-winning approach to problem-solving that sets us apart.

If you're ready to change the world, then take your consulting career to the Nth°.

TO THE N^{th°}

Newton
The science of performance

Making the Most of Work Experience

By **Etta Parkes**
Director of Student Employability, Aston University

Ten years ago, the majority of employers regarded work experience as something of a 'luxury item' when they were recruiting graduates. If students applying for places on a graduate programme had done a work placement or other experience it was usually seen by recruiters as a bonus, but not a prerequisite for their application. And few employers who ran work experience schemes linked them directly to their graduate recruitment. The emphasis was on helping students try out different roles, career sectors and industries before they applied for their first graduate job.

Today, more than half the recruiters at *The Times Top 100 Graduate Employers* warn that students who've not had any work experience at all whilst at university now have little or no chance of getting a graduate job offer. And virtually every major employer offers a variety of different internships, work placements and introductory courses, all designed to encourage students onto their graduate programme.

So why is there so much emphasis on work experience and how can you make the most of it while you're at university?

One of the key reasons that it's become so important is that recruiters see work experience as a way to spot the best graduate talent earlier.

> *Whatever type of work experience you do, it's essential to reflect carefully on what you've done and what you've learnt from it.*

And it gives employers the opportunity to 'try before they buy' when they're recruiting, before they commit to making a student a graduate job offer. Each year, around a third of graduate vacancies at the top employers are now filled by graduates who've done work experience with the organisation beforehand.

There are several different types of work experience available, depending on the type of degree course that you're studying and which year you're in. Many employers offer short 'taster' experiences for first year students, often during the Christmas or Easter holidays. This could be a day's work shadowing, a site visit or a training course. Quite a few employers also use competitions, business games or skills training events during term-time to introduce their organisations.

They may only be brief experiences, but they can tell you a lot about individual career areas and are a great way to find out about the types of graduate jobs that are available. If you're one of the many students who arrive at university with little idea of what you want to do afterwards, these first steps will help give you an idea of what interests you and the skills you'll need to develop to be successful.

Don't be afraid to explore as many different employers as you can, it'll be a lot harder to try

AMBITIOUS
SMART
FAST-PACED
INSPIRING
DRIVING
CHANGE
SHARP
UNITED
PIONEERING
VERSATILE CHALLENGING
LIFE-SAVING PERCEPTIONS

THIS IS HOW IT FEELS HELPING TO BEAT CANCER.
For your chance to experience it, go to cruk.org/graduates

CANCER
RESEARCH
UK

other options once you're working full-time as a graduate. And even if you're someone with a very clear career plan, looking into a few alternatives during your first year can reassure you that you're heading in the right direction and the additional experience will make you more employable.

As you progress through your degree, longer periods of work experience can give you a deeper understanding of particular graduate roles.

Aston University, which is celebrating its 50th anniversary in 2016, is one of many universities around the UK that offers a formal placement year as part of its undergraduate degrees. These are typically in the third year of four-year courses and are designed to help students really understand the workplace and develop their employability skills. For many, this will be their first taste of doing a 'real' job and all of the practicalities it brings – experiencing commuting to work, dressing appropriately and paying taxes can be just as valuable as the work itself.

The choice of placements is usually very broad, from small local businesses to major multinationals, but your university will ensure that the employer you join provides the right experiences to compliment your degree studies. Whatever you choose, the experience is likely to

make a big impact on you. It's not unusual for students to go into a sector that they think they're really going to enjoy, only to find it wasn't what they were expecting at all. Whilst it may sound like a disappointing outcome, this is a really powerful learning experience and it's far better to discover that you're not suited to a particular role or industry during a placement, rather than when you start your first graduate job.

If your degree doesn't include a placement year, then a good alternative would be to do an internship or summer vacation placement, usually at the end of your penultimate year. Your university careers service can help you research which opportunities are available and many of the better-known employers will promote their internships or vacation placements through local careers fairs and other campus events. You can also access your careers service's alumni database, LinkedIn and other social media to contact previous graduates from your university who may be useful contacts for work experience.

There is stiff competition for places on the most popular internship schemes and the application process can be just as demanding as if you were applying for a graduate job. This often means you'll need to fill in a detailed online application

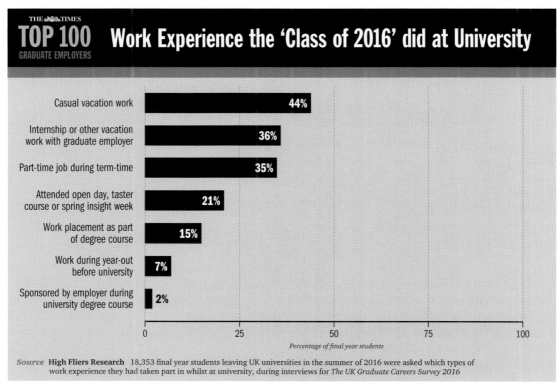

THE TIMES TOP 100 GRADUATE EMPLOYERS
Work Experience the 'Class of 2016' did at University

Work experience type	Percentage
Casual vacation work	44%
Internship or other vacation work with graduate employer	36%
Part-time job during term-time	35%
Attended open day, taster course or spring insight week	21%
Work placement as part of degree course	15%
Work during year-out before university	7%
Sponsored by employer during university degree course	2%

Percentage of final year students

Source **High Fliers Research** 18,353 final year students leaving UK universities in the summer of 2016 were asked which types of work experience they had taken part in whilst at university, during interviews for *The UK Graduate Careers Survey 2016*

form, do a Skype or telephone interview, complete a selection of tests and even attend an assessment day. This is deliberately tough because as well as offering an internship, employers are looking for students who have the potential to join their graduate programmes after their final year.

The encouraging news is that if you pass the selection process and your work placement is successful, then the employer may well offer you a place on their graduate programme without any further assessments, or fast-track you to a final-round interview for a graduate job. They might even be prepared to sponsor you during your final year at university or employ you as a student brand manager. And going through the internship recruitment process is also excellent practice for your future graduate job applications.

Almost all the work placements offered by major employers, such as those appearing in *The Times Top 100 Graduate Employers*, are usually paid roles, but there are a number of sectors such as journalism, fashion, charities and some areas of healthcare, where the work is either unpaid or just pays travel expenses. Many universities won't advertise work placements unless they do offer a salary. If you are thinking about doing an unpaid

placement, you need to weigh up how valuable the experience is likely to be to you and whether you can afford to support yourself during the placement. Your university careers service can support you in negotiating with companies to help secure payment and reimbursement of expenses, and also to encourage employers to be flexible with working hours to give you the option to mix paid with unpaid work.

It isn't just the large, well-known employers who provide work placements. Many small and medium-sized businesses are also keen to recruit undergraduates for projects at different times of the year – either during the university holidays or on a part-time basis during term-time – and can offer greater responsibility or a wider range of experiences because of the size of the organisation.

Whatever type of work experience you do before your final year, it's essential to reflect carefully on what you've done and what you've learnt from it. Part of this process is about understanding whether you've enjoyed the role and the work, and if you'd be keen to do something similar for a full-time graduate job. You should also think about whether the culture of the organisation you've worked for is a good 'fit' for you and what you're looking for.

THE TIMES
TOP 100 Work Experience for First Year Students in 2017
GRADUATE EMPLOYERS

EMPLOYER, TYPE OF WORK EXPERIENCE, LENGTH	EMPLOYER, TYPE OF WORK EXPERIENCE, LENGTH
AECOM Summer Internships *8-12 weeks*	**J.P. MORGAN** Spring Week *1 Week*
ALLEN & OVERY A&O First *See website for full details*	**KPMG** Insight Programme *2 days*, Women in Technology Insight Week *1 week*
ATKINS Summer Internships *8-12 weeks*	**LINKLATERS** Pathfinder *2 days*
BAE SYSTEMS Summer Internships *12 weeks*	**L'OREAL** Summer Internships *10 weeks*, Spring Insight Programme *1 week*
BANK OF ENGLAND First Year Internships *6 weeks*	**MARS** Summer Internships *12 weeks*
BARCLAYS Spring Insight Programme *1-2 weeks*	**MORGAN STANLEY** Spring Insight Programme *3 days-1 week*
BLACKROCK Spring Insight Week *1 week*, Technology Insight Programme *1 week*	**MOTT MACDONALD** Summer Internships *6-12 weeks*
BP Discovery Week *1 week*, Discovery Days *1 day*	**NORTON ROSE FULBRIGHT** First Step *1 week*
CANCER RESEARCH UK Internships *3 months*	**PENGUIN RANDOM HOUSE** Summer Internships *10 weeks*, Work Experience *2 weeks*
CIVIL SERVICE FAST STREAM Early Diversity Internships *1 week*	**PWC** Talent Academy *2-3 days*, Women in Business *1 week*, Tech Academy *1 week*
CREDIT SUISSE Spring Insight Program *1 week*, Autumn Internships *10 weeks*	**SAVILLS** Insight Programme *1 week*
DELOITTE Spring into Deloitte *2 days*	**SKY** Work Experience *1-2 weeks*
EY Summer Internships *6 weeks*, Discover EY *2 days*	**SLAUGHTER AND MAY** Open Day *1 day*
FRONTLINE Insight Day *1 Day*	**TRANSPORT FOR LONDON** Summer Internships *12 weeks*
GOLDMAN SACHS Spring Programme *2 weeks*	**UBS** Insights Week *5 days*
GOOGLE Internship Programme *Minimum of 10 weeks*	**UNILEVER** Spring Programme *3 days*
HERBERT SMITH FREEHILLS First Year Workshops *2 days*	**WELLCOME** Summer Internships *8 weeks*
HSBC Spring Insight Programme *4 days*, First Year Internships *8 weeks*	

Source **The Times Top 100 Graduate Employers** For full details of these work experience programmes for first year students in 2017 and other opportunities, see employers' individual graduate recruitment websites, as listed on page 240.

Remember, there's no such thing as 'bad' work experience, even something that you've not enjoyed can help you understand what motivates you, where your skills lie and what's going to work for you in the long term. If you can learn from the experience, you'll be more likely to find a graduate job that's right for you in the future and that in turn means that you're more likely to be successful and stay longer with your first employer.

If you're in the happy position that your work experience leads to a graduate job offer, then you'll need to think through whether to accept it or continue job hunting. The employer will obviously be keen to know whether you plan to join their graduate programme but don't feel pressurised into taking the job just because it's the only offer you've received. If you're not sure that it's right for you, either ask for more time to consider your options, or be brave and turn it down. It's important to be aware that once you've accepted a graduate job offer from an employer, it is a legally binding contract.

Regardless of whether you get a graduate job offer from it or not, the work experience you do at university will open your eyes to the possibilities for life after graduation and help you decide what kind of career to aim for, as well as giving you the knowledge, insight and employability skills that graduate employers are looking for.

In total, the employers featured within this edition of *The Times Top 100 Graduate Employers* offered a record 14,058 paid vacation placements, internships or other work experience opportunities during 2016 for university students and recent graduates, and that number may well rise further for 2017.

THE TIMES TOP 100 GRADUATE EMPLOYERS — Work Experience for Penultimate Year Students in 2017

EMPLOYER, TYPE OF WORK EXPERIENCE, LENGTH	EMPLOYER, TYPE OF WORK EXPERIENCE, LENGTH
AECOM Summer Internships *8-12 weeks*	**HSBC** Summer Internships *8-12 weeks*
ALLEN & OVERY Summer & Winter Vacation Schemes *2 weeks*	**IBM** Summer Internships *12 weeks*
AMAZON Summer Internships *12 weeks*	**IRWIN MITCHELL** Legal Work Placements *2 weeks*
ATKINS Summer Internships *8-12 weeks*	**J.P. MORGAN** Summer Internships *10 weeks*
BAE SYSTEMS Summer Internships *12 weeks*	**KPMG** Summer Vacation Programme *4-8 weeks*, Summer Internships *10 weeks*
BANK OF ENGLAND Penultimate Year Internships *8 weeks*	**LINKLATERS** Summer Vacation Scheme *4 weeks*
BBC Summer Work Placements *3 months*	**LLOYD'S** Summer Internship Programme *8 weeks*
BDO Internships *6 weeks*	**LLOYDS BANKING GROUP** Summer Internships *10 weeks*
BLACKROCK Summer Internships *8 weeks*	**MARS** Summer Internships *12 weeks*
BP Summer Internships *11 weeks*	**MCKINSEY & COMPANY** Summer Business Analyst *6-8 weeks*
BT Summer Internships *12 weeks*	**MORGAN STANLEY** Summer Analyst Programme *10 weeks*
CANCER RESEARCH UK Internships *3 months*	**MOTT MACDONALD** Summer Internships *6-12 weeks*
CIVIL SERVICE FAST STREAM Summer Diversity Internships *6-9 weeks*	**NORTON ROSE FULBRIGHT** Open Days *1 day*, Summer Vacation Scheme *3 weeks*
CREDIT SUISSE Summer Internships *10 weeks*	**PENGUIN RANDOM HOUSE** Summer Internships *10 weeks*, Work Experience *2 weeks*
DELOITTE Summer Internships *3-6 weeks*	**PWC** Women in Business *1 week*, Tech Academy *1 week*, Summer Internships *2-11 weeks*
DIAGEO Summer Internships *8-12 weeks*	**SAVILLS** Summer Scheme *4 weeks*
DLA PIPER Summer Vacation Scheme *2 weeks*	**SHELL** Assessed Internship Programme *10-12 weeks*
EXXONMOBIL Summer Placements *8 weeks*	**SKY** Work Experience *1-2 weeks*
EY Summer Internships *4-6 weeks*, Discover EY *1-2 days*	**SLAUGHTER AND MAY** Easter & Summer Work Experience *1-3 weeks*
FRONTLINE Summer Internships *3 weeks*	**STANDARD LIFE** Summer Internships *10 weeks*
GOLDMAN SACHS Summer Analyst Programme *10 weeks*	**TEACH FIRST** Insight Programme *2 weeks*
GOOGLE Internship Programme *Minimum of 10 weeks*	**TRANSPORT FOR LONDON** Summer Internships *12 weeks*
GRANT THORNTON Internships *4-6 weeks*	**UBS** Summer Internships *9 weeks*
GSK Summer Placements *10-12 weeks*	**UNILEVER** Summer Placements *12 weeks*
HERBERT SMITH FREEHILLS Vacation Placements *2-3 weeks*	**WELLCOME** Summer Internships *8 weeks*
HOGAN LOVELLS Vacation Schemes *2-3 weeks*	

Source **The Times Top 100 Graduate Employers** For full details of these work experience programmes for penultimate year students in 2017 and other opportunities, see employers' individual graduate recruitment websites, as listed on page 240.

> The skills and knowledge you build up as an ICAEW Chartered Accountant will open more doors than you realise.

ICAEW

Helen Wright
ICAEW Chartered Accountant
Finance Director
at Comic Relief

ICAEW Chartered Accountants are recognised globally as leaders in accountancy, finance and business. They are at the heart of business; making decisions that affect the strategy, direction and profitability of organisations all over the world. Helen Wright, Finance Director at Comic Relief, explains how her career has been influenced by being an ICAEW Chartered Accountant.

I was attracted to accountancy because of the variety it offers and the reputation of the ACA, ICAEW's leading qualification. I trained at PwC, where I got to work with some amazing people on big name brands. I progressed quickly as there was an emphasis on personal development which was incredibly valuable. I had the opportunity to manage and train junior staff in my second year of work – something that few of my friends in other careers had the chance to do so early on.

I'm now the Finance Director at Comic Relief, where I am responsible for the finance and legal teams. These teams have a great impact on the future direction and strategy of Comic Relief.

No two days are the same. I have been lucky enough to have had some very interesting experiences at Comic Relief.

On my first Red Nose Day, Comic Relief passed the £1billion raised mark during the live BBC TV show which was amazing to be part of. My role during the live TV show is to verify the numbers before they go on screen, which on this occasion included reading the number out in words to be loaded onto the autocue for Sir Lenny Henry – the show producer was worried about getting it wrong.

I have no idea where I'll be in the future – the joy of a career like this is that it could be anywhere! My peers are now doing a wide variety of things; several are Finance Managers and Directors, one is a Chief Executive Officer, some made Partner. Others are running their own businesses or have moved into training, consultancy or general management. The commercial awareness, logical, critical thought processes and communication skills you develop through ACA training are immensely transferable. It is a highly respected qualification, which has helped me throughout my career – whatever the job has thrown at me!

Successful Job Applications

By **James Darley**
Graduate Recruitment Director, Teach First

Employers featured in *The Times Top 100 Graduate Employers* are offering a record number of vacancies for new graduates in 2017, but competition for places on the most popular graduate programmes remains intense.

With several thousand applications to consider, many of the best-known employers now use a four-stage process to select the right recruits for their graduate programmes, beginning with an online application form. A typical form will ask you for your standard biographical details – the schools you attended, your GCSE and A-level results, a summary of your academic results so far at university, plus your predicted degree result.

It's really important to be completely honest when you complete this section. Employers are very likely to check the details later in the recruitment process and if you've exaggerated your achievements, you could well have a job offer withdrawn.

For example, if your first year university results weren't as good as you'd hoped because you were enjoying yourself a little too much, you still need to include them but explain that you don't feel they are representative of what you're going to achieve.

The next part of the application form will often ask about the work experience you've done.

> **66** *Some employers will literally strike your application out if you've made spelling or grammatical errors.* **99**

Again it's very important to give employers a true reflection of what you've done and an accurate description of what the work experience involved. Don't be tempted to fill in gaps in your CV to make it sound like you've done more than you have. But if you've worked part-time through university to pay your way, make sure you include those details as they can be valuable experiences too.

Bear in mind that recruiters aren't looking for a long-winded description of the activities that you did in a job, they're trying to find out what you've learned, and how you've developed.

They don't want a long list of activities – 'I did the mail every day', 'I did the photocopying', 'I answered the telephone' – it won't help them understand the insights that the work experience has given you. By all means explain that you did administrative tasks during a placement but follow it up with what you found out about the firm you were working for and why it encouraged you to apply to them for a graduate role.

Most application forms will also include either 'competency' or 'strengths' questions. Competency questions ask you to write about a time where you overcame a particular problem or rose to a challenge, whereas strengths-based questions describe a situation and ask you what you would

Inventive engineering requires more than inventive engineers.

It doesn't just take engineers to make a Dyson machine work. We need problem solvers in all sorts of areas – including Finance, Marketing and IT. It is a broad combination of different skill sets that makes Dyson a successful technology company. So if you see problems as opportunities, whether you're an engineer or not, apply here: **www.careers.dyson.com**

dyson

do about it. These types of questions are asking you to reflect on things you've done, what the outcome was and what you've learnt by doing them. Try and find examples that will be relevant to the workplace, rather than from your academic studies – talking about getting a bad mark in a tough essay and then working harder to get a better mark next time isn't going to impress a graduate recruiter.

When you're answering these questions, remember not to go over the word limit and make sure you check what you've written. Some employers will literally strike your application out if you've made spelling or grammatical errors, or used 'text speak' in your answers.

There's usually also a question around your interest and passion for the organisation and the job you're applying for. Here's an important warning – don't just cut and paste between different application forms for this, however tempting this seems. Recruiters will be able to tell straightaway if you've used the same standard answer to every accountancy firm you've applied to. Your answer should be bespoke and carefully articulate why you think the organisation is the one for you and why you believe that your skills, knowledge and experience are right for the role you're applying for.

This inevitably means doing some research. The day-to-day content of work for a graduate role in banking or finance is likely to be similar from one employer to the next but culturally they could be very different. Is it an American investment bank versus a European commercial bank? Knowing the differences can help you show that you have a real understanding of why that organisation is right for you and why you want to join it.

Once your application is in, the next step in the selection process is likely to be one or more online tests. Testing is incredibly popular with employers and you'll be hard-pressed to find a graduate programme that won't include some form of testing before you progress further. And don't be fooled, just because you've been invited to do the tests, doesn't mean your application has been successful. Many organisations use automated processes that test everyone who applies and use the results to determine which candidates' application forms are then read by a recruiter.

There are several categories of tests that employers use regularly, from ability tests such as verbal or numerical reasoning, to personality and psychometric tests.

Preparing in advance is the key to all of them because they are unfamiliar experiences and can seem very alien at first. Although from a psychology point of view you're not supposed to be able to do better at tests if you practice, familiarity with the structure of the tests and the different types of questions can be very helpful. It can be a real shock if you're sent an email from an employer, you click on a link and the test starts immediately – you could find yourself having to do it in a situation where it's not quiet, you can't concentrate and you've only got one chance to attempt the test.

Verbal or numerical reasoning tests may be reminiscent of English exams or GCSE maths questions, but situational judgement tests introduce what it's like working for an employer. You'll be on a computer during the test and lots of things will come into your in-box and you'll have to work out 'do I tell my manager about that one'? Or do I delegate it, or just file it? Is this just for reading or do I need to action it? It's a good simulation of the real world and tests your decision-making under time pressure. Your university careers service can help you practice different types of tests and some employers include sample tests on their recruitment websites.

If you perform well in an employer's tests, then you'll progress to the interview stage. Check beforehand what type of interview it will be. Is it a competency or strengths-based interview and how is it being conducted? More than half the employers featured in *The Times Top 100 Graduate Employers* either do face-to-face or telephone interviews but a third of recruiters now use recorded online interviews.

These can be a weird experience because the question will flash up on the screen saying 'give an example of a leadership position that you've had' and you'll see a clock counting down the time you've got left to answer it. It can be very, very off-putting and artificial, so it's essential to get as much practice as you can.

Although recruiters will be listening to your answers, they'll also be watching you too. So if you're very reserved, quiet and looking insecure, constantly looking down, that's not going to bode well. To help make the best impression, make sure you're at a desk, in a quiet place, dressed smartly and think about your background too – no dodgy posters or too much distracting clutter. And try to imagine there's a real human being across the desk from you, so that you are as animated as possible when you're answering the questions.

The final stage of the selection process at most organisations is an assessment centre. These can last for a half day, a full day or, in some cases, include an overnight stay, and can feature a range of exercises, presentations, testing and further interviews.

The crucial thing to remember is that you're being assessed from the second that you walk in the door. Some recruiters will talk to the receptionist to see if anyone was late or rude when they arrived. And if there is a dinner or drinks reception when you're told it's your time to have fun and relax, remember what you say and do during the evening – including overindulging in the free hospitality – is likely to be noted by recruiters.

Part of the assessment centre is often a group exercise where you're thrown into a team of other candidates and a set a challenge. Many people struggle with this because they think they have to be the leader and talk all the time to show how impressive they are. It's not necessary and it's more important that you do something within the team that helps get the task done and ensures that there is a positive outcome.

You definitely don't want an *Apprentice*-style battle during one of these exercises. Graduate recruiters will be just as impressed if you're a calming influence who brings people back on message, rather than someone who tries to lead the whole process. But remember, staying silent isn't an option – you need to actively contribute otherwise recruiters won't have any evidence of your strengths and abilities.

Throughout this final selection stage, it's vital to keep thinking about what the assessors and recruiters are expecting from you. At Teach First our assessment centre wouldn't include a business presentation but we would ask you to prepare and teach a 7-minute lesson. What should the key outcome be? At the end of the lesson, the students in front of you should have enjoyed the lesson and have learned something.

You could prepare the best presentation and the most impressive content, but if you're thrown off course with a difficult question all of that can go out of the window. Thinking on your feet and staying focused on the outcome of the task will help you get back on track and reassure recruiters that you're the right person for the job.

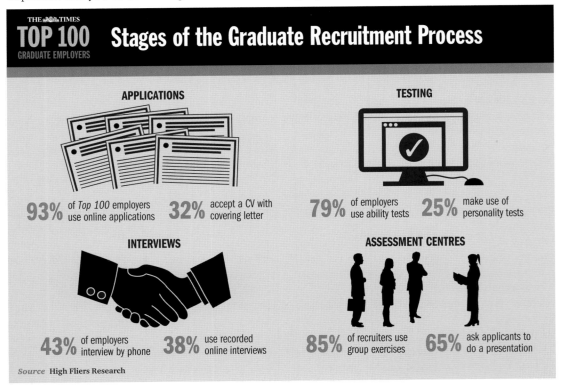

THE TIMES
TOP 100
GRADUATE EMPLOYERS
Stages of the Graduate Recruitment Process

APPLICATIONS

93% of Top 100 employers use online applications

32% accept a CV with covering letter

TESTING

79% of employers use ability tests

25% make use of personality tests

INTERVIEWS

43% of employers interview by phone

38% use recorded online interviews

ASSESSMENT CENTRES

85% of recruiters use group exercises

65% ask applicants to do a presentation

Source High Fliers Research

BOLD. BOLDER. BOLDEST.

GRADUATE & UNDERGRADUATE OPPORTUNITIES
ENGINEERING & COMMERCIAL BUSINESS AREAS

We're on a journey. A journey to redefine the benchmark for excellence. With ambitions to set pulses racing in more countries and more markets than ever before, there's never been a more exciting time to join it. The scale of our ambition is reflected by the ever-expanding breadth of our graduate programmes and undergraduate placements. From our Manufacturing and Engineering disciplines to our Commercial and Business functions, this is a place where you'll continually push the boundaries of your own potential. Where you'll develop specialist and commercial skills working alongside an industry-revered team. Where your achievements, and ours, will only go from strength to strength to strength.

Discover careers that move at **jaguarlandrovercareers.com**

Flt Lt Andrew Longbottom is an Aerosystems Engineering Officer in the Royal Air Force. His current role involves him being in charge of Typhoon aircraft. He joined after getting sponsorship from the RAF to complete his engineering degree and has been lucky enough to travel the world as part of his role.

"The Royal Air Force sponsored me through my undergraduate master's degree in Aerospace Engineering. Now I'm being sponsored through a master's degree, this time in Airworthiness."

"I have served on operational deployments in Afghanistan, Cyprus and the Falkland Islands, and have spent up to three months on exercises in Norway, California, Las Vegas – with 31 Sqn on Tornados and Oman with XI Sqn on Typhoon aircraft. I have also spent time in France, Denmark, Germany, Holland, Italy and Greece."

"I lead a three week, RAF sponsored, expedition to Chilean Patagonia. Leading a 6 man team, we completed the Torres del Paine National Park circuit, a 140km self-supported trek, in seven days before kayaking in the regions lakes and rivers wild camping as we went."

"The RAF has afforded me the opportunity to see and experience some amazing things, killer wales hunting and elephant seals birthing in the Falklands Islands, to kayaking amongst icebergs in Patagonia. But the best experiences have come from the sense of satisfaction and camaraderie when the team pulls together and completes a task which at first seemed almost impossible."

⊙ ROYAL AIR FORCE
REGULAR & RESERVE

Flight Lieutenant Nosheen Chaudry is an Aerosystems Engineering Officer who has worked on several Squadrons including a GR4 Tornado Sqn at RAF Marham and on the Royal Air Force Aerobatic Team (RAFAT), The Red Arrows.

From early childhood Nosheen had a fascination with aircraft and the idea of flight. She was offered a RAF scholarship to be sponsored through Birmingham University to study engineering and now works around the cutting-edge aircraft used by the RAF.

"I fulfil a variety of roles, with responsibility for the teams maintaining aircraft within our fleet. It's challenging work but I like the fact I get posted from one station to another every two years to work on other related and sometimes different projects."

"One of the big attractions for me about the Royal Air Force is the sports and adventurous training on offer. I am really keen on athletics and have competed for the RAF Athletics Team for the last eight years." The RAF requires its personnel to keep physically fit and actively encourages adventurous training.

"I knew from an early age that this is the kind of thing I wanted to do and my family were very supportive in my career choice. In fact, they encouraged me to apply for the University Bursary which certainly helps with the cost of getting a degree."

For information about all of the roles available in the RAF, as well as sponsorship opportunities, visit the RAF Recruitment website. Search online for RAF Recruitment.

KNOW YOUR PARTIES

FROM YOUR PARTIES

The Student Subscription

Access quality journalism online and on your mobile.
Plus enjoy a range of benefits, including 2-for-1 cinema
tickets and half-price meals with a tastecard. You'll even
get a free gift when you subscribe. **Only £20 a year**

Sign up at thetimes.co.uk/studentsubscription

THE TIMES
THE SUNDAY TIMES
Know your times

THE TIMES

TOP 100

GRADUATE EMPLOYERS

Index

EMPLOYER	TOP 100 RANKING	ACCOUNTANCY	CONSULTING	ENGINEERING	FINANCE	GENERAL MANAGEMENT	HUMAN RESOURCES	INVESTMENT BANKING	IT	LAW	LOGISTICS	MARKETING	MEDIA	PROPERTY	PURCHASING	RESEARCH & DEVELOPMENT	RETAILING	SALES	NUMBER OF VACANCIES	PAGE
JAGUAR LAND ROVER	19	●		●	●				●		●	●		●	●	●		●	250	152
JOHN LEWIS PARTNERSHIP	18					●											●		30+	154
J.P. MORGAN	12				●		●	●	●										No fixed quota	156
KPMG	6	●	●		●		●		●						●				1,000	158
L'ORÉAL	22				●						●	●						●	28	160
LIDL	14					●					●			●	●		●		240+	162
LINKLATERS	39									●									110	164
LLOYD'S	79				●		●		●		●								25	166
LLOYDS BANKING GROUP	25	●	●		●	●	●	●	●	●								●	400+	168
M&S	54				●	●	●		●		●	●		●	●	●	●		200	170
MARS	45			●	●	●	●		●					●	●				40	172
MCDONALD'S	98				●														100	174
MCKINSEY & COMPANY	21		●																No fixed quota	176
MI5 – THE SECURITY SERVICE	55				●				●										150	178
MORGAN STANLEY	31				●			●	●										No fixed quota	180
MOTT MACDONALD	75		●	●										●					250+	182
NETWORK RAIL	76			●	●	●	●							●					125-175	184
NEWTON EUROPE	53		●																120	186
NGDP FOR LOCAL GOVERNMENT	88					●													120	188
NHS	8	●			●	●	●		●						●				100+	190
NORTON ROSE FULBRIGHT	78									●									Up to 50	192
OXFAM	84	●				●			●			●	●		●	●			50+ (voluntary)	194
P&G	34			●	●		●		●		●	●			●		●		100	196
PENGUIN RANDOM HOUSE	61	●			●		●		●		●	●					●		50+	198
POLICE NOW	62																		250	200
PWC	1	●	●		●				●	●									1,500	202
RBS	35	●			●	●	●	●	●			●					●		300+	204
ROYAL AIR FORCE	73	●		●	●	●	●		●	●	●				●		●		500-600	206
ROYAL NAVY	67			●	●	●	●		●	●	●				●				No fixed quota	208
SANTANDER	63				●	●										●			Up to 50	210
SAVILLS	94													●					170	212
SHELL	27			●	●		●		●		●	●			●				70+	214
SIEMENS	83			●	●				●						●	●			70-80	216
SKY	41				●						●								90+	218
SLAUGHTER AND MAY	56									●									80	220
STANDARD LIFE	95	●			●	●	●		●	●		●							50	222
TEACH FIRST	3	●	●	●	●	●	●	●	●	●	●	●	●	●	●	●	●	●	1,750	224
TESCO	32			●	●	●	●		●		●	●		●	●		●		150-200	226
TRANSPORT FOR LONDON	48	●		●	●	●			●					●	●				150	228
UBS	92					●	●	●	●			●							300	230
UNILEVER	11			●	●	●			●		●	●			●				50	232
VIRGIN MEDIA	64	●		●	●	●	●					●					●		50+	234
WELLCOME	72			●	●	●	●	●	●			●	●						10-12	236
WPP	49											●	●						1-10	238

accenture.com/timestop100

As one of the world's leading consulting and technology organisations, Accenture achieves amazing things for its clients every day – whether that's increasing profits, gaining a greater market share, redefining strategies, working with new technologies or offering better customer experiences.

Accenture examines a client's organisation, works out how best to improve it using the latest technology and digital solutions, and implements agreed actions to bring about positive, lasting and profitable change. For Accenture, it's not just about coming up with great ideas, it's also about successfully delivering and implementing them.

To manage the broad spectrum of challenges Accenture's clients face, their business needs to be diverse, which is why they've set up their organisation across five key business areas. These are Accenture Strategy; Accenture Consulting; Accenture Digital; Accenture Technology, and Accenture Operations.

This has enabled Accenture to deliver some ground-breaking solutions; such as the RBS 6 Nations Championship app that delivers in-game statistics direct to a person's phone and new technology that impacts millions of lives every day; visit accenture.com/accentureinyourday to discover more of the surprising and innovative things the organisation does every day to make people's lives better.

There are a variety of ways that graduates can join Accenture. Whichever programme they join, graduates will enjoy the perfect mix of intensive training, expert support, live project experience and great benefits.

Graduates are able to make the most of their talents and get the variety and scope of opportunities they deserve. They can be an integral part of projects that impact the way the world thinks, works and plays, and they're able to enjoy the responsibility that helps them get ahead, fast.

GRADUATE VACANCIES IN 2017
CONSULTING
IT

NUMBER OF VACANCIES
500+ graduate jobs

LOCATIONS OF VACANCIES

STARTING SALARY FOR 2017
£Competitive

UNIVERSITY VISITS IN 2016-17
ASTON, BATH, BIRMINGHAM, BRISTOL, BRUNEL, CAMBRIDGE, CITY, DURHAM, EDINBURGH, EXETER, IMPERIAL COLLEGE LONDON, KING'S COLLEGE LONDON, KENT, LANCASTER, LEEDS, LONDON SCHOOL OF ECONOMICS, LOUGHBOROUGH, MANCHESTER, NEWCASTLE, NORTHUMBRIA, NOTTINGHAM, OXFORD, QUEEN MARY LONDON, ROYAL HOLLOWAY, SHEFFIELD, SOUTHAMPTON, ST ANDREWS, STRATHCLYDE, UNIVERSITY COLLEGE LONDON, WARWICK
Please check with your university careers service for full details of local events.

MINIMUM ENTRY REQUIREMENTS
Relevant degree required for some roles.

APPLICATION DEADLINE
Year-round recriutment
Early application advised.

FURTHER INFORMATION
www.Top100GraduateEmployers.com
Register now for the latest news, campus events, work experience and graduate vacancies at Accenture.

Ready for an adventure?

We're looking for future leaders.
Idea generators. And strategic thinkers.

We're looking for future leaders. Idea generators. And strategic thinkers. Put your degree and skills to work. We'll help you build the roadmap that's right for your career – including a few twists and turns to keep things interesting. If you have passion, a brilliant mind and an appetite to grow every day, this is the place for you.

Begin your journey: accenture.com/timestop100

Strategy | Consulting | Digital | Technology | Operations

High performance. Delivered.

GRADUATE VACANCIES IN 2017
CONSULTING
ENGINEERING
FINANCE
HUMAN RESOURCES
PROPERTY

NUMBER OF VACANCIES
400 graduate jobs

LOCATIONS OF VACANCIES

STARTING SALARY FOR 2017
£23,000-£26,000

UNIVERSITY VISITS IN 2016-17
ASTON, BATH, BELFAST, BIRMINGHAM, BRISTOL, CAMBRIDGE, CARDIFF, DURHAM, EDINBURGH, EXETER, GLASGOW, HERIOT-WATT, IMPERIAL COLLEGE LONDON, KING'S COLLEGE LONDON, LEEDS, LEICESTER, LIVERPOOL, LOUGHBOROUGH, MANCHESTER, NEWCASTLE, NORTHUMBRIA, NOTTINGHAM, NOTTINGHAM TRENT, OXFORD, OXFORD BROOKES, PLYMOUTH, READING, SHEFFIELD, SOUTHAMPTON, STRATHCLYDE, SURREY, TRINITY COLLEGE DUBLIN, ULSTER, UNIVERSITY COLLEGE DUBLIN, UNIVERSITY COLLEGE LONDON, WARWICK, YORK
Please check with your university careers service for full details of local events.

MINIMUM ENTRY REQUIREMENTS
2.2 Degree

APPLICATION DEADLINE
Year-round recruitment
Early application advised.

FURTHER INFORMATION
www.Top100GraduateEmployers.com
Register now for the latest news, campus events, work experience and graduate vacancies at AECOM.

AECOM is built to deliver a better world. AECOM design, build, finance and operate infrastructure assets for governments, businesses and organisations in more than 150 countries. From high-performance buildings and infrastructure, to resilient communities and environments, to stable and secure nations.

As a company AECOM are responding fast to the fact that since we live in an interconnected and challenging world, new thinking is called for. As a fully integrated firm, AECOM connect knowledge and experience across a global network of experts to help clients solve their most complex challenges. From high-performance buildings and infrastructure, to resilient communities and environments, to stable and secure nations, the work AECOM does is transformative, differentiated and vital.

AECOM is a leader in all of the key markets it serves, including transportation, facilities, environmental, energy, oil and gas, water, high-rise buildings and government. AECOM provides a blend of global reach, local knowledge, innovation and technical excellence in delivering solutions that create, enhance and sustain the world's built, natural and social environments. AECOM bring together creative, technical and management specialists to work on projects at every scale.

AECOM engineer energy-efficient buildings and build new links between cities, design new communities and regenerate existing ones. AECOM are the first whole environments business, going beyond buildings and infrastructure.

AECOM are looking for graduates from a wide range of disciplines including civil, structural, mechanical, electrical, planning, surveying, project management, building services, sustainable buildings engineering, ecology, environmental engineering, water related disciplines, and energy related disciplines.

AIRBUS GROUP

www.jobs.airbusgroup.com

facebook.com/AirbusGroupCareers graduates@airbus.com

linkedin.com/company/AirbusGroup twitter.com/AirbusGroup

instagram.com/airbus_group youtube.com/AirbusGroup

Airbus Group is a global pioneer in aeronautics, space and related services. Uniting the capabilities of three market leaders – Airbus, Airbus Defence and Space, and Airbus Helicopters – it strives towards amazing innovation, from the double-deck Airbus A380, to the comet explorer Rosetta.

Airbus is a leading aircraft manufacturer offering a complete range of aircraft families, from 100 to well over 500 passenger seats, as well as the most modern, comprehensive and fuel-efficient product line on the market.

Airbus Defence and Space is No.1 in Europe and No.2 in the world's space industry. That's because their people are driven to find new and better ways to protect the world, and to explore beyond it, for everyone's benefit.

Airbus Group looks for graduates with passionate drive and sound commercial awareness to join the Airbus and Airbus Defence and Space UK Graduate Programmes. These programmes offer unrivalled opportunities for graduates to learn and hone their talents, providing the support they need to grow.

The two/three-year programmes consist of structured rotational placements, so graduates will learn and develop technical and management skills, gaining a rounded picture of their division's work. With the training and support of Airbus Group, graduates will drive their development in the direction they choose, building a career of outstanding opportunities. For those looking for a direct role, there are also graduate openings available within Airbus Defence and Space.

Whatever their chosen path, successful applicants will join a team dedicated to creating a better future for everyone. They'll explore new ideas, think innovatively, and help Airbus Group achieve incredible things on the ground, in the air, and in space.

GRADUATE VACANCIES IN 2017

ENGINEERING

FINANCE

IT

LOGISTICS

PURCHASING

RESEARCH & DEVELOPMENT

NUMBER OF VACANCIES
80+ graduate jobs

LOCATIONS OF VACANCIES

STARTING SALARY FOR 2017
£26,000+
Plus a £2,000 welcome payment.

UNIVERSITY VISITS IN 2016-17
ASTON, BATH, BRISTOL, CARDIFF, IMPERIAL COLLEGE LONDON, LIVERPOOL, LOUGHBOROUGH, MANCHESTER, NOTTINGHAM, SHEFFIELD, SOUTHAMPTON, SURREY, SWANSEA
Please check with your university careers service for full details of local events.

MINIMUM ENTRY REQUIREMENTS
2.2 Degree

APPLICATION DEADLINE
25th November 2016

FURTHER INFORMATION
www.Top100GraduateEmployers.com
Register now for the latest news, campus events, work experience and graduate vacancies at Airbus.

With roots dating back to 1913, Aldi (short for Albrecht Discount) came to the UK in 1990 and customers were amazed to see a fantastic example of 'no frills' shopping. Aldi are now one of the UK's fastest-growing supermarkets and one of the world's most successful retailers.

All graduates enter the business on their Area Manager Training Programme. It's gained a reputation for being tough, and rightly so. Graduates have an enormous amount of responsibility very early on and after 12 months, they'll take control of a multi-million pound area of three to four stores. Graduates receive incredible support throughout their training, with a dedicated mentor and regular one-to-one sessions with talented colleagues.

It's the perfect introduction to Aldi and a superb foundation for future success. It gives graduates a wider lens to make critical business decisions later on in their journey. Two to three years into the programme, secondments are available with many graduates having the chance to spend time in other parts of the UK, the US or even Australia. After five or so years as an Area Manager, high-performing graduates can then move into a Director role within (for example) Buying, Finance or Operations.

Aldi is built on an attitude. It's about never giving up; always striving for smarter, simpler ways of doing things. They're a business with integrity: they're fair to their partners and suppliers, and everything they do is for the benefit of their customers and their people. They look for graduates who are incredibly hardworking with a positive, 'roll their sleeves up' attitude. Those who join Aldi will blend intellect with a practical, business-focused mindset as they achieve impressive results with a world-class team.

GRADUATE VACANCIES IN 2017
GENERAL MANAGEMENT
RETAILING

NUMBER OF VACANCIES
150 graduate jobs

LOCATIONS OF VACANCIES

STARTING SALARY FOR 2017
£42,000

UNIVERSITY VISITS IN 2016-17
ABERDEEN, ASTON, BATH, BIRMINGHAM, CARDIFF, DURHAM, EAST ANGLIA, EDINBURGH, EXETER, GLASGOW, LANCASTER, LEEDS, LEICESTER, LIVERPOOL, LONDON SCHOOL OF ECONOMICS, LOUGHBOROUGH, MANCHESTER, NEWCASTLE, NORTHUMBRIA, NOTTINGHAM, READING, SHEFFIELD, SOUTHAMPTON, ST ANDREWS, STRATHCLYDE, SWANSEA, WARWICK, YORK
Please check with your university careers service for full details of local events.

MINIMUM ENTRY REQUIREMENTS
2.1 Degree
240 UCAS points

APPLICATION DEADLINE
Year-round recruitment

FURTHER INFORMATION
www.Top100GraduateEmployers.com
Register now for the latest news, campus events, work experience and graduate vacancies at Aldi.

It's tougher than you think. **Turns out I'm tougher than I thought.**

Graduate Area Manager Programme

- **£42,000 starting salary (rising to £72,000 after four years) • Pension • Healthcare • Audi A4**
- **All-year round recruitment but places fill quickly**

The Area Manager role gives graduates real responsibility and fast progression. From day one, I knew that my skills, determination and strength of character were contributing to the success of one of the UK's fastest-growing supermarkets. Amazing when you think about it.
aldirecruitment.co.uk/graduates

BECAUSE I'M ALDI. AND I'M LIKE NO OTHER.

ALLEN & OVERY

Allen & Overy is a pioneering legal practice operating around the world at the frontline of developing business. By helping companies, institutions and governments tackle ever-more complex issues and transactions on a global stage, it is leading the way and extending what is possible in law.

With 44 offices in 31 countries, plus a network of relationship firms in other locations, Allen & Overy is one of the few legal practices that can genuinely claim to be global, covering 99% of the world's economy.

For the firm's clients this means global reach and access to high-calibre, internationally minded local expertise. For trainees, it means exposure to multinational work, collaboration with colleagues from around the world and, in many cases, the opportunity to travel. In 2015, 73% of its transactional work involved two or more countries and 48% involved three or more.

Trainee lawyers joining the firm enter an environment characterised by innovative thinking and a global vision. They are exposed to challenging and meaningful work from the outset, supporting a partner or senior associate in each of their training 'seats'. In addition, they are encouraged to spend six months in one of the firm's overseas offices, or on secondment to one of its corporate clients – currently approximately 80% of its trainees take up this opportunity.

Alongside a rich and exciting experience, graduates can also look forward to world-class training and working in an open and supportive culture that values both teamwork and independent thought. Allen & Overy has established a reputation for combining the very highest professional standards with warmth and approachability.

Regardless of their degree discipline – and around half of the firm's trainees study subjects other than law – joining Allen & Overy puts graduates at the forefront of the rapidly-evolving global legal sector.

GRADUATE VACANCIES IN 2017

LAW

NUMBER OF VACANCIES
90 graduate jobs
For training contracts starting in 2019.

LOCATIONS OF VACANCIES

STARTING SALARY FOR 2017
£42,000

UNIVERSITY VISITS IN 2016-17
BATH, BELFAST, BIRMINGHAM, BRISTOL, CAMBRIDGE, CARDIFF, DURHAM, EDINBURGH, EXETER, IMPERIAL COLLEGE LONDON, LANCASTER, LEEDS, LEICESTER, LONDON SCHOOL OF ECONOMICS, MANCHESTER, NEWCASTLE, NOTTINGHAM, OXFORD, SHEFFIELD, SOUTHAMPTON, ST ANDREWS, TRINITY COLLEGE DUBLIN, UNIVERSITY COLLEGE DUBLIN, UNIVERSITY COLLEGE LONDON, WARWICK, YORK
Please check with your university careers service for full details of local events.

MINIMUM ENTRY REQUIREMENTS
2.1 Degree
340 UCAS points

APPLICATION DEADLINE
Please see website for full details.

FURTHER INFORMATION
www.Top100GraduateEmployers.com
*Register now for the latest news, campus events, work experience and graduate vacancies at **Allen & Overy**.*

ALLEN & OVERY

A career in law

Setting precedents, not following them… Because tomorrow will not be like today.

The practice of law is constantly evolving, and we take pride in being pioneers, in challenging the status quo and looking beyond what has been done before to create innovative solutions for our clients. It is this culture of forward thinking that has resulted in us being the only law firm to have featured in the top three of the Financial Times Innovative Law Firm ranking every year and to have topped the list four times.

Last year we were named Graduate Employer of Choice in law by TARGETjobs for the 11th year in a row and Times High Fliers Graduate Employer of Choice in law for a 6th year. There's a reason for that. As a trainee at Allen & Overy you'll be part of a truly global and collaborative team, working with big-name clients on the deals that make the front pages. Above all, your A&O Training Contract will give you a platform of skills and experiences on which to build a long-term career and our people agree: last year 98% said there were opportunities to grow and develop their skills here.

Find out more at **aograduate.com**

 Follow the conversation @AllenOveryGrads | www.facebook.com/allenoverygrads

Amazon's mission is to be Earth's most customer-centric company where people can find and discover anything they want to buy online. Amazon's evolution from website to e-commerce and publishing partner to development platform is driven by the pioneering spirit that is part of Amazon's DNA.

The world's brightest technology minds come to Amazon to research and develop new technologies that improve the lives of our customers, shoppers, sellers, content creators, and developers around the world. Because that's what being Earth's most customer-centric company is all about, and it's still Day 1 at Amazon.

Amazon is looking for analytical and entrepreneurial thinkers, who like to be challenged and are able to keep pace in a fast-moving business. In return they'll give graduates responsibility and hands-on training to help them succeed. Amazon has opportunities available across areas such as Retail, Finance, Design, and Amazon Media Group. They also have software development engineering opportunities at Amazon's Development Centres supporting businesses including Amazon Instant Video and Amazon Data Services. Amazon's operations network also offers graduate roles within Engineering, Finance, HR, IT, Logistics, and Operations.

For example, Area Managers are in charge of a department within warehouses, also known as Fulfillment Centres. They manage the day-to-day operations to deliver on the targeted key performance indicators. They are also responsible for leading a team whilst driving process improvement within their area. Through their work they will continuously improve the functionality and service level Amazon provides their customers. The Area Manager role is one of many exciting opportunities for graduates to grow their career at Amazon!

GRADUATE VACANCIES IN 2017
ENGINEERING
FINANCE
GENERAL MANAGEMENT
HUMAN RESOURCES
IT
LOGISTICS
MARKETING
PURCHASING
SALES

NUMBER OF VACANCIES
500+ graduate jobs

LOCATIONS OF VACANCIES

Vacancies also available in Europe.

STARTING SALARY FOR 2017
£Competitive

UNIVERSITY VISITS IN 2016-17
ASTON, BATH, BIRMINGHAM, BRISTOL, CAMBRIDGE, CARDIFF, CITY, DURHAM, EDINBURGH, EXETER, GLASGOW, IMPERIAL COLLEGE LONDON, KING'S COLLEGE LONDON, LANCASTER, LEEDS, LEICESTER, LIVERPOOL, LONDON SCHOOL OF ECONOMICS, LOUGHBOROUGH, MANCHESTER, NEWCASTLE, NOTTINGHAM, OXFORD, SHEFFIELD, SOUTHAMPTON, ST ANDREWS, STRATHCLYDE, SURREY, SWANSEA, TRINITY COLLEGE DUBLIN, UNIVERSITY COLLEGE LONDON, WARWICK
Please check with your university careers service for full details of local events.

MINIMUM ENTRY REQUIREMENTS
2.1 Degree

APPLICATION DEADLINE
Year-round recruitment

FURTHER INFORMATION
www.Top100GraduateEmployers.com
Register now for the latest news, campus events, work experience and graduate vacancies at Amazon.

We're a company of Pioneers.

It's our job to make bold bets, and we get our energy from inventing on behalf of customers.

There's more inside.
Begin your career with Amazon.

If you want to go a step beyond thinking outside the box, come to Amazon where we *invent* our way out.

Find your opportunity at amazon.jobs
Search for #AmazonGradsPioneer

amazon
we pioneer

WE CAME AS
CODERS, RESEARCHERS,
ENGINEERS, ECONOMISTS,
RISK ANALYSTS AND LINGUISTS.
AFTER SANDHURST TRAINING
WE BECAME LEADERS.
WE LEAD A LIFE OF SERVICE.
WITH HEART. WITH MIND.
ARMY OFFICER.

#WITHHEARTWITHMIND
SEARCH
ARMY OFFICER

ARMY
BE THE BEST

Becoming an Army Officer can teach graduates many things. It teaches them to work harder, see further, stand taller. It teaches them skills in leadership, management and communication. Professional skills and skills for life. A life of achievement, purpose and opportunity. A life full of adventure.

The route from university to becoming an Army Officer starts at the Royal Military Academy Sandhurst. This elite training academy has welcomed graduates in Geography, French, IT, Engineering, Law, Management Accounting and many other subjects. The 44 weeks of Officer training provided here prepares graduates to apply their knowledge in ways they never imagined: leading projects of incredible scope and scale; leading humanitarian relief efforts; and leading life-saving missions.

Sandhurst is also the place where graduates get their first taste of Army Adventurous Training. This is an opportunity to participate in, and gain qualifications in, a broad range of outdoor activities from skiing in Canada to skydiving in the Bahamas whilst earning a training salary of £25,727.

When graduates complete their Officer training, they are commissioned as a Second Lieutenant. They then move to their chosen Regiment or Corps for further specialist training and to take immediate responsibility for leading a team of around 30 soldiers as well as having a salary increase to £30,922.

The best leadership training in the world together with the support needed to make the most of it, a clear path for promotion, and challenge and adventure all the way. Life as an Army Officer offers everything people with leadership potential, a strong sense of moral direction and focused ambition could want.

Bring people together. Bring a nation to its feet. With heart. With mind. Army Officer.

GRADUATE VACANCIES IN 2017

ENGINEERING
GENERAL MANAGEMENT
HUMAN RESOURCES
IT
LAW
LOGISTICS

NUMBER OF VACANCIES
650 graduate jobs

LOCATIONS OF VACANCIES

STARTING SALARY FOR 2017
£25,727
Rising to £30,922 upon completion of training.

UNIVERSITY VISITS IN 2016-17
ABERDEEN, BATH, BELFAST, BIRMINGHAM, BRISTOL, CARDIFF, DURHAM, EDINBURGH, EXETER, LEEDS, LIVERPOOL, LOUGHBOROUGH, MANCHESTER, NEWCASTLE, NORTHUMBRIA, NOTTINGHAM, OXFORD BROOKES, READING, SHEFFIELD, SWANSEA, YORK
Please check with your university careers service for full details of local events.

MINIMUM ENTRY REQUIREMENTS
180 UCAS points

APPLICATION DEADLINE
Year-round recruitment

FURTHER INFORMATION
www.Top100GraduateEmployers.com
Register now for the latest news, campus events, work experience and graduate vacancies at the British Army.

www.astrazenecacareers.com/students

facebook.com/astrazenecacareers

linkedin.com/company/astrazeneca/careers   twitter.com/AstraZenecaJobs

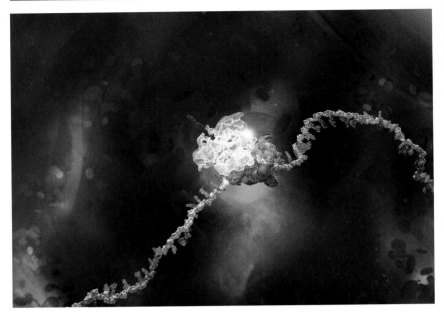

AstraZeneca pushes the boundaries of science to deliver life-changing medicines. A global, innovation-driven biopharmaceutical business, they invest very heavily in their scientific & clinical capabilities, and are proud to have a unique workplace culture that inspires innovation and collaboration.

AstraZeneca offers graduates the opportunity to thrive in an international and diverse organisation with numerous stakeholders, and take real responsibility from day one. Throughout the graduate programme, graduates will have frequent opportunities to review their progress as they train, experience groundbreaking projects, and build a strong support network, gaining an extensive understanding of the pharmaceutical industry whatever their degree. The company provides many paths towards the achievement of graduates' career objectives, and outstanding personal development plans, devised with managers, and incorporating a formal performance management process.

Some programmes will give graduates the chance to work abroad, and whichever excellent learning and development route they take, they'll find this is a company with a diverse range of perspectives, challenges and ideas.

Proud to have gained a host of awards for their progressive and diverse working practices, AstraZeneca is always reaching for more. Each award pushes them further, and strengthens the connections between fellow employees, patients, stakeholders and the communities in which they work.

At AstraZeneca, graduates find an energised, supportive environment, stoked by innovation and exemplary leaders at every level. This is the chance to collaborate with people whose ideas are as diverse as the cultures that have helped shape them.

GRADUATE VACANCIES IN 2017
GENERAL MANAGEMENT
IT
LOGISTICS
PURCHASING
RESEARCH & DEVELOPMENT

NUMBER OF VACANCIES
80+ graduate jobs

LOCATIONS OF VACANCIES

Vacancies also available in Europe, Asia, the USA and elsewhere in the world.

STARTING SALARY FOR 2017
£28,000
Plus bonus, benefits and relocation (if applicable).

UNIVERSITY VISITS IN 2016-17
BRISTOL, CAMBRIDGE, DURHAM, IMPERIAL COLLEGE LONDON, KING'S COLLEGE LONDON, LEEDS, LONDON SCHOOL OF ECONOMICS, MANCHESTER, OXFORD, UNIVERSITY COLLEGE LONDON, WARWICK, YORK
Please check with your university careers service for full details of local events.

MINIMUM ENTRY REQUIREMENTS
2.1 Degree

APPLICATION DEADLINE
Varies by function

FURTHER INFORMATION
www.Top100GraduateEmployers.com
Register now for the latest news, campus events, work experience and graduate vacancies at AstraZeneca.

Exciting challenges on a global scale.
How will you make a difference?

Active in over 100 countries, AstraZeneca pushes the boundaries of science to deliver life-changing medicines which are already used by millions of patients worldwide. Our ambition is to improve the lives of 200 million people, and be a $50 billion company, by 2025. Right now we have opportunities for high-calibre graduates to join our Graduate Programmes in 2017.

These programmes offer you myriad possibilities for development, enabling you to excel as a graduate in your chosen field. You'll find AstraZeneca is ideally placed to help you build a satisfying career, where learning, growing and meeting exciting challenges are all in a day's work.

We offer programmes within:

- **Global Operations**
- **Information Technology**
- **Innovative Medicines and Early Development**
- **Pharmaceutical Development**

As we build on our strengths, to continue to meet the needs of a changing world, you'll also find we have a diverse workforce, with employees drawn from all backgrounds and cultures. This helps us to better reflect and understand our patients and the healthcare professionals we serve, in increasingly global markets - and ultimately, develop the medicines the world needs.

AstraZeneca welcomes applications from all sections of the community.

An Equal Opportunity Employer Minorities/Women/Protected Veterans/Disabled/Sexual Orientation/Gender Identity.

To find out more, please visit:
www.astrazenecacareers.com/students

What science can do

Oncology combination therapies
AstraZeneca is investigating combinations of biologic and small molecule therapies for the treatment of cancer. These combinations target the tumour directly and some help boost the body's own immune system to induce tumour cell death.

graduates@atkinsglobal.com
twitter.com/AtkinsGraduates   facebook.com/AtkinsGlobalCareers
plus.google.com/+wsatkins/posts   linkedin.com/company/atkins/careers
instagram.com/atkins_global   youtube.com/wsatkinsplc

ATKINS

As one of the world's most respected design, engineering and project management consultancies, Atkins is well placed to invest in the development of its graduates and support them in becoming experts in whatever inspires them most. Their imaginations could help to transform the future.

With Atkins, graduates join teams who help to create a world where lives are enriched through the implementation of the organisation's ideas, from moving people across London faster on Crossrail through to solving the energy challenges of the future.

Atkins's work covers a range of sectors including Transportation, Water, Defence, Energy and the Built Environment. They're looking for talented engineering graduates from civil, structural, mechanical, electrical, chemical, aerospace and aeronautical, systems and communications as well as IT, physics, geography and maths.

Atkins is looking for bright and ambitious graduates to join their award-winning Graduate Development Programme. Applicants will be passionate about addressing challenges with creative thinking, and be able to demonstrate flexibility, resilience and drive. Atkins offers an environment in which engineers, planners, architects and a myriad of related professionals flourish. Graduates on the scheme will have access to extensive opportunities across a range of geographical locations, functional disciplines and business areas. They will be responsible for driving their own development, but with plenty of support.

Atkins also offers a range of undergraduate opportunities too. Year-long placements and summer internships to help explore career ideas and focus on future plans, so undergraduates can spend some time with Atkins and get valuable experience and ideas.

GRADUATE VACANCIES IN 2017

CONSULTING
ENGINEERING

NUMBER OF VACANCIES
350 graduate jobs

LOCATIONS OF VACANCIES

STARTING SALARY FOR 2017
£22,000
Plus a settling-in allowance of £2,500.

UNIVERSITY VISITS IN 2016-17
BATH, BIRMINGHAM, BRISTOL, CAMBRIDGE, CARDIFF, HERIOT-WATT, IMPERIAL COLLEGE LONDON, LEEDS, LIVERPOOL, LOUGHBOROUGH, MANCHESTER, NEWCASTLE, NOTTINGHAM, NOTTINGHAM TRENT, OXFORD, SHEFFIELD, SOUTHAMPTON, SURREY
Please check with your university careers service for full details of local events.

MINIMUM ENTRY REQUIREMENTS
2.1 Degree

APPLICATION DEADLINE
21st December 2016

FURTHER INFORMATION
www.Top100GraduateEmployers.com
Register now for the latest news, campus events, work experience and graduate vacancies at Atkins.

twitter.com/BAESGraduates
facebook.com/BAESGraduates
youtube.com/user/BAESystemsplc
linkedin.com/company/bae-systems

"There's support from managers, senior mentors and colleagues, which means there's a lot of opportunity to reach my career goals"

GRADUATE VACANCIES IN 2017

ACCOUNTANCY
CONSULTING
ENGINEERING
FINANCE
HUMAN RESOURCES
IT
RESEARCH & DEVELOPMENT

NUMBER OF VACANCIES
350+ graduate jobs

LOCATIONS OF VACANCIES

BAE Systems is one of the world's most innovative companies, delivering a range of services from technology-led defence and aerospace systems to cyber security. The company's Graduate Development Framework (GDF) enables talented graduates to develop their potential.

With over 18,000 engineers in the UK, the company supports professional accreditation and offers opportunities across a wide range of engineering disciplines. Openings in the defence and aerospace business cover everything from civil, electrical, manufacturing and naval architecture, to research, software and systems.

Alongside this, BAE Systems Applied Intelligence offers more than 120 positions each year in software engineering, technical consulting, electronic engineering, delivery management and business consulting roles. Over 18 months, it equips people to contribute to a world-class reputation for developing innovative, cutting edge solutions.

There is also a continual need for people who can add real value in the fields of business development, commercial, human resources, information technology, procurement and project management.

Then there's the five-year, fast-track finance graduate scheme, preparing individuals to become Finance Directors of the future. The programme includes a structured and fully supported route to the highly respected Chartered Institute of Management Accountants (CIMA) qualification.

Finally, Sigma is a three-year, fast-track leadership programme for people with the very highest potential. With only a few places available each year, it is unique, fast-paced and designed to give individuals breadth and depth of knowledge across multiple areas in business or engineering.

STARTING SALARY FOR 2017
£28,000-£30,000
Plus a £2,000 welcome payment.

UNIVERSITY VISITS IN 2016-17
BATH, BIRMINGHAM, BRISTOL, BRUNEL,
CAMBRIDGE, CARDIFF, DURHAM,
EDINBURGH, GLASGOW, HERIOT-WATT,
IMPERIAL COLLEGE LONDON, KENT,
LANCASTER, LEEDS, LIVERPOOL,
LOUGHBOROUGH, MANCHESTER,
NEWCASTLE, NOTTINGHAM, OXFORD,
SHEFFIELD, SOUTHAMPTON, STRATHCLYDE,
SURREY, UNIVERSITY COLLEGE LONDON,
WARWICK, YORK
Please check with your university careers service for full details of local events.

MINIMUM ENTRY REQUIREMENTS
2.1 Degree
Relevant degree required for some roles.

APPLICATION DEADLINE
Year-round recruitment
Early application advised.

FURTHER INFORMATION
www.Top100GraduateEmployers.com
Register now for the latest news, campus events, work experience and graduate vacancies at BAE Systems.

Remarkable people
doing work that matters

At BAE Systems, we provide some of the world's most advanced, technology-led defence, aerospace and security solutions, employing a skilled workforce of some 83,400 people in over 40 countries. Working with customers and local partners, we develop, engineer, manufacture and support products and systems to deliver military capability, protect national security and people and keep critical information and infrastructure secure. That's work that inspires us.

We're always looking out for people who can add real value to our business. That's why we offer exciting and challenging career opportunities to enthusiastic, driven graduates and undergraduates.

If you're aspiring to develop professional excellence, you can join our Graduate Development Framework in a business or engineering role, ranging from human resources to naval architecture. For those who want to be part of a team that builds solutions of the future, there's Applied Intelligence, with roles ranging from cyber security to software engineering. For individuals with the capability and determination to take up a senior finance role in the future, there's the Finance Leader Development Programme. Or there's the Sigma Leadership Programme, designed to develop those with the highest leadership potential into a business or engineering leader of the future. We also welcome ambitious undergraduates looking to take up an Industrial Placement or Summer Internship.

BAIN & COMPANY

Bain & Company is one of the world's leading management consulting firms. They work with top executives to help them make better decisions, convert those decisions to actions and deliver the sustainable success they desire. For 40 years, they've been passionate about achieving better results for their clients.

Bain & Company advise global leaders on their most critical issues and opportunities: strategy, marketing, organisation, operations, technology, digital, advanced analytics, transformations, sustainability and mergers & acquisitions, across all industries and geographies. Bain have a unique approach to traditional change management, called Results Delivery®, which helps clients measure and manage risk and overcome the odds to realise results.

Associate Consultants (ACs) are responsible for solving business problems and helping the team work on clients' critical issues. In addition, ACs learn how to develop and implement practical solutions to drive tangible financial results for clients. Bain offers unparalleled flexibility – ACs have the opportunity to pursue an MBA, go on externship or take a leave of absence to do charity work or travel.

Throughout a career at Bain, excellent training is offered. The first year starts with two weeks of detailed training in the office and a further two-week global training programme, alongside international colleagues. In addition, ACs are assigned a mentor to help guide them through their career as well as receive ongoing coaching, both informal and formal, from senior case members and peer group sessions to ensure continual skill development.

Bain people are dynamic, entrepreneurial and thrive on early responsibility. Bain look for exceptional graduates and postgraduates from any degree discipline who demonstrate strong analytical and communication skills, initiative, and leadership.

GRADUATE VACANCIES IN 2017
CONSULTING

NUMBER OF VACANCIES
No fixed quota

LOCATIONS OF VACANCIES

STARTING SALARY FOR 2017
£Competitive
Plus a starting bonus and performance-related annual bonus.

UNIVERSITY VISITS IN 2016-17
BATH, BRISTOL, CAMBRIDGE, DURHAM, EDINBURGH, IMPERIAL COLLEGE LONDON, KING'S COLLEGE LONDON, LONDON SCHOOL OF ECONOMICS, OXFORD, TRINITY COLLEGE DUBLIN, UNIVERSITY COLLEGE DUBLIN, UNIVERSITY COLLEGE LONDON, WARWICK
Please check with your university careers service for full details of local events.

MINIMUM ENTRY REQUIREMENTS
2.1 Degree

APPLICATION DEADLINE
28th October 2016

FURTHER INFORMATION
www.Top100GraduateEmployers.com
Register now for the latest news, campus events, work experience and graduate vacancies at Bain & Company.

WORLD-CHANGERS WANTED.

We have a proud 40+ year track record of helping the world's most influential organizations solve their toughest challenges. Our success is simple — we hire immensely talented people and give them everything they could possibly need to be brilliant at what they do. Introduce yourself to us at **joinbain.com** — we'd love to chat with you.

BAIN & COMPANY

joinbain.com

Go –places–

Baker & McKenzie prides itself on being the global law firm that offers a personal and professional approach to its graduates and clients alike. It's this approach that ensures the firm is ideally placed to offer graduates the best possible start to their legal career.

Baker & McKenzie is a leading global law firm based in over 75 locations in nearly 50 countries and has a presence in all of the world's leading financial centres. The London office, which has been established for over 50 years, is the largest. From here over 400 legal professionals serve a wide and varied network of clients, both in the UK and across the globe.

The global nature of the firm means it offers a great deal of variety to its graduates. It works hard to combine its local legal expertise with the wider experience of its international offices, providing clients with a consistent service and legal professionals the opportunity to interact with colleagues from across the world.

In terms of its client base, Baker & McKenzie works principally with venture capital funds, investment banks, technology powerhouses and household name brands. Its international scope means the firm is well equipped to act on cross-border transactions and disputes. Baker & McKenzie in London provides the practices that one would expect from one of the world's leading law firms, and is the recognised market leader in many of these.

The firm thrives on new talent. So it makes a significant investment in its graduates' potential through tailored training and development. Those who enjoy an intellectual challenge, are problem solvers and team players with a personable approach will feel at home at this friendly and supportive firm. A career with Baker & McKenzie can really go places.

GRADUATE VACANCIES IN 2017
LAW

NUMBER OF VACANCIES
30 graduate jobs
For training contracts starting in 2019.

LOCATIONS OF VACANCIES

STARTING SALARY FOR 2017
£45,000

UNIVERSITY VISITS IN 2016-17
BELFAST, BRISTOL, CAMBRIDGE, DURHAM, EDINBURGH, EXETER, KING'S COLLEGE LONDON, LEEDS, LEICESTER, LONDON SCHOOL OF ECONOMICS, MANCHESTER, NOTTINGHAM, OXFORD, QUEEN MARY LONDON, SOUTHAMPTON, ST ANDREWS, UNIVERSITY COLLEGE LONDON, WARWICK, YORK
Please check with your university careers service for full details of local events.

MINIMUM ENTRY REQUIREMENTS
2.1 Degree

APPLICATION DEADLINE
Varies by function

FURTHER INFORMATION
www.Top100GraduateEmployers.com
Register now for the latest news, campus events, work experience and graduate vacancies at Baker & McKenzie.

Graduate careers
– in Law –

Training Contract

Vacation Scheme

International Vacation Scheme

First Year Programme

Open Days

At Baker & McKenzie, we pride ourselves on being a global law firm with a personal touch, and a friendly approach that will make your career really go places.

We're looking for the best and brightest talent to turn into the well-rounded commercial lawyers that make our Firm stand out from the crowd.

bakermckenzie.com/londongraduates

Journeys can begin anywhere. Yours begins at Baker & McKenzie.

BANK OF ENGLAND

The impact of the Bank of England's work is uniquely far-reaching. As the country's central bank, they promote the good of the people of the UK by maintaining monetary and financial stability. The work they do, and the decisions they make, influences the daily lives of millions of people.

The Bank's primary role hasn't changed for over 300 years. But the range of work they do, and the ways they deliver it, is changing all the time. It's changing quicker than ever before and graduates are a key part of this progress.

Wherever they work – from Economics, Regulation and Policy Analysis to Project Management, Technology and Communications – they'll take on complex work that they can be proud of. They'll be involved in projects that support, shape and challenge the biggest ideas in the economy. And the work graduates do will benefit every single person in the UK.

Despite the nature of the Bank's work, economics is not the only way in. They welcome graduates from all degree disciplines, because quality of thinking is what counts there. Their culture is open and collaborative, where ideas are shared freely and people at every level are empowered to speak up. It is refreshingly diverse too. The Bank looks for people from all backgrounds, and individual perspectives are embraced. Graduates will find a wide range of societies, clubs and employee networks open to them.

As training is at the heart of the Bank's programme, they'll be able to grow into real experts in their field. Equally, the support is there to explore other parts of the Bank if they wish. There are many and varied pathways available. For graduates keen to broaden their horizons, they'll have every opportunity to define their own future as the Bank itself moves forward.

GRADUATE VACANCIES IN 2017

CONSULTING
FINANCE
HUMAN RESOURCES
IT
RESEARCH & DEVELOPMENT

NUMBER OF VACANCIES
60+ graduate jobs

LOCATIONS OF VACANCIES

STARTING SALARY FOR 2017
£30,000

UNIVERSITY VISITS IN 2016-17
Please check with your university careers service for full details of local events.

MINIMUM ENTRY REQUIREMENTS
2.1 Degree

APPLICATION DEADLINE
Varies by function

FURTHER INFORMATION
www.Top100GraduateEmployers.com
*Register now for the latest news, campus events, work experience and graduate vacancies at the **Bank of England**.*

BANK OF ENGLAND

CHOOSE A PATH THAT FASCINATES YOU
THEN FOLLOW IT

We have one clear aim – to ensure stability at the heart of the UK's economy. But there are countless ways in which you could help us achieve this. From HR and Technology to Economics and Risk, you'll be encouraged and supported to follow the path that inspires you the most. And you'll enjoy real influence – not just over the projects you're involved in, but also over where your future with us goes next.

The Bank of England is changing today. **You define tomorrow.**

bankofenglandearlycareers.co.uk

GRADUATE VACANCIES IN 2017

FINANCE
GENERAL MANAGEMENT
HUMAN RESOURCES
INVESTMENT BANKING
IT
MARKETING
SALES

NUMBER OF VACANCIES
300+ graduate jobs

LOCATIONS OF VACANCIES

Vacancies also available in Europe, the USA, Asia and elsewhere in the world.

STARTING SALARY FOR 2017
£Competitive

UNIVERSITY VISITS IN 2016-17
Please check with your university careers service for full details of local events.

APPLICATION DEADLINE
Varies by function

FURTHER INFORMATION
www.Top100GraduateEmployers.com
Register now for the latest news, campus events, work experience and graduate vacancies at Barclays.

Healthy economies need strong banks to drive economic and social progress. Barclays' Shared Growth Ambition is simple. When their customers and clients thrive, so do they. When the communities they work in thrive, so do they. Interns and graduates at Barclays have the opportunity to contribute something vital. Something momentous.

With home markets in the UK and US, Barclays is a transatlantic consumer, corporate and investment bank offering products and services across personal, corporate and investment banking, credit cards and wealth management.

With over 325 years of expertise in banking, Barclays operates in over 40 countries, employing around 130,000 people to help move, lend, invest and protect money for customers and clients worldwide.

Barclays was the first bank to appoint a female bank manager, introduce ATMs, launch credit cards and contactless payment. From the products and services they develop to the partnerships they build, they seek to improve lives and drive growth that benefits everyone.

Those joining can expect immediate responsibility. Challenging work and collaborative projects will build their know-how, while ongoing training will build their momentum, providing the expertise that drives the banking profession.

Barclays offers a wealth of opportunities for students from all degree disciplines. All they need is a commercial outlook, relationship skills, and the initiative, integrity, and ambition to help Barclays evolve to become the best bank it can be.

It's time to start a career that fosters real development – for Barclays and for society. In a positive, supportive environment, graduates will find the momentum to achieve great things. The chance to be momentous.

Other companies promise the world. We'll give you the opportunity to change it.

In partnership with WildHearts, Barclays are proud to announce the Micro-Tyco competition. Open to all UK university students, we're looking for aspiring entrepreneurs with real momentum. Invest £1 and you'll have four weeks to generate as much money as you can, all for charity. And the prize? A portfolio internship – both with Barclays and other leading graduate employers.

Ready to be momentous?
Sign up at joinus.barclays.com/microtyco

GRADUATE VACANCIES IN 2017
ENGINEERING
GENERAL MANAGEMENT
IT
MEDIA
RESEARCH & DEVELOPMENT

NUMBER OF VACANCIES
35-40 graduate jobs

LOCATIONS OF VACANCIES

STARTING SALARY FOR 2017
£22,000+

UNIVERSITY VISITS IN 2016-17
ABERYSTWYTH, CARDIFF, LEEDS,
LIVERPOOL, OXFORD, YORK
*Please check with your university careers
service for full details of local events.*

MINIMUM ENTRY REQUIREMENTS
2.1 Degree

APPLICATION DEADLINE
Varies by function

FURTHER INFORMATION
www.Top100GraduateEmployers.com
*Register now for the latest news, campus
events, work experience and graduate
vacancies at the BBC.*

The BBC is the world's leading public service broadcaster. It is different from other broadcasters. It is funded by the licence fee and guided by a unique set of principles and values. Its mission is to enrich people's lives with programmes that inform, educate and entertain. People know it and are passionate about what it produces.

BBC graduate schemes are equally different and range from software engineering through to production and cyber security.

Software Engineering graduates have the unique chance to work on some of the nation's most innovative and popular digital products, including BBC News and Sport apps and of course BBC iPlayer, its pioneering on-demand service.

The work that Research & Development graduates are involved in is at the heart of the BBC's commitment to innovate, UX Design graduates gain unparalleled experience in user research, information architecture, content analysis, interaction design, visual design, prototyping and much more.

BBC Production graduates are taught the skills to turn creative ideas into brilliant programmes and of course work on some of the BBC's best loved programmes and channels, including EastEnders, Doctor Who and Radio 1, to name but a few.

And that's just a very small taste… no matter which scheme is chosen, BBC graduates can be certain of being part of something genuinely special – making things that are enjoyed by millions. Almost everyone in the UK spends time with BBC content each week and it feels great to be part of something that reaches so many people. BBC graduates also have amazing training and development opportunities, courtesy of its award-winning in-house training facility, and will work alongside top industry specialists.

Be part of something special. Join the BBC
Graduate Opportunities | UK Wide | £22,000 – £29,000 pa

The BBC is the world's leading public service broadcaster, known and loved internationally for its radio, television and online content.

Our aim is simple – to enrich people's lives with programmes and services that inform, educate and entertain by being the most creative organisation in the world.

Creativity is the lifeblood of our organisation. We're brave. We innovate and demonstrate creative ambition, trying new things and embracing new technology.

We're looking for the next generation of talent to keep the BBC at its very best with fresh ideas and different perspectives. The more diverse our workforce, the better able we are to respond to and reflect our audiences in all their diversity.

As a BBC graduate you will be making a difference, working on products and services that are enjoyed every day by millions of people. Our graduate schemes include software engineering, broadcast engineering, research & development, legal and production to name a few.

Be part of something special and join the BBC.

To find out more visit **www.bbc.co.uk/careers/trainee-schemes-and-apprenticeships**

The world's watching

www.bdograduaterecruitment.co.uk
Student.Recruitment@BDO.co.uk
twitter.com/BDO_Trainees_UK facebook.com/BDOTraineesUK

SHOW YOUR TRUE COLOURS

BDO are a leading accountancy and business advisory firm, aimed at mid-market businesses. They work with retail brands, manufacturing companies, growing technology and media companies, hotel and restaurant chains and many more, both in the UK and internationally.

BDO know how to make sure their people give their best. Quite simply, they let them. They hire those who show potential and then help them put it to work, turning business dreams into realities.

BDO is about exceptional client service. This means getting to know their clients well and understanding what they want to achieve. So the company chooses people who can rise to this challenge, who have colourful personalities as well as brilliant skills, and who can take the initiative and be creative.

If graduates want to work in a firm where they can make real progress, then BDO is the ideal size – combining nationwide presence with local expertise and a personal touch. They have 18 regional offices across the British Isles, and their international network is the world's fifth largest, with 1,400 offices in 154 countries.

BDO offer a whole spectrum of different services, and they'll encourage graduates to find their specialist area. Possible choices include Audit, Tax, Advisory and Financial Services. BDO are experts in a huge variety of other sectors too, with clients ranging from family businesses to multi-national companies, to public sector organisations and charities.

BDO gives graduates all the training they need to attain their professional qualifications, along with extensive practical experience that includes on-site client work. The firm also offers constant support to make sure graduates are never out of their depth. It all adds up to a colourful world of choice.

GRADUATE VACANCIES IN 2017
ACCOUNTANCY
FINANCE

NUMBER OF VACANCIES
250 graduate jobs

LOCATIONS OF VACANCIES

STARTING SALARY FOR 2017
£Competitive
Plus a range of core and voluntary benefits.

UNIVERSITY VISITS IN 2016-17
BELFAST, BIRMINGHAM, BRISTOL, CAMBRIDGE, CARDIFF, CITY, DURHAM, EDINBURGH, EXETER, GLASGOW, LEEDS, LEICESTER, LIVERPOOL, LONDON SCHOOL OF ECONOMICS, MANCHESTER, NEWCASTLE, NOTTINGHAM, NOTTINGHAM TRENT, OXFORD, SHEFFIELD, SOUTHAMPTON, UNIVERSITY COLLEGE LONDON, YORK
Please check with your university careers service for full details of local events.

MINIMUM ENTRY REQUIREMENTS
2.2 Degree

APPLICATION DEADLINE
Year-round recruitment
Early application advised.

FURTHER INFORMATION
www.Top100GraduateEmployers.com
Register now for the latest news, campus events, work experience and graduate vacancies at BDO.

SHOW YOUR
TRUE COLOURS

We're BDO. Welcome to our world.

It's a world where the only predictable thing is that today will be different. It's bright people turning professional solutions into an art form. It's a place to be yourself and give your best.

We give you all the training you need to attain your professional qualifications, along with extensive practical experience that includes on-site client work. And given the size of our firm, the rewards and benefits are of course highly competitive.

COLOURFUL CAREERS | COLOURFUL CHARACTERS

FIND OUT A SHADE MORE ABOUT BDO

f BDO-TraineesUK   🄴 @BDO_TraineesUK
www: bdo.co.uk/careers | e: student.recruitment@bdo.co.uk

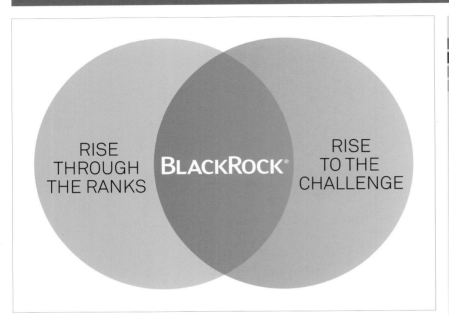

RISE THROUGH THE RANKS

BlackRock®

RISE TO THE CHALLENGE

BlackRock was founded 28 years ago by eight entrepreneurs who wanted to start a very different company. One that combined the best of a financial leader and a technology pioneer. One that focused on a singular purpose: making a difference in the lives of the parents and grandparents, the doctors and teachers who entrust them with their money – and their futures – every day.

Today, as the world's largest asset manager, with more than $4.9 trillion under management, BlackRock brings together financial leadership, worldwide reach and state-of-the-art technology to provide answers to the millions of investors who entrust their financial futures to the company.

The story of BlackRock's success rests not just with its founders, but with the thousands of talented people who have brought their ideas and energy to the firm every day since. That's why BlackRock always looks for fresh perspectives, new ideas and views its differences as strengths. It knows that its success depends on its ability to use collective experiences and ideas to achieve more for its clients and the business. BlackRock strongly believes that diverse skill sets and perspectives lead to more innovative solutions and better results.

BlackRock's programmes are an ideal opportunity for natural-born problem solvers, innovators and future leaders to work for a firm that has been called in by some of the world's largest companies and governments to find solutions for their most pressing financial challenges.

BlackRock is committed to harnessing every graduate's potential. The programme begins with an orientation in New York, followed by a structured curriculum of ongoing training designed to maximise business knowledge and individual effectiveness. The work is diverse with opportunities across Advisory & Strategy, Analytics & Risk, Client Businesses, Corporate, Investment and Technology.

MAKE A
LIVING

BLACKROCK®

MAKE A
DIFFERENCE

The world is more complex than ever before. And with the financial futures of millions in our hands, we're looking for the best and brightest talent – the future leaders that will help make a difference for our clients and the larger world around us. From Advisory and Client Support to Investment Management and Technology – no matter what you're looking to do, there are many exciting challenges waiting for you at BlackRock.

Meet our people and find out how you can make a difference at BlackRock at **blackrockoncampus.com**

BLACKROCK®
INVESTING FOR A NEW WORLD™

Bloomberg unleashes the power of information to inspire people who want to change the world. Well-established yet dynamic and disruptive at heart, Bloomberg is truly global, connecting influential decision-makers to a network of news, people and ideas.

It all starts with data. Anchored by the Bloomberg Professional® service (the Terminal), which offers real-time financial information to more than 325,000 subscribers globally, Bloomberg solves a variety of challenges for clients through an ever-expanding array of technology, data, news and media services that add value to information. Global Data provides the foundation for innovation as the company continues to evolve beyond traditional data analysis to provide clients with unique, meaningful and actionable information delivered through a variety of technologies and platforms.

The Enterprise Solutions business delivers the tools companies need to improve efficiency, minimise operational costs, comply with mounting regulations and achieve meaningful transparency. Bloomberg's approach helps clients not just access data, but capitalize on it in the most agile ways possible.

Bloomberg Media – digital, television, print, mobile and radio – is a critical input that reaches influential business decision makers around the world in over 150 bureaus across 73 countries. Through Bloomberg Government (BGOV), Bloomberg New Energy Finance (BNEF) and Bloomberg Bureau of National Affairs (BNA), Bloomberg provides data, news and analytics to decision makers in government, clean energy and legal markets.

Bloomberg takes care to foster a culture of community, and are dedicated to employees' well-being, offering generous benefits, training and opportunities for meaningful volunteerism.

GRADUATE VACANCIES IN 2017

ENGINEERING

FINANCE

IT

NUMBER OF VACANCIES
250+ graduate jobs

LOCATIONS OF VACANCIES

Vacancies also available in USA.

STARTING SALARY FOR 2017
£Competitive
Plus benefits and an annual bonus.

UNIVERSITY VISITS IN 2016-17
BRISTOL, CAMBRIDGE, CITY, EDINBURGH, IMPERIAL COLLEGE LONDON, KING'S COLLEGE LONDON, LONDON SCHOOL OF ECONOMICS, MANCHESTER, OXFORD, QUEEN MARY LONDON, SOUTHAMPTON, ST ANDREWS, UNIVERSITY COLLEGE LONDON, WARWICK
Please check with your university careers service for full details of local events.

APPLICATION DEADLINE
Year-round recruitment

FURTHER INFORMATION
www.Top100GraduateEmployers.com
Register now for the latest news, campus events, work experience and graduate vacancies at Bloomberg.

MY SKILLS ARE MOVING FORWARD, NOT STANDING STILL.

Make your mark.

The world's top investors,
traders and leaders depend
on our information and news.
We need your ideas and passion
to help us meet some of the
biggest challenges around.
How will you make your mark?

bloomberg.com/careers

Bloomberg

/company/bloomberg-lp/careers

 **Rolls-Royce** Motor Cars Limited

www.bmwgroup.jobs/uk
hr.services.recruitment@bmwgroup.co.uk
facebook.com/BmwCareersUK

The BMW Group, with its 31 production and assembly facilities in 14 countries as well as a global sales network, is the world's leading manufacturer of premium automobiles and motorcycles, and provider of premium financial and mobility services. Recent graduates looking to jump-start their career are sure to find exciting and fulfilling opportunities with them.

As a global leader in their field, BMW Group are always looking for passionate graduates who are interested in developing their business experience and strengthening their strategic and operational competencies. Their 24-month graduate programme, offered across a variety of disciplines, is a unique chance for graduates to strengthen their business profile through involvement in a range of projects and placements. Supervised by mentors and surrounded by fellow graduates, they'll gain valuable insights into business processes and strategy, as well as the opportunity to get to know BMW's culture and brand from the inside.

There are many paths to success. Why not consider BMW's Global Leader Development Programme (GLDP)? This talent development opportunity will equip successful applicants step-by-step with the skills they need to succeed. Supported by an experienced mentor, they'll be able to benefit from this structured programme in several ways: having the chance to work abroad, sharing know-how across borders, joining teams to tackle exciting and varied projects and building their own global network of contacts are only some of the programme's integral parts.

For graduates who share BMW Group's passion for future mobility solutions and would welcome the opportunity to take on new responsibilities, the 24-month graduate programme and GLDP will open doors. Graduates who are passionate about mobility solutions and enjoy taking on responsibility are in good company.

GRADUATE VACANCIES IN 2017
ENGINEERING
FINANCE
HUMAN RESOURCES
LOGISTICS
MARKETING
SALES

NUMBER OF VACANCIES
20-30 graduate jobs

LOCATIONS OF VACANCIES

STARTING SALARY FOR 2017
£31,000

UNIVERSITY VISITS IN 2016-17
ASTON, BATH, BIRMINGHAM, BRISTOL, LEEDS, LONDON SCHOOL OF ECONOMICS, LOUGHBOROUGH, NOTTINGHAM TRENT, OXFORD BROOKES, READING, SHEFFIELD, SURREY, SUSSEX
Please check with your university careers service for full details of local events.

MINIMUM ENTRY REQUIREMENTS
2.1 Degree

APPLICATION DEADLINE
Year-round recruitment
Early application advised.

FURTHER INFORMATION
www.Top100GraduateEmployers.com
Register now for the latest news, campus events, work experience and graduate vacancies at the BMW Group.

THOSE WHO DARE TO MAKE DECISIONS ARE IN GOOD COMPANY.

GET THE SKILLS TO SUCCEED – THE BMW GROUP UK GRADUATE PROGRAMME AND THE GLOBAL LEADER DEVELOPMENT PROGRAMME.

As a global leader in our field, we're constantly searching for motivated graduates to join us in shaping the future of the automotive industry. If you are prepared to take on responsibility, and enjoy working within innovative teams - then there are engaging assignments and valuable, individually-tailored development opportunities awaiting you with the BMW Group. Joining us as a graduate will help you to quickly build up your network, take full advantage of the numerous professional opportunities within the company and lay the foundation for a rewarding and successful long-term career.

There are many opportunities for recent graduates with us, such as our 24-month Graduate Programme or our Global Leader Development Programme.

Are you looking for an exciting challenge? Then join our team. We look forward to receiving your application. You can find detailed information and apply online at **www.bmwgroup.jobs/uk**

Interested in our opportunities?
Then go to **facebook.com/BmwCareersUK**

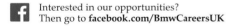

early careers

#boots360

Boots is the UK's leading health and beauty retailer, and it's on a mission to make the nation feel healthier and happier. It continues to evolve in the ever-changing world of retail, and is always on the lookout for potential future leaders to drive business performance with innovative, fresh new ideas.

Boots UK is part of a global enterprise, Walgreens Boots Alliance, which has a presence in over 25 countries. By joining the programme, graduates get to take a closer look inside the global health and wellbeing industry. Offering various graduate programmes, Boots is on the search for innovative minds and proactive go-getters to help grow the business.

On the Global Commercial Programme, graduates get to learn a wide range of commercial skills: understanding customer insights, trends and behaviours, sourcing products, interacting with customers, and trading in changing markets.

The Technology Programme gives graduates the opportunity to join the creative labs and help create new and innovative ways to operate the Boots retail business by using the latest technology.

Joining the Finance team, graduates are able to do much more than just financial accounting. They'll get to shape future finance planning, gain an industry-recognised qualification, and have the opportunity to do an international placement in their third year.

The Supply Chain and Operations graduates help make Boots UK one of the best retailers out there using the most efficient techniques to meet the exciting challenge of moving products around the UK and internationally.

All graduates at Boots can be sure of receiving all the support they need to develop their business knowledge, progress their career and see the bigger picture of retail with one of the nation's most trusted household names.

GRADUATE VACANCIES IN 2017

FINANCE
GENERAL MANAGEMENT
IT
LOGISTICS
MARKETING
RETAILING

NUMBER OF VACANCIES
40-60 graduate jobs

LOCATIONS OF VACANCIES

STARTING SALARY FOR 2017
£25,000
Plus a £1,000 welcome payment.

UNIVERSITY VISITS IN 2016-17
BIRMINGHAM, EXETER, LANCASTER, LEEDS,
LEICESTER, LIVERPOOL, LOUGHBOROUGH,
NEWCASTLE, NOTTINGHAM, NOTTINGHAM
TRENT, OXFORD, SHEFFIELD, WARWICK
Please check with your university careers service for full details of local events.

MINIMUM ENTRY REQUIREMENTS
2.1 Degree

APPLICATION DEADLINE
Varies by function

FURTHER INFORMATION
www.Top100GraduateEmployers.com
Register now for the latest news, campus events, work experience and graduate vacancies at Boots.

the bigger picture

whichever way you look at it
#boots360

feel good

BUILD. CONNECT. GROW.

BCG
THE BOSTON CONSULTING GROUP

The Boston Consulting Group (BCG) is a global management consulting firm with more than 12,000 employees, working in over 85 offices in 48 countries. BCG partners with clients in solving the hardest problems challenging their businesses – and the world.

BCG hires talented graduates from diverse academic backgrounds, including business, engineering, economics, science and the humanities. BCG seeks people with strong drive, relentless curiosity, the desire to create their own path, and the passion and leadership to make an impact. At the core of BCG's business is close collaboration – among employees at all levels and with the firm's clients. Challenged by mentors and supported by teams, employees at BCG join a diverse group of highly driven, exceptional individuals who respect and trust each other.

A career at BCG offers opportunities to work in many different fields and industries, learning how to navigate complexity, draw unique insights, facilitate change and become a leader responsible for real and lasting impact. Exposure to both breadth and depth of experiences enables employees to pursue any number of career paths.

With on-the-job experience combined with extensive training and mentorship programs, employees develop analytical, conceptual, and leadership skills, increasing their value at BCG and beyond. The opportunities for educational support, international mobility, social impact work, and connections to the organisation's vast alumni network help graduates find deep personal meaning as they develop a platform for future success. Become a part of BCG's heritage of game-changing ideas, business model innovation, and reshaping landscapes.

bp

www.bp.com/grads/uk

facebook.com/bpcareers
linkedin.com/company/bp [in]   twitter.com/bp_careers
youtube.com/BPplc   plus.google.com/+bp

BP develops and produces energy resources that benefit people across the world. Constantly pushing the boundaries of what's achievable, they rely on their vast team of talented individuals to come together and make it possible. Together, their future has no limits.

Geoscientists sending sound waves through the earth to find new oil and gas reserves. Engineers building platforms in the ocean for extraction. Traders anticipating and reacting to changes in the markets. BP take on graduates and interns at every stage of the energy life cycle. So whichever route a student or graduate chooses, they'll be starting a career path that can really take them places.

Whether applicants want to be a business leader, a world-class scientist or a ground-breaking engineer, BP have a programme to suit. For graduates, their 2-3 year 'Challenge' and supply and trading programmes will provide the skills and experience they need to succeed – whatever field they're in. For penultimate-year undergraduates and postgraduates, they offer paid internships that last for a full 12 months or for 11 weeks over the summer months – providing a chance to gain valuable insights into how BP works as a business.

It's possible to learn a lot as a BP graduate or intern. But most important of all, it's the start of a career path that can really take them places. At BP, it's about more than just academic achievements. Their approach is built on teamwork and respect, inclusion and ambition. It's this approach that enables them to deliver excellent energy safely. And it's these values that graduates will share.

To understand what life as a BP graduate or intern is really like, hear from the people who live it. Visit their careers site to get graduate perspectives on the things that matter. Or, to find the right role, use BP's online degree matcher tool – find it at bp.com/degreematcher.

GRADUATE VACANCIES IN 2017

ACCOUNTANCY
ENGINEERING
FINANCE
HUMAN RESOURCES
IT
LOGISTICS
PURCHASING
RESEARCH & DEVELOPMENT
RETAILING
SALES

NUMBER OF VACANCIES
100+ graduate jobs

LOCATIONS OF VACANCIES

STARTING SALARY FOR 2017
£33,000+
Plus £3,000 settling in allowance.

UNIVERSITY VISITS IN 2016-17
ABERDEEN, BATH, BIRMINGHAM, CAMBRIDGE, DURHAM, HERIOT-WATT, IMPERIAL COLLEGE LONDON, LONDON SCHOOL OF ECONOMICS, MANCHESTER, NOTTINGHAM, OXFORD, STRATHCLYDE, UNIVERSITY COLLEGE LONDON
Please check with your university careers service for full details of local events.

MINIMUM ENTRY REQUIREMENTS
2.1 Degree

APPLICATION DEADLINE
Varies by function

FURTHER INFORMATION
www.Top100GraduateEmployers.com
Register now for the latest news, campus events, work experience and graduate vacancies at BP.

"Taking on responsibility and owning projects is really exciting."

LeAnn's perspective on opportunity

Intern and graduate opportunities

From creating world-class products to developing secure, sustainable energy for the future, there's more to BP than you might think. As a graduate, you'll make a difference from day one, embarking on a real career with real responsibilities. So from business and trading, to engineering and science, whatever it is you're doing, you'll be playing your part in our success.

To find out more visit bp.com/grads/uk

bp

As part of International Airlines Group, British Airways is one of the world's leading global premium airlines and the largest international carrier in the UK. The carrier has its home base at London Heathrow, the world's busiest international airport, and flies to almost 200 destinations in over 75 countries.

This is a business worth getting to know. With over 40 million customers and a fleet of more than 280 aircraft, British Airways is a major player in global air travel. It is a complex and diverse organisation, but at its heart are its people. The airline's 40,000 employees work together in a wide variety of roles, drawn together from a surprisingly diverse range of disciplines. The opportunities for graduates can be varied, and the list of fascinating challenges is endless.

All British Airways employees play a key part of fulfilling a profound purpose, the promise British Airways makes to its customers – 'To Fly. To Serve.'

These words describe the passion and expertise that British Airways sets out to demonstrate every day, delivering a unique personalised service to its customers.

Any graduate joining British Airways can expect real jobs with real responsibilities. This takes ambition, resilience, and the drive to go above and beyond. There is a need to work smart, think innovatively and have the will to be the best. Graduates can expect to work across different business areas, be involved in key business decisions, and have opportunities to travel and work in different locations. Working on live projects with real impact, their placements see them making the most of their innovative thinking and problem-solving capabilities.

With a comprehensive induction and a structured development plan, British Airways graduates will have all the support and opportunities they need to develop and fulfil their potential.

Think you know us?

Adventure Dispensers

Graduate Opportunities

At British Airways, we bring together a wide variety of brilliant people in a range of fascinating roles. From people managers and business leaders, to researchers, consultants and engineers, this is a place where all kinds of careers take off. Join us and you'll immerse yourself in eye-opening and uniquely complex challenges, to help us achieve one unwavering goal – a premium, seamless customer experience from start to finish. You'll be surprised by where and how far your adventure with us could take you. So if you thought you knew everything we do, maybe you'd like to get to know us a little better?

Every day BT's people touch the lives of millions, providing services that help customers get the most out of their working and personal lives. That's a privilege and a responsibility. At BT, they use the power of communications to make a better world. Helping people, businesses and communities create possibilities.

BT is one of the world's leading providers of communications services and solutions, with customers in 180 countries. BT operates globally and delivers locally. BT's unique breadth of scope, reach and capability helps solve the most complex business communications requirements on a global scale. They're innovative in their thinking and dependable in their delivery.

Across the globe BT makes amazing things happen. They have a proven track record in inventions that change the world. But, ground-breaking innovations don't just happen – it takes drive, passion and a thirst for knowledge and solutions in every area of BT and some of the most amazing graduates.

Diversity is at the very heart of the company. In order to provide the very best products and services to a varied customer base they need a diverse workforce to imagine, create and deliver the solutions required both now and into the future. This means creating and maintaining a working environment that includes and values diversity.

BT's graduates are personable, straightforward and brilliant. BT looks for all of these qualities. And more. They look for people who don't wait to be told what to do, and who can't wait to get involved. BT's amazing graduate programme focusses on developing the future leaders. They will make sure successful applicants get all the training and development they need to become whatever they want to be. So join BT's ongoing quest to 'make amazing things happen'.

GRADUATE VACANCIES IN 2017

CONSULTING
ENGINEERING
GENERAL MANAGEMENT
HUMAN RESOURCES
IT
LAW
MARKETING
RESEARCH & DEVELOPMENT
SALES

NUMBER OF VACANCIES
250 graduate jobs

LOCATIONS OF VACANCIES

STARTING SALARY FOR 2017
£27,500-£31,500

UNIVERSITY VISITS IN 2016-17
BELFAST, BIRMINGHAM, CAMBRIDGE, DURHAM, MANCHESTER, NOTTINGHAM, OXFORD, SHEFFIELD, SOUTHAMPTON, UNIVERSITY COLLEGE LONDON, YORK
Please check with your university careers service for full details of local events.

MINIMUM ENTRY REQUIREMENTS
2.1 Degree
320 UCAS points

APPLICATION DEADLINE
Varies by function

FURTHER INFORMATION
www.Top100GraduateEmployers.com
Register now for the latest news, campus events, work experience and graduate vacancies at BT.

Make amazing things happen

Change the world

Life today is built on connectivity. As a global innovations company, we use the power of communications to make a better world.

From broadband and TV to mobile, we're driven by the exhilaration of building an ever-growing range of services that help our customers get more out of life. But there's so much more to BT than that. Our research and development teams help vehicle manufactures make smarter cars, let consultants treat patients remotely and provide secure finger print technology for festival goers.

Our history is all about shaping the future with ground breaking ideas. Today, we're proud to be the UK's number one tech sector investor in R&D, with 14,000 scientists and technologists leading innovation in BT. If you share our passion for putting customers at the heart of what we do, we'll invest in your future too.

So, join our relentless quest for innovation in one of the following areas:

Business Management, Customer First & Sales, Human Resources, Legal, Marketing, Networking Engineering, Research & Innovation, Security, Software Engineering.

Whichever programme you decide upon you could make amazing things happen. For more information and how to apply, visit:

www.btgraduates.com

CANCER RESEARCH UK

GRADUATE VACANCIES IN 2017

IT

MARKETING

RESEARCH & DEVELOPMENT

SALES

NUMBER OF VACANCIES
8 graduate jobs

LOCATIONS OF VACANCIES

STARTING SALARY FOR 2017
£25,000

UNIVERSITY VISITS IN 2016-17
ASTON, BATH, BIRMINGHAM, BRISTOL, BRUNEL, CARDIFF, CITY, DURHAM, EDINBURGH, EXETER, GLASGOW, IMPERIAL COLLEGE LONDON, KING'S COLLEGE LONDON, LEEDS, LEICESTER, LIVERPOOL, LONDON SCHOOL OF ECONOMICS, MANCHESTER, NEWCASTLE, NOTTINGHAM, QUEEN MARY LONDON, SHEFFIELD, SUSSEX, UNIVERSITY COLLEGE LONDON
Please check with your university careers service for full details of local events.

MINIMUM ENTRY REQUIREMENTS
2.1 Degree
Relevant degree required for some roles.

APPLICATION DEADLINE
October/November 2016

FURTHER INFORMATION
www.Top100GraduateEmployers.com
Register now for the latest news, campus events, work experience and graduate vacancies at Cancer Research UK.

Cancer. Be afraid. CRUK is a world-leading organisation funding science through exceptional fundraising efforts, raising £520m last year. Its ambition is to see three-quarters of people surviving within the next 20 years – focusing on prevention, early diagnosis, and development and personalising treatments to be more effective.

Graduates who join CRUK do something different, something extraordinary. They're changing lives. CRUK are looking for smart, sharp minded graduates to help achieve their goals. Its graduates are passionate in their work, determined, unafraid to challenge, stand out communicators and effective relationship builders.

What does a graduate scheme at an organisation like this offer? All graduates are put through their paces from the very beginning. Whether joining Fundraising & Marketing; Scientific Strategy and Funding; Technology; or Policy, Information and Communications streams, they will have the exciting opportunity to rotate across four diverse business areas over the course of two years.

Graduates receive support and challenge from senior mentors, peers and placement managers along their journey with formal training whilst transitioning between placements. Placements are varied, stretching and business critical. From day one they will be working on high profile projects with leaders across the organisation; drawing on and developing their individual strengths, talents and experience. CRUK invest in their talent, therefore all of their graduate placements are permanent roles.

As well as graduate opportunities, Cancer Research UK offers a vast array of entry level jobs for recent graduates and volunteering opportunities including award-winning twelve-week internships.

CRUK wants like minds, and the best minds, to help beat cancer sooner.

AMBITIOUS
SMART FAST-PACED
INSPIRING
DRIVING
CHANGE SHARP
UNITED
PIONEERING
VERSATILE CHALLENGING
LIFE-SAVING PERCEPTIONS

THIS IS HOW IT FEELS HELPING TO BEAT CANCER.
For your chance to experience it, go to cruk.org/graduates

"Working to create
life changing services
is immensely rewarding."

Sijuwade Salami, Fast Streamer

GRADUATE VACANCIES IN 2017
FINANCE
GENERAL MANAGEMENT
HUMAN RESOURCES
IT
MARKETING
PURCHASING
RESEARCH & DEVELOPMENT

NUMBER OF VACANCIES
900+ graduate jobs

LOCATIONS OF VACANCIES

Vacancies also available in Europe.

STARTING SALARY FOR 2017
£25,000-£27,000

UNIVERSITY VISITS IN 2016-17
Please check with your university careers
service for full details of local events.

MINIMUM ENTRY REQUIREMENTS
2.2 Degree

APPLICATION DEADLINE
End November 2016

FURTHER INFORMATION
www.Top100GraduateEmployers.com
Register now for the latest news, campus
events, work experience and graduate
vacancies at the **Civil Service Fast Stream**.

The Fast Stream is an unrivalled opportunity to lead changes that count and build a career that matters. At the heart of government, Fast Streamers work on some of the most vital and challenging issues facing Britain now and in the future. With a diversity of roles offering incredible professional development.

The Fast Stream is an accelerated learning and development programme for graduates with the motivation and the potential to become the future leaders of the Civil Service. Fast Streamers are given considerable responsibility from the outset: they are stretched and challenged on a daily basis, and they move regularly between posts to gain a wide range of contrasting experiences and build up an impressive portfolio of skills and knowledge.

Work ranges across professional areas including digital, communications, policy development, corporate services, people management, commercial awareness, financial management and project management, giving Fast Streamers a wide understanding of how government delivers public services.

Comprehensive training and development combined with on-the-job learning and support is provided. Successful applicants will receive an excellent package of benefits.

There's no such thing as a typical Fast Streamer, and graduates from widely diverse backgrounds are excited by the idea of making a positive and highly visible impact on the most important and exciting issues facing the country. Society is best served by a Civil Service which is as diverse as itself.

There are opportunities available across the UK in all areas of government, offering graduates a unique perspective of work at the heart of current affairs and key government agendas. There's no limit to where they could lead on the Civil Service Fast Stream. All degree disciplines are welcome.

'Where will you lead?'

Education. Health. Justice. Commercial. Human Resources. Defence. Transport. Climate change. International development. Foreign affairs. If the government has a policy on something, it is guaranteed that Fast Streamers are working at the heart of it, putting their brains and their skills at the disposal of the whole of society.

The Civil Service Fast Stream offers the kind of variety of roles and leadership training you simply can't have anywhere else. Choose from an exciting range of generalist and specialist streams with a programme that's ranked among the top five of The Times Top 100 Graduate Employers.

Learn more: www.gov.uk/faststream

Civil Service
Fast Stream

CREDIT SUISSE

the
future
at work

Credit Suisse is a leading global wealth manager with strong investment banking and asset management capabilities. Since its founding in 1856, Credit Suisse has expanded to be a global force, employing over 48,000 people in more than 50 countries.

With their new leadership, new strategy and streamlined global organisation, Credit Suisse are set for growth. They partner across businesses, divisions and regions to create innovative solutions to meet the needs of their clients – and to help their employees grow.

There is a distinct culture at Credit Suisse, with a core set of common values, based on a commitment to principled behavior, and a desire to stay close to its clients. They act as a trusted partner who proactively seeks solutions to its clients' needs and are committed to collaborating with their colleagues in a dynamic yet supportive environment.

Credit Suisse look for people with a wide range of experiences, interests and degrees who will add fresh perspectives to their business. They offer entry-level programs in a variety of business areas. The organisation's programs give graduates the chance to make a difference from day one, and provide world-class training and support to help them develop into future business leaders.

Whichever program successful candidates choose, they'll contribute to projects that have a significant impact on the business, while building their own expertise. At Credit Suisse it is a high priority to continually invest in its employees by providing ongoing opportunities for training, networking and mobility. A graduate career with Credit Suisse can help shape the future of the organisation.

GRADUATE VACANCIES IN 2017

INVESTMENT BANKING
IT
SALES

NUMBER OF VACANCIES
No fixed quota

LOCATIONS OF VACANCIES

Vacancies also available elsewhere in the world.

STARTING SALARY FOR 2017
£Competitive

UNIVERSITY VISITS IN 2016-17
CAMBRIDGE, IMPERIAL COLLEGE LONDON, KING'S COLLEGE LONDON, LONDON SCHOOL OF ECONOMICS, MANCHESTER, OXFORD, UNIVERSITY COLLEGE LONDON, WARWICK
Please check with your university careers service for full details of local events.

MINIMUM ENTRY REQUIREMENTS
2.1 Degree

APPLICATION DEADLINE
20th November 2016

FURTHER INFORMATION
www.Top100GraduateEmployers.com
Register now for the latest news, campus events, work experience and graduate vacancies at Credit Suisse.

CREDIT SUISSE

Calling all...
Idea Igniters
Industry Shapers
Market Leaders

We look for a wide range of interests, backgrounds and degrees. We look for future leaders.

To learn more about careers in financial services and how to apply visit:

credit-suisse.com/careers

the future at work

DANONE

> "I HAVE BUILT MY CAREER IN DANONE, DEVELOPING FROM A RAW GRADUATE TO LEADING A TEAM ON THE OTHER SIDE OF THE WORLD"

PAUL TILSDALE
HEAD OF MODERN TRADE, DANONE ELN MALAYSIA

For over 100 years, a unique purpose to 'bring health through food and beverages to as many people as possible', has inspired world leading brands such as Evian, Activia, Cow&Gate and Nutricia. Today, this purpose unites 100,000 Danone employees behind products that reach nine million consumers worldwide.

The UK Danone graduate scheme is designed for motivated individuals who are passionate about Danone's mission and values. In return, Danone provides them with the essential skills and behaviours needed to grow into committed and inspirational leaders.

Although a global business, Danone has a non-hierarchical structure that ensures every employee is equally valued, respected and empowered to make a difference. For graduates, that means they are placed in influential roles, with independence and autonomy, gaining extensive experience to support their personal progression. Graduates will be at the cutting edge of the business, playing a key role from the start.

Individual growth and development are an integral part of the company's DNA. A graduate's learning journey is completely personalised, based on their career aspirations and developmental targets. Along the way, they are fully supported by an internal coach and a network of key individuals who are committed to helping them achieve their goals.

Danone was built on the pioneering spirit of its founders. It's their spirit that underpins the core values of the entire organisation and their legacy is the development of a business that began and remains at the forefront of innovation. In its graduates, Danone is looking for new and exciting visionaries to continue this legacy and to contribute to a healthier world.

GRADUATE VACANCIES IN 2017
FINANCE
HUMAN RESOURCES
LOGISTICS
MARKETING
SALES

NUMBER OF VACANCIES
25-30 graduate jobs

LOCATIONS OF VACANCIES

STARTING SALARY FOR 2017
£28,500
Plus a 5-10% bonus and flexible benefits.

UNIVERSITY VISITS IN 2016-17
ASTON, BATH, BIRMINGHAM, BRISTOL, DURHAM, EXETER, KING'S COLLEGE LONDON, LANCASTER, LOUGHBOROUGH, MANCHESTER, NOTTINGHAM
Please check with your university careers service for full details of local events.

MINIMUM ENTRY REQUIREMENTS
2.1 Degree
Relevant degree required for some roles.

APPLICATION DEADLINE
31st October 2016

FURTHER INFORMATION
www.Top100GraduateEmployers.com
Register now for the latest news, campus events, work experience and graduate vacancies at Danone.

THERE'S MORE TO DANONE THAN YOU THINK

We bring health through food to as many people as possible... Find out how you can make a difference and be part of it all.

Deloitte.

The business and technology landscape is, every year, more ambiguous and disruptive. Solving the problems of today takes more creativity and empathy than ever before. It also requires a broader set of skills and different ways of thinking; the ability to find simple answers to complex questions.

For the influencers, the challengers, the explorers – for those who are true thinkers – they'll find Deloitte is a business that doesn't just recognise the need for diversity, but fully embraces it. A firm of problem solvers, Deloitte's hunger for smarter solutions lies at the heart of all they do. At Deloitte, it's the mind-set that shapes the role, not vice versa. It's this attitude, shared by everyone who works there, that is helping to shape a better world.

Covering the entire professional spectrum, there are opportunities in all areas candidates would expect, and in those they wouldn't, like Management Consulting & Technology. All paths offer the chance to work with the best minds in the industry, guidance from inspirational and supportive senior managers, and every opportunity to grow and progress.

Often described as the firm's greatest assets, Deloitte's people think boldly, act commercially, and make decisions based on the impact they'll have for clients, colleagues and the communities they live in. Which means they're looking for both a sharp mind and a generous spirit, true open-mindedness along with unshakable integrity. Deloitte commits to those who possess these qualities. Every year, they invest more in learning and development. Agile working is a way of life. People are deeply respected for their individuality. Ownership is highly rewarded. Leadership is visible at every level. And, with offices recruiting across the UK, each with a global, multi-industry portfolio of clients, there are plenty of reasons why Deloitte really is, for the curious.

GRADUATE VACANCIES IN 2017

ACCOUNTANCY
CONSULTING
FINANCE
IT
PROPERTY

NUMBER OF VACANCIES
1,200 graduate jobs

LOCATIONS OF VACANCIES

STARTING SALARY FOR 2017
£Competitive
Plus 25 days holiday, pension, life assurance, accident insurance and mobile phone.

UNIVERSITY VISITS IN 2016-17
ABERDEEN, ASTON, BATH, BIRMINGHAM, BRISTOL, BRUNEL, CAMBRIDGE, CARDIFF, CITY, DURHAM, EAST ANGLIA, EDINBURGH, EXETER, GLASGOW, IMPERIAL COLLEGE LONDON, KING'S COLLEGE LONDON, LANCASTER, LEEDS, LEICESTER, LIVERPOOL, LONDON SCHOOL OF ECONOMICS, LOUGHBOROUGH, MANCHESTER, NEWCASTLE, NOTTINGHAM, NOTTINGHAM TRENT, OXFORD, OXFORD BROOKES, QUEEN MARY LONDON, READING, SHEFFIELD, SOUTHAMPTON, ST ANDREWS, STRATHCLYDE, SURREY, ULSTER, UNIVERSITY COLLEGE LONDON, WARWICK, YORK
Please check with your university careers service for full details of local events.

MINIMUM ENTRY REQUIREMENTS
2.1 Degree
280-360 UCAS points

APPLICATION DEADLINE
Year-round recruitment
Early application advised.

FURTHER INFORMATION
www.Top100GraduateEmployers.com
Register now for the latest news, campus events, work experience and graduate vacancies at Deloitte.

Deloitte.

This is for the **thinkers.** The problem solvers. The **challengers.** Those who question the now. And want to influence the new. This is for the **caring.** The **explorers.** The **visionaries.** The ones who see simplicity in complexity. And **bright** solutions in **big** ideas. This is for the **imaginative.** The **bold** ones. The brave ones. The **inspired** ones. The ones who ask themselves and others... What **impact** will **you** make ?

For the curious.

careers.deloitte.com

DIAGEO

Diageo is the world's leading premium drinks company. Their roots are found in entrepreneurs, philanthropists and people of extraordinary character; Guinness®, Smirnoff®, Johnnie Walker® and Tanqueray® and hundreds more iconic brands are part of their organisation full of heritage and passion.

With a company purpose to celebrate life every day, everywhere; Diageo are passionate about their customers and consumers. They are proud of what they do. At Diageo, they believe that everyone should have the opportunity to learn and grow at work. Their award-winning Global Graduate Programme is designed to challenge and inspire graduates to reach their full potential.

The programme accelerates functional and leadership skills, across a global platform. Not only do graduates make a real contribution to the business, but they will also be able to dip into a global network to enhance their career journey both now and in the future.

Diageo find the broader the experience, the better equipped graduates are to face challenges. Throughout the three-year programme, graduates are placed in a variety of roles that will give them the breadth of skills and knowledge to become the next leaders across the business.

In Marketing, Sales, HR, Supply or Finance, graduates will experience an environment where they can be themselves, be open, collaborative, deliver their best ideas and build a personal legacy.

While on the programme graduates get access to a formal development curriculum. They experience different parts of the business, support local CSR projects, sign up to an International Buddy Scheme and connect to mentors across the world. Diageo will support every step of the way, but a natural drive and enthusiasm will ensure the most is made of all the opportunities available.

GRADUATE VACANCIES IN 2017

ENGINEERING
FINANCE
HUMAN RESOURCES
LOGISTICS
MARKETING
SALES

NUMBER OF VACANCIES
50+ graduate jobs

LOCATIONS OF VACANCIES

Vacancies also available in Europe.

STARTING SALARY FOR 2017
£Competitive
Plus an impressive reward package.

UNIVERSITY VISITS IN 2016-17
ASTON, BATH, BELFAST, BIRMINGHAM, BRISTOL, BRUNEL, EDINBURGH, EXETER, GLASGOW, HERIOT-WATT, LEICESTER, LONDON SCHOOL OF ECONOMICS, LOUGHBOROUGH, MANCHESTER, NOTTINGHAM, SHEFFIELD, ST ANDREWS, STRATHCLYDE, TRINITY COLLEGE DUBLIN, UNIVERSITY COLLEGE DUBLIN, UNIVERSITY COLLEGE LONDON, WARWICK
Please check with your university careers service for full details of local events.

MINIMUM ENTRY REQUIREMENTS
2.1 Degree

APPLICATION DEADLINE
Varies by function

FURTHER INFORMATION
www.Top100GraduateEmployers.com
Register now for the latest news, campus events, work experience and graduate vacancies at Diageo.

DLA PIPER

www.dlapipergraduates.co.uk

facebook.com/dlapiperukgraduates   recruitment_graduate@dlapiper.com

linkedin.com/company/dla-piper-uk-graduates   twitter.com/DLA_Piper_Grads

GRADUATE VACANCIES IN 2017
LAW

NUMBER OF VACANCIES
75-80 graduate jobs
For training contracts starting in 2019.

LOCATIONS OF VACANCIES

STARTING SALARY FOR 2017
£24,000-£42,000

UNIVERSITY VISITS IN 2016-17
ABERDEEN, BIRMINGHAM, BRISTOL, CAMBRIDGE, CITY, DUNDEE, DURHAM, EDINBURGH, EXETER, GLASGOW, KING'S COLLEGE LONDON, LANCASTER, LEEDS, LIVERPOOL, LONDON SCHOOL OF ECONOMICS, MANCHESTER, NEWCASTLE, NOTTINGHAM, OXFORD, QUEEN MARY LONDON, SHEFFIELD, ST ANDREWS, STRATHCLYDE, UNIVERSITY COLLEGE LONDON, WARWICK, YORK
Please check with your university careers service for full details of local events.

MINIMUM ENTRY REQUIREMENTS
2.1 Degree

APPLICATION DEADLINE
28th July 2017

FURTHER INFORMATION
www.Top100GraduateEmployers.com
Register now for the latest news, campus events, work experience and graduate vacancies at DLA Piper.

DLA Piper is a global law firm with lawyers located in more than 30 countries throughout the Americas, Asia Pacific, Europe and the Middle East, positioning the firm to help companies with their legal needs anywhere in the world. In the UK, it provides legal advice from London and the other major centres.

Unlike many law firms, DLA Piper is organised to provide clients with a range of essential business advice, not just on large scale mergers and acquisitions and banking deals but also on people and employment, commercial dealings, litigation, insurance, real estate, IT, intellectual property, plans for restructuring and tax. It has a comprehensive, award winning client relationship management programme and the brand is built upon local legal excellence and global capability.

DLA Piper looks for opportunities to use its strength as a leading business law firm to make a positive contribution in their local and global communities. The firm's Corporate Responsibility initiatives demonstrate how their values are embedded in the way the firm engages with its people, its clients and its communities.

Within its trainee cohort the firm needs a diverse group of highly talented individuals who have a consistently strong academic performance, formidable commercial acumen, who are articulate, ambitious and driven with sharp minds, enthusiasm and intellectual curiosity. In return, DLA Piper offers a dynamic and diverse environment in which people can build a long and fruitful career and have their success rewarded.

Trainees complete four six-month seats and are given an opportunity to express what areas of law they would like to experience during their training contracts. They have the opportunity to do a seat abroad, or a client secondment.

BIGGER

OPPORTUNITIES

· ·

DLA Piper offers big opportunities to ambitious graduates – big firm, big clients, big careers.

Don't just take our word for it. Find out more at
www.dlapipergraduates.co.uk

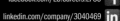

GRADUATE VACANCIES IN 2017
FINANCE
GENERAL MANAGEMENT
HUMAN RESOURCES
IT
LAW
MARKETING
MEDIA
RESEARCH & DEVELOPMENT

NUMBER OF VACANCIES
No fixed quota

LOCATIONS OF VACANCIES

Vacancies available in Europe.

STARTING SALARY FOR 2017
£41,500+

UNIVERSITY VISITS IN 2016-17
Please check with your university careers service for full details of local events.

APPLICATION DEADLINE
Varies by function

FURTHER INFORMATION
www.Top100GraduateEmployers.com
Register now for the latest news, campus events, work experience and graduate vacancies at the European Commission.

Looking for a challenging career in a dynamic environment? Based in the heart of Europe, the EU Institutions offer a truly international career to ambitious and capable graduates. Serving 500 million citizens, a range of options are available, all with the chance to make a real and lasting difference.

For final-year students and graduates, entry-level positions are available in various fields, from law to economics or languages, as well as more general policy or project management roles. New recruits could be drafting legislation, helping to implement EU law, developing communication strategies, or managing projects and resources.

Most positions are based either in Brussels or Luxembourg, with around 20% of staff based in offices throughout the world. Applying for an EU Career could in practice mean working for the European Commission, Council of the EU, European Parliament, European External Action Service, European Court of Justice, European Court of Auditors, as well as other EU bodies and agencies or any of the other main EU Institutions or Agencies.

Interested applicants will need to prove their strong analytical, organisational and communication skills, a drive to deliver the best possible results, the ability to work effectively as part of a multi-cultural team, and a potential for leadership and personal development.

Candidates are selected through a process of open competition, which generally consists of a first round of computer-based tests in centres throughout the EU, followed by an assessment centre in Brussels or Luxembourg for the best performers. The main graduate recruitment cycle normally opens in the spring, but all of the EU Institutions offer paid graduate traineeships throughout the year – a great way to gain a first taste of a future EU career.

FACE A BIGGER CHALLENGE

"What I really love about my job is that I'm working right at the heart of international politics and at the top of the news agenda. One day I might be live tweeting from a European Council summit or the G7, and the next working on the Council's long-term social media strategy or advising upcoming Council presidencies on their social media activities.

"I get to travel a lot, speak different languages, and meet new people from all over the world. But what I really appreciate is how the EU institutions invest in their staff, and the opportunities to build my career through new skills and experiences."

Alexandra coordinates social media for the Council of the European Union. She studied History.

eu
careers

eu-careers.eu

ExxonMobil

ExxonMobil.com/UKRecruitment

twitter.com/ExxonMobil_UK   UK.Campus.Recruitment@ExxonMobil.com

youtube.com/ExxonMobil   linkedin.com/company/exxonmobil

Global fundamentals

Consider how modern energy enriches your life. Now consider the 7 billion other people on earth who also use energy each day to make their own lives richer, more productive, safer and healthier. Then you will recognize what is perhaps the biggest driver of energy demand: the human desire to sustain and improve the well-being of ourselves, our families and our communities. Through 2040, population and economic growth will drive demand higher, but the world will use energy more efficiently and shift toward lower-carbon fuels.

25%

The world's population will rise by more than 25 percent from 2010 to 2040, reaching nearly 9 billion people. Population and economic growth are key factors behind increasing demand for energy.

 Imagine working for the world's largest publicly traded oil and gas company, on tasks that affect nearly everyone in the world today and for future generations to come. ExxonMobil in the UK is better known for its Esso and Mobil brands due to the success of its service stations and high performance lubricants.

ExxonMobil offers challenging long-term careers to high performing graduates, as well as summer and year placements with real responsibility!

There's no such thing as an average day at ExxonMobil and there are many different career paths available from a technical career to a leadership position to a commercial role. For graduates who are looking for a long-term career that will be challenging, rewarding and certainly varied, then a career with ExxonMobil might just be for them.

What are ExxonMobil looking for? For the technical schemes, applications are welcomed from Chemical, Electrical and Mechanical Engineers with a 2:1 minimum. For the commercial schemes, applications from a number of disciplines including Science/Engineering/IT/Business degrees with a 2:1 minimum are accepted.

In addition to the competitive base salary and relocation allowance, employees are also offered a matched 2-for-1 share scheme, final salary pension plan, private health care scheme, 33 days holiday per annum (including public holidays), interest-free loan, tailored graduate training and continuous development, support towards studying for professional qualifications such as CIMA and IChemE, free sports facilities and subsidised dining facilities at most locations, voluntary community activities, international opportunities and regular job rotations (typically every one to three years) with opportunities to develop and hone skills.

GRADUATE VACANCIES IN 2017

ENGINEERING
HUMAN RESOURCES
IT
MARKETING
SALES

NUMBER OF VACANCIES
No fixed quota

LOCATIONS OF VACANCIES

STARTING SALARY FOR 2017
£37,500+
Plus a relocation allowance.

UNIVERSITY VISITS IN 2016-17
BATH, BIRMINGHAM, CAMBRIDGE, EDINBURGH, IMPERIAL COLLEGE LONDON, LOUGHBOROUGH, MANCHESTER, NEWCASTLE, NOTTINGHAM, STRATHCLYDE, UNIVERSITY COLLEGE LONDON
Please check with your university careers service for full details of local events.

MINIMUM ENTRY REQUIREMENTS
2.1 Degree
Relevant degree required for some roles.

APPLICATION DEADLINE
Varies by function

FURTHER INFORMATION
www.Top100GraduateEmployers.com
Register now for the latest news, campus events, work experience and graduate vacancies at ExxonMobil.

ukcareers.ey.com/graduates

facebook.com/EYUKcareers
linkedin.com/company/ernstandyoung twitter.com/EY_StudentsUK
instagram.com/eyukcareers youtube.com/user/EYUKCareers

Banking or biotech?

Office-based or remote worker?

Analysis or action?

Exams or experiences?

Science or Law?

Qualifications or qualities?

Strategy or execution?

London or Leeds?

EY is a global professional services organisation. By asking better questions, they provide their clients with better answers, helping them solve complex business issues. For smart, curious graduates, working at EY offers the opportunity to change how world-leading organisations do business.

EY depends on high performing teams of people from a huge range of cultures and backgrounds to help clients make better decisions and find better solutions. They operate across four service lines: Assurance, Consulting, Tax and Transactions.

The firm drives itself and its clients forward with technological innovation and disruptive thinking. Graduates who thrive on change and challenge will be in their element here. With 212,000 people in more than 150 countries, and an unrivalled breadth of opportunities, along with a vision to double revenues by 2020, at EY, graduates can shape their career their way.

EY supports graduates at every stage of their studies and career thinking, helping them understand their own qualities to make the right choice about their future in business. As well as hosting on-campus sessions, they publish a wealth of useful content containing advice on career decision-making, employability and up-skilling.

EY recruits graduates on the basis of their strengths and potential, not just their academic backgrounds. Exceptional training and development makes the most of these strengths, and a team-based business culture gives people the support they need to thrive from the moment they join the organisation.

For graduates who see the change the world needs and are smart enough to be part of it, EY is a great place to build the career they want, and make their own contribution to EY's purpose of building a better working world.

GRADUATE VACANCIES IN 2017
ACCOUNTANCY
CONSULTING
FINANCE
IT

NUMBER OF VACANCIES
900 graduate jobs

LOCATIONS OF VACANCIES

STARTING SALARY FOR 2017
£Competitive

UNIVERSITY VISITS IN 2016-17
ABERDEEN, ASTON, BATH, BIRMINGHAM, BRISTOL, CAMBRIDGE, CARDIFF, CITY, DURHAM, EAST ANGLIA, EDINBURGH, EXETER, GLASGOW, HERIOT-WATT, HULL, IMPERIAL COLLEGE LONDON, KING'S COLLEGE LONDON, KENT, LANCASTER, LEEDS, LEICESTER, LIVERPOOL, LONDON SCHOOL OF ECONOMICS, LOUGHBOROUGH, MANCHESTER, NEWCASTLE, NORTHUMBRIA, NOTTINGHAM, NOTTINGHAM TRENT, OXFORD, OXFORD BROOKES, QUEEN MARY LONDON, READING, SHEFFIELD, SOUTHAMPTON, ST ANDREWS, STRATHCLYDE, ULSTER, UNIVERSITY COLLEGE LONDON, WARWICK, YORK
Please check with your university careers service for full details of local events.

APPLICATION DEADLINE
Year-round recruitment

FURTHER INFORMATION
www.Top100GraduateEmployers.com
Register now for the latest news, campus events, work experience and graduate vacancies at EY.

As a start-up where do you want to end up?
Build the career you want at EY and change business for the better.
Start today. Change tomorrow.
ukcareers.ey.com/graduates
The better the question. The better the answer. The better the world works.

FRONTLINE
CHANGING LIVES

www.thefrontline.org.uk

recruitment@thefrontline.org.uk ✉

twitter.com/FrontlineSW 🐦   facebook.com/FrontlineChangingLives **f**

youtube.com/FrontlineSW ▶️   linkedin.com/company/frontline-org **in**

There are lots of graduate programmes out there. Most of them involve nice, comfortable office jobs. Frontline is different. The programme represents the only career where graduates can work with all agents across the breadth of a child's life. Participants work with children, families, schools and the police to change lives.

Changing lives isn't easy. Being a social worker takes resolve, dedication and qualities graduates didn't even know they had. Most people would probably run in the opposite direction. But for graduates who dare to change; who want one of Britain's most challenging jobs, then Frontline is for them.

Frontline's two-year leadership programme is a unique opportunity for exceptional individuals to join one of Britain's toughest and most rewarding professions – child protection social work. Taking an innovative approach to social work, participants will work in child protection teams in Greater London, Greater Manchester, the South East of England, the North East and the West Midlands.

The programme begins with a five-week summer residential where a team of world-leading academics and individuals with care experience deliver master classes in social work practice. In September, participants join a local authority and start their first year, learning 'on-the-job' while receiving ongoing academic tuition. Upon qualification, the second year consists of 12 months guaranteed employment as a children's social worker and the opportunity to study towards a fully funded Masters qualification.

Frontline is committed to developing leadership skills amongst participants so they can drive positive change both in social work and in broader society, whatever their future career path.

Frontline welcomes applicants with a range of experiences from any discipline.

GRADUATE VACANCIES IN 2017
GENERAL MANAGEMENT
HUMAN RESOURCES
LAW

NUMBER OF VACANCIES
300 graduate jobs

LOCATIONS OF VACANCIES

STARTING SALARY FOR 2017
£Competitive

UNIVERSITY VISITS IN 2016-17
ASTON, BATH, BIRMINGHAM, BRISTOL, BRUNEL, CAMBRIDGE, CARDIFF, DURHAM, EAST ANGLIA, EDINBURGH, ESSEX, EXETER, GLASGOW, IMPERIAL COLLEGE LONDON, KEELE, KING'S COLLEGE LONDON, KENT, LANCASTER, LEEDS, LEICESTER, LIVERPOOL, LONDON SCHOOL OF ECONOMICS, LOUGHBOROUGH, MANCHESTER, NEWCASTLE, NORTHUMBRIA, NOTTINGHAM, OXFORD, QUEEN MARY LONDON, READING, SHEFFIELD, SOUTHAMPTON, ST ANDREWS, STRATHCLYDE, SURREY, SUSSEX, UNIVERSITY COLLEGE LONDON, WARWICK, YORK
Please check with your university careers service for full details of local events.

MINIMUM ENTRY REQUIREMENTS
2.1 Degree

APPLICATION DEADLINE
November 2016

FURTHER INFORMATION
www.Top100GraduateEmployers.com
Register now for the latest news, campus events, work experience and graduate vacancies at Frontline.

BRAVE ENOUGH TO DO SOMETHING DIFFERENT?

MAKE REAL CHANGE FOR CHILDREN AND FAMILIES.

FRONTLINE
CHANGING LIVES

Frontline is an initiative designed to recruit outstanding individuals to be leaders in social work and broader society. Successful applicants will take part in an intensive and innovative two year leadership programme and gain a master's degree. But most importantly, they'll be working to transform the lives of vulnerable children and young people.
www.thefrontline.org.uk

 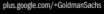

GRADUATE VACANCIES IN 2017

ACCOUNTANCY
FINANCE
HUMAN RESOURCES
INVESTMENT BANKING
IT
LAW

NUMBER OF VACANCIES
Around 300 graduate jobs

LOCATIONS OF VACANCIES

Vacancies also available in Europe.

Goldman Sachs is a leading global investment banking, securities and investment management firm that provides a wide range of financial services to a substantial and diversified client base, including corporations, financial institutions, governments and individuals.

At Goldman Sachs, graduates have many opportunities to make an impact. The unique perspectives that its people bring to the firm and their shared passion for working on projects of great global, economic and social significance, help drive progress and create results.

Goldman Sachs is structured in a series of divisions: Executive Office, Finance, Global Compliance, Global Investment Research, GS Bank, Human Capital Management, Internal Audit, Investment Banking, Investment Management, Legal, Merchant Banking, Operations, Realty Management, Securities, Services and Technology.

From the very first day, graduates will be immersed in a collaborative environment with people of all levels who share the firm's values. Nearly everyone – from junior analysts to the most senior leaders – is actively involved in recruiting talented people from a variety of backgrounds, because Goldman Sachs recognises that a diverse workforce enables the bank to serve its clients most effectively and in the most innovative ways.

The diversity of talents and educational backgrounds in Goldman Sachs's people is crucial to its performance and business success. To that end, the firm is committed to an environment that values diversity, promotes inclusion and encourages teamwork. Whatever the background or area of academic study, Goldman Sachs values the intellect, personality and integrity of an individual. While an interest in and appreciation for finance is important, one's personal qualities are key.

STARTING SALARY FOR 2017
£Competitive

UNIVERSITY VISITS IN 2016-17
Please check with your university careers service for full details of local events.

APPLICATION DEADLINE
Please see website for full details.

FURTHER INFORMATION
www.Top100GraduateEmployers.com
*Register now for the latest news, campus events, work experience and graduate vacancies at **Goldman Sachs**.*

Goldman Sachs

HOW WILL YOU
MAKE AN IMPACT

CONTRIBUTE, COLLABORATE AND SUCCEED WITH A CAREER AT GOLDMAN SACHS

If you're the kind of person who can't wait to make a difference, consider a career at Goldman Sachs. We believe that good ideas and innovations can come from anyone, at any level. We offer meaningful opportunities, best-in-class training and a wide variety of career paths for talented people from all academic backgrounds. Plus, with access to important clients and projects, you'll have the chance to make an impact with global significance.

APPLICATION DEADLINES

NEW ANALYST: 30 October 2016
SUMMER ANALYST: 4 December 2016
SPRING PROGRAMME: 4 January 2017
WORK PLACEMENT PROGRAMME: 4 January 2017

Submit your application at
goldmansachs.com/careers

Goldman Sachs Careers
DOWNLOAD OUR APP to learn more about how you can make an impact.

goldmansachs.com/careers
 @GSCareers

www.google.com/careers/students

plus.google.com/+GoogleStudents G+
twitter.com/googlestudents facebook.com/GoogleStudents f
youtube.com/GoogleStudents linkedin.com/company/google/careers in

Google

Founders Larry Page and Sergey Brin met at Stanford University in 1995. By 1996, they had built a search engine that used links to determine the importance of individual web pages. Today, Google is a tech company that helps businesses of all kinds succeed on and off the web.

It's really the people that make Google the kind of company it is. Google hire people who are smart and determined, and favour ability over experience.

University graduates joining Google will enter either the Small-to-Medium Business (SMB) Sales or Global Customer Experience teams. As small business experts, Googlers in SMB help to get local entrepreneurs on the map, and deliver a beautifully simple, intuitive experience that enables customers to grow their businesses. By spotting and analysing customer needs and trends, Google's innovative teams of strategists, account developers and customer experience specialists work together on scalable solutions for each business, no matter its age or size.

Google hires graduates from all disciplines, from humanities and business related courses to engineering and computer science. The ideal candidate is someone who can demonstrate a passion for the online industry and someone who has made the most of their time at university through involvement in clubs, societies or relevant internships. Google hires graduates who have a variety of strengths and passions, not just isolated skill sets. For technical roles within engineering teams, specific skills will be required.

The Google Business Associate Programme is a two-year developmental programme that supplements a Googler's core role in SMB. It offers world-class training, equipping new joiners with the business, analytical and leadership skills needed to be successful at Google.

GRADUATE VACANCIES IN 2017
CONSULTING
ENGINEERING
HUMAN RESOURCES
IT
MARKETING
MEDIA
SALES

NUMBER OF VACANCIES
No fixed quota

LOCATIONS OF VACANCIES

Vacancies also available in Europe and the USA.

STARTING SALARY FOR 2017
£Competitive
Plus world-renowned perks and benefits.

UNIVERSITY VISITS IN 2016-17
Please check with your university careers service for full details of local events.

MINIMUM ENTRY REQUIREMENTS
2.1 Degree

APPLICATION DEADLINE
Year-round recruitment

FURTHER INFORMATION
www.Top100GraduateEmployers.com
Register now for the latest news, campus events, work experience and graduate vacancies at Google.

Google

www.google.com/careers/students

How to sum up a complex and exciting business like Grant Thornton? Simply put, they're part of a global organisation providing business and financial advice to dynamic organisations right at the heart of growth. In the UK alone, they deliver solutions to 40,000 clients in over 100 countries.

Grant Thornton are a shared enterprise – meaning their people share ideas, share responsibility and share reward. It's never been a more exciting time to be a part of a firm that are passionate about their higher purpose – unlocking growth for clients and driving a vibrant economy. Business and the way we do it is changing, Grant Thornton are at the start of an exciting journey and they recognise the need for agility and collaboration in today's environment. They're starting from within – all 4,500 people thinking and behaving according to their shared mindset for growth.

Over 400 ambitious graduates, interns and placement students join Grant Thornton each year. They enjoy variety and responsibility from the start on exciting client assignments, from multinationals to fast-growth companies such as start-ups. The structured training, varied on-the-ground client experience and supportive working environment gives trainees the chance to develop and grow as trusted advisers with a deep understanding of business, as well as achieving a respected professional qualification and a competitive salary.

So what makes a business adviser at the go-to firm for growth? People with a passion for business, who combine technical thinking with their shared insight to give the kind of advice that makes a real difference to the organisations they work with and the wider economy. They listen critically and have the confidence to challenge assumptions right from day one. They seek out opportunities, collaborate and add real value to clients by unlocking their potential for growth.

GRADUATE VACANCIES IN 2017

ACCOUNTANCY
CONSULTING
FINANCE

NUMBER OF VACANCIES
200+ graduate jobs

LOCATIONS OF VACANCIES

STARTING SALARY FOR 2017
£Competitive

UNIVERSITY VISITS IN 2016-17
ASTON, BATH, BIRMINGHAM, BRISTOL, CARDIFF, DURHAM, EAST ANGLIA, EDINBURGH, EXETER, GLASGOW, KING'S COLLEGE LONDON, KENT, LEEDS, LEICESTER, LIVERPOOL, LONDON SCHOOL OF ECONOMICS, LOUGHBOROUGH, MANCHESTER, NOTTINGHAM, NOTTINGHAM TRENT, OXFORD BROOKES, READING, SHEFFIELD, SOUTHAMPTON, WARWICK, YORK
Please check with your university careers service for full details of local events.

APPLICATION DEADLINE
Year-round recruitment
Early application advised.

FURTHER INFORMATION
www.Top100GraduateEmployers.com
Register now for the latest news, campus events, work experience and graduate vacancies at Grant Thornton.

DON'T EAT YELLOW SNOW

What will your advice be?

Some advice just states the obvious. But the kind of insight that adds real value to dynamic organisations and drives a vibrant economy requires you to think and behave like an owner from day one. We've introduced a culture of shared enterprise. Shared ideas, shared responsibility and shared reward. If you want to kick start a career as a respected business adviser at the go to firm for growth, here's our advice, visit:

Grant Thornton

An instinct for growth™

Careers in audit, tax and advisory

www.grant-thornton.co.uk/trainees

do more
feel better
live longer

GSK is a science-led global healthcare company of over 100,000 individuals united by their mission and four values of patient focus, integrity, respect for people and transparency. GSK put these values at the heart of everything they do to better help meet their patients and consumers needs.

Based in the UK, with operations in over 115 countries, GSK research and develop a broad range of healthcare products from lifesaving prescription medicines and vaccines to popular consumer products such as Beechams, Sensodyne, Savlon and Panadol. Every year GSK screens millions of compounds and make billions of packs of medicines and consumer healthcare products, with a commitment to widening access to their products, so more people can benefit, no matter where they live in the world or what they can afford to pay.

Dedicated to helping millions of people around the world to do more, feel better and live longer, GSK is revolutionising its business to meet changing global healthcare needs. GSK invested £3.1 billion in R&D in 2015 and has consistently topped the Access to Medicine Index, reinforcing the company's commitment to tackle some of the world's worst diseases by embracing new, open and innovative ways of working.

GSK is deeply committed to developing people through a range of ongoing opportunities that includes tailored 2-3 year rotational graduate Future Leaders programmes, industrial or summer placements. Successful graduates will be stretched to forge new relationships, seek out new experiences and be responsible for driving their own development. GSK will be there every step of the way, helping to build the skills that will allow them to reach their potential.

Most of all, GSK graduates enjoy the sense of purpose that comes from leading change in an industry that touches millions every day.

**Lead change.
Benefit millions of lives.**

Join our Future Leaders Programme
and you'll be part of a leading
global business tackling the world's
biggest healthcare challenges. Bring
your curiosity. Share our ambition.
We'll give you the opportunities
to build the future you want.

Find out more at
www.futureleaders.gsk.com

gsk
do more
feel better
live longer

Yazmin
IT Future Leaders Programme.
Ensuring leading IT systems
protect patient safety.

HERBERT SMITH FREEHILLS

Corporate and litigation. Arbitration and advocacy. Herbert Smith Freehills has it all. And as one of the world's leading law firms, Herbert Smith Freehills works with some of the biggest and most ambitious organisations across the globe on some of their biggest and most ambitious projects.

The firm is a global force with more than 2,900 lawyers across Asia, Australia, Europe, the Middle East and the USA. The quality of Herbert Smith Freehills international network means it can provide integrated cross-border services to its high-profile clients.

Herbert Smith Freehills' dispute resolution practice is number one in the UK, Asia and Australia, and includes both the firm's leading international arbitration practice and award-winning in-house advocacy unit. The firm has a market-leading corporate practice plus other quality practices like finance, competition and regulation and trade. Herbert Smith Freehills prides itself on being a world class law firm that brings together the best people to achieve the best results for clients.

And Herbert Smith Freehills trainees can be a part of it all. The training contract balances contentious and non-contentious work with pro bono opportunities and real responsibility. Trainees rotate around four six-month seats with the opportunity to go on secondment either to a client, or to one of the firm's international offices.

Herbert Smith Freehills looks for people with the drive to become brilliant lawyers. As well as a great academic record, applicants should be commercially minded and willing to build relationships with clients and colleagues alike. For people who are assured, perceptive, empathetic and ambitious, Herbert Smith Freehills offers more than the chance to experience everything. It offers the chance to be a part of it.

GRADUATE VACANCIES IN 2017
LAW

NUMBER OF VACANCIES
70 graduate jobs
For training contracts starting in 2019.

LOCATIONS OF VACANCIES

Vacancies also available in Europe, the USA, Asia and elsewhere in the world.

STARTING SALARY FOR 2017
£44,000

UNIVERSITY VISITS IN 2016-17
BATH, BELFAST, BIRMINGHAM, BRISTOL, CAMBRIDGE, CARDIFF, CITY, DURHAM, EDINBURGH, EXETER, GLASGOW, IMPERIAL COLLEGE LONDON, KING'S COLLEGE LONDON, KENT, LANCASTER, LEEDS, LEICESTER, LONDON SCHOOL OF ECONOMICS, MANCHESTER, NEWCASTLE, NOTTINGHAM, OXFORD, QUEEN MARY LONDON, READING, SCHOOL OF AFRICAN STUDIES, SHEFFIELD, SOUTHAMPTON, ST ANDREWS, TRINITY COLLEGE DUBLIN, UNIVERSITY COLLEGE DUBLIN, UNIVERSITY COLLEGE LONDON, WARWICK, YORK
Please check with your university careers service for full details of local events.

MINIMUM ENTRY REQUIREMENTS
2.1 Degree

APPLICATION DEADLINE
Please see website for full details.

FURTHER INFORMATION
www.Top100GraduateEmployers.com
Register now for the latest news, campus events, work experience and graduate vacancies at Herbert Smith Freehills.

CAPITALS AND COLLABORATION

BE A PART OF EVERYTHING

HERBERT SMITH FREEHILLS

INTERNATIONAL GRADUATE CAREERS IN LAW

Finalising a bid in a competitive auction process in Moscow. Being recognised for your outstanding contribution on a deal. We'll give you the support you need to become a brilliant lawyer. And help you get the best from your career.

When you join Herbert Smith Freehills you get so much more than a job. You'll have the chance to gain the skills and experience you'll need to become a brilliant lawyer. As a full service global firm, our work is incredibly varied and there is no limit to where your career could take you. From first-year workshops to vacation schemes and training contracts, we have a wide variety of opportunities for you.

Don't just experience everything, be a part of it.

careers.herbertsmithfreehills.com/uk/grads

SEARCH HSF GRADUATES FOR MORE

 26 OFFICES GLOBALLY

 22 INTERNATIONAL SECONDMENTS

 £44k IN FIRST YEAR

**THIS IS
THE NEW DYNAMIC**

CAREERS IN LAW

A practical, straight-talking approach to law. Open, honest and deep relationships with clients. Training that keeps on evolving. A global community where everyone is on the same wavelength – but always encouraged to be themselves. All of this gives Hogan Lovells a different dynamic to other global law firms.

It's why many prestigious, forward-thinking clients choose to work with us. The firm has a reputation not just for the consistently high quality of its 2,500 lawyers, but also for its sense of community. The network of 45 global offices collaborates closely and constructively. Together, our teams of corporate, finance, dispute resolution, government regulatory and intellectual property lawyers tackle some of the most intricate legal and commercial issues that businesses face.

Here, trainee solicitors don't just master law. They develop industry expertise and explore the principles of business, entrepreneurship and social enterprise.

Each year, the firm takes on 60 trainee solicitors – both law and non-law graduates. The two-year training contract is split into four six-month 'seats'. During this time, trainee solicitors move around four different practice areas, including corporate, finance, and dispute resolution. Graduates will gain exposure to and develop a rounded understanding of international law, and they will have an opportunity to apply for an international or client secondment.

Hogan Lovells also runs highly-regarded spring, summer and winter vacation schemes. Up to 90 places are available in total. Each lasts up to three weeks, and gives participants the chance to work alongside partners, associates and trainees in major practice areas. Students are exposed to two or three practice areas and learn to draft documents, carry out legal research, attend meetings and in some cases attend court. This hands-on learning is complemented by tailored workshops, case studies and social events.

GRADUATE VACANCIES IN 2017

LAW

NUMBER OF VACANCIES
60 graduate jobs
For training contracts starting in 2019.

LOCATIONS OF VACANCIES

STARTING SALARY FOR 2017
£43,000

UNIVERSITY VISITS IN 2016-17
BELFAST, BIRMINGHAM, BRISTOL, CAMBRIDGE, CARDIFF, DURHAM, EAST ANGLIA, EXETER, GLASGOW, HULL, KING'S COLLEGE LONDON, LANCASTER, LEICESTER, LONDON SCHOOL OF ECONOMICS, MANCHESTER, NOTTINGHAM, ST ANDREWS, UNIVERSITY COLLEGE LONDON, WARWICK, YORK
Please check with your university careers service for full details of local events.

MINIMUM ENTRY REQUIREMENTS
2.1 Degree

APPLICATION DEADLINE
Law: 30th June 2017
Non-law: 31st January 2017

FURTHER INFORMATION
www.Top100GraduateEmployers.com
Register now for the latest news, campus events, work experience and graduate vacancies at Hogan Lovells.

BE YOURSELF.
BE RESPECTED.
BE INSPIRED.
BE AMONG EXPERTS.
DISCOVER YOUR POTENTIAL.
THIS IS THE NEW DYNAMIC.

Most firms can give you part of this.
Here, you can have it all. See how
our new dynamic could open up your
career at hoganlovells.com/graduates.

www.hsbc.com/careers/students-and-graduates

facebook.com/hsbccareers

campus.recruitment@hsbc.com

youtube.com/hsbc

linkedin.com/company/hsbc

HSBC aims to be the world's leading international bank. With around 6,000 offices in 71 countries and territories, serving more than 47 million customers, their ambition is to be where the growth is, connecting customers to opportunities and enabling businesses to thrive and economies to prosper.

HSBC seeks forward-thinking, driven and perceptive students and graduates who are open to different ideas and cultures, who enjoy being part of a team and have the ambition to become future leaders.

HSBC recognises that the talent and diversity of its people are the foundation of its success. It hires, develops and promotes employees based on merit and provides an open, supportive and inclusive working environment. This is an organisation where everyone can be themselves and achieve their potential. HSBC is committed to building its business for the long-term by balancing social, environmental and economic considerations in the decisions it makes.

Graduates can apply to join one of HSBC's global programmes in one of its four global businesses: Commercial Banking, Global Banking and Markets, Global Private Banking or Retail Banking and Wealth Management, including Global Asset Management. The journey will begin with a global discovery induction and will be followed by four 6-month rotations across the business. The bank has a strong focus on professional and personal development; successful applicants will benefit from working with exceptional colleagues and mentors in addition to a development programme which will support them as their career progresses. They also offer a wide range of internship programmes to undergraduate students, which includes a first year internship, penultimate year internships and a spring week. They welcome applicants from all degree disciplines.

GRADUATE VACANCIES IN 2017

FINANCE

INVESTMENT BANKING

RETAILING

SALES

NUMBER OF VACANCIES
500+ graduate jobs

LOCATIONS OF VACANCIES

Vacancies also available in Europe, the USA, Asia and elsewhere in the world.

STARTING SALARY FOR 2017
£Competitive

UNIVERSITY VISITS IN 2016-17
ASTON, BATH, BIRMINGHAM, BRISTOL, CAMBRIDGE, CARDIFF, CITY, DURHAM, EDINBURGH, EXETER, GLASGOW, IMPERIAL COLLEGE LONDON, KING'S COLLEGE LONDON, LEEDS, LEICESTER, LIVERPOOL, LONDON SCHOOL OF ECONOMICS, LOUGHBOROUGH, MANCHESTER, NEWCASTLE, NOTTINGHAM, OXFORD, QUEEN MARY LONDON, SHEFFIELD, UNIVERSITY COLLEGE LONDON, WARWICK, YORK
Please check with your university careers service for full details of local events.

MINIMUM ENTRY REQUIREMENTS
2.1 Degree
300 UCAS points

APPLICATION DEADLINE
Varies by function

FURTHER INFORMATION
www.Top100GraduateEmployers.com
Register now for the latest news, campus events, work experience and graduate vacancies at HSBC.

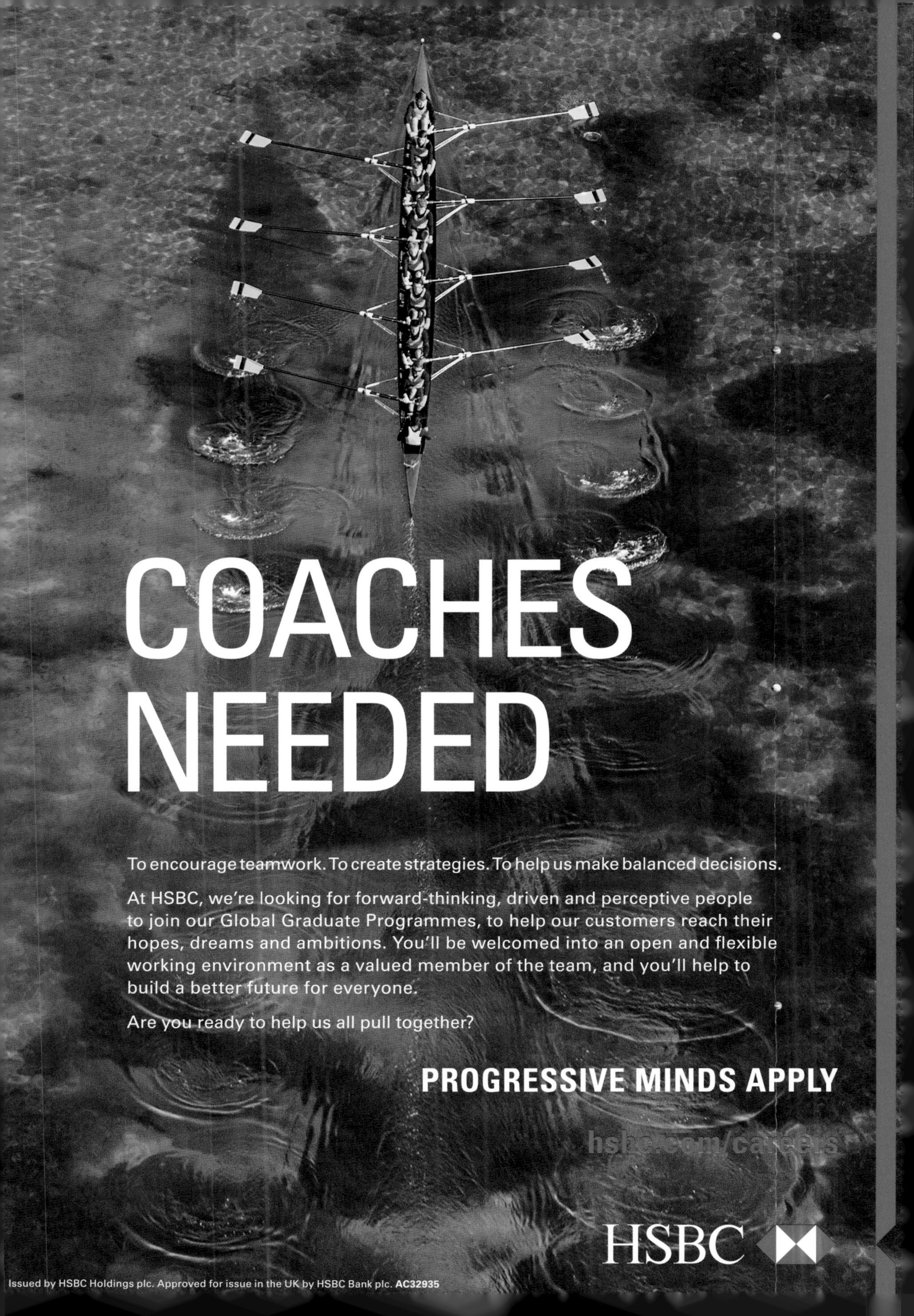

COACHES NEEDED
To encourage teamwork. To create strategies. To help us make balanced decisions.
At HSBC, we're looking for forward-thinking, driven and perceptive people to join our Global Graduate Programmes, to help our customers reach their hopes, dreams and ambitions. You'll be welcomed into an open and flexible working environment as a valued member of the team, and you'll help to build a better future for everyone.
Are you ready to help us all pull together?
PROGRESSIVE MINDS APPLY
hsbc.com/careers
HSBC
Issued by HSBC Holdings plc. Approved for issue in the UK by HSBC Bank plc. AC32935

IBM are looking for passionate graduates interested in developing their skills and building their career with a global leader. At IBM graduates get the support needed to make a real impact and most importantly they will have the opportunity to do work that matters.

IBM work with some of the greatest and best known names on the planet, providing IT services and consultancy across all industries including retail, sport, business, finance, health, media and entertainment.

IBM look for the best and brightest graduates, from all universities, degree backgrounds and abilities. They want creative and passionate people who will share their dedication to tackling the world's toughest problems. Whether graduates want to pursue a career in consulting, technology, business, design or sales they'll have the chance to collaborate with extraordinary people in a creative environment to make the world work better.

IBM are dedicated to giving graduates every opportunity to enhance their career development. They'll work in an environment that cultivates creativity and individual differences, rewarding their best work.

IBM's award-winning, bespoke training is designed to give graduates the personal, business and technical skills to take their career wherever they want to go. Graduates will continuously learn and develop new skills and have the opportunity to contribute to the enhancement of their field.

IBM will encourage graduates to extend their expertise through customised professional development and leadership training, allocating every graduate a professional development manager and a mentor to ensure graduates get the most out of the programme.

Be part of a global transformation and join IBM.

GRADUATE VACANCIES IN 2017

CONSULTING

IT

SALES

NUMBER OF VACANCIES
300+ graduate jobs

LOCATIONS OF VACANCIES

STARTING SALARY FOR 2017
£30,000+

UNIVERSITY VISITS IN 2016-17
ASTON, BATH, BIRMINGHAM, BRISTOL, CAMBRIDGE, CARDIFF, DURHAM, EDINBURGH, EXETER, GLASGOW, IMPERIAL COLLEGE LONDON, KING'S COLLEGE LONDON, LANCASTER, LEEDS, LIVERPOOL, LONDON SCHOOL OF ECONOMICS, LOUGHBOROUGH, MANCHESTER, NEWCASTLE, NOTTINGHAM, OXFORD, SHEFFIELD, SOUTHAMPTON, UNIVERSITY COLLEGE LONDON, WARWICK, YORK
Please check with your university careers service for full details of local events.

MINIMUM ENTRY REQUIREMENTS
2.1 Degree

APPLICATION DEADLINE
Year-round recruitment

FURTHER INFORMATION
www.Top100GraduateEmployers.com
Register now for the latest news, campus events, work experience and graduate vacancies at IBM.

I work where my ideas can help change the world.

Outthink ordinary. Don't settle for feeling like a cog in a machine. You matter at IBM – your voice and ideas are heard loud and clear to bring the best ideas to exciting projects. Be a part of technologies that change the world, revolutionizing everything from social services to healthcare and beyond. IBM gives you the opportunity to bring your ideas to life.

Discover what you can do at IBM.
ibm.com/jobs/uk

outthink

GRADUATE VACANCIES IN 2017

LAW

NUMBER OF VACANCIES
50 graduate jobs
For training contracts starting in 2019.

LOCATIONS OF VACANCIES

The Irwin Mitchell Group is one of a few law firms to provide a diverse range of legal services to business and private clients. It has a strong customer service culture and a high level of client retention. Following the merger with Thomas Eggar in December 2015 national presence has increased to 15 locations.

The firm's training contracts are streamed so that a trainee solicitor would either undertake a training contract based within the Personal Legal Services or Business Legal Services division. As a national firm, there is opportunity to undertake a training contract in one or more locations in the UK. Trainees will have three training seats and a qualification seat, giving them the chance to gain practical experience in diverse areas of law, whilst maximising retention opportunities. Whatever division is chosen, trainees will enjoy a fantastic training contract at a truly unique and innovative firm.

Irwin Mitchell seek to provide opportunities to those who have the ability to work under pressure in a fast-paced environment. The trainees will be creatively minded, use their initiative and have strong organisational and problem-solving skills.

From the moment a trainee joins Irwin Mitchell they will receive a dedicated training and development programme. The firm invests in the future of employees, as this could build their journey to the very top of the firm.

Each summer the firm runs a formal work placement programme which is a great way to get a real insight into what life is like as a trainee at Irwin Mitchell, along with the culture. An increasing number of training contracts are offered to those who have undertaken a Legal Work Placement, so all those interested in joining should apply via this route.

STARTING SALARY FOR 2017
£25,000+
Plus GDL/LPC fees and a maintenance grant.

UNIVERSITY VISITS IN 2016-17
BIRMINGHAM, BRISTOL, CAMBRIDGE, CARDIFF, DURHAM, EXETER, KING'S COLLEGE LONDON, KENT, LEEDS, MANCHESTER, NEWCASTLE, NOTTINGHAM, READING, SHEFFIELD, SOUTHAMPTON, SURREY, SUSSEX, UNIVERSITY COLLEGE LONDON, WARWICK, YORK
Please check with your university careers service for full details of local events.

MINIMUM ENTRY REQUIREMENTS
2.1 Degree
300 UCAS points

APPLICATION DEADLINE
30th June 2017

FURTHER INFORMATION
www.Top100GraduateEmployers.com
Register now for the latest news, campus events, work experience and graduate vacancies at Irwin Mitchell.

Through revolutionary technologies, performance and craftsmanship, Jaguar Land Rover have pushed the boundaries of what the industry considers possible over and over again. Now, their ambitions are bolder than ever before – to reimagine the next generation of innovative vehicles and redefine the standards for excellence in the industry and beyond.

Home to some of the most iconic nameplates ever to take to the road, Jaguar Land Rover has a proud and enviable heritage. But it's their future that excites most. With continued investment in the development of new products, processes and facilities, and expansion into new markets gaining momentum, they need to find the next generation of innovators and creative thinkers that will ensure they continue to set the standards others can only follow.

Reflecting the scale of their ambition is Jaguar Land Rover's extensive and expanding graduate offering. Opportunities lie right across the business in everything from Engineering and Manufacturing disciplines to their Commercial and Business areas. Graduates joining will develop specialist and commercial skills while pushing the boundaries of their potential, possessing the autonomy to make a real impact on real projects. With ongoing support to gain further professional qualifications and accreditation, in-house training and a thorough induction programme, the graduate scheme has been designed to be as inspiring as the pioneering vehicles they'll help produce.

As would be expected from two of the world's most revered brands, a range of rewards and benefits await those who have initiative, vision and drive to contribute to the organisation's global success – including a competitive salary, joining bonus, pension scheme and discount car purchase scheme. All this and more makes Jaguar Land Rover an enviable place to start their journey.

GRADUATE VACANCIES IN 2017

ACCOUNTANCY
ENGINEERING
FINANCE
IT
LOGISTICS
MARKETING
PROPERTY
PURCHASING
RESEARCH & DEVELOPMENT
SALES

NUMBER OF VACANCIES
250 graduate jobs

LOCATIONS OF VACANCIES

STARTING SALARY FOR 2017
£29,000
Plus a £2,000 joining bonus.

UNIVERSITY VISITS IN 2016-17
ASTON, BATH, BELFAST, BIRMINGHAM, BRISTOL, CAMBRIDGE, CARDIFF, DURHAM, EDINBURGH, EXETER, IMPERIAL COLLEGE LONDON, LANCASTER, LEEDS, LEICESTER, LIVERPOOL, LOUGHBOROUGH, MANCHESTER, NEWCASTLE, NOTTINGHAM, OXFORD, SHEFFIELD, SOUTHAMPTON, STRATHCLYDE, TRINITY COLLEGE DUBLIN, WARWICK
Please check with your university careers service for full details of local events.

MINIMUM ENTRY REQUIREMENTS
2.2 Degree

APPLICATION DEADLINE
31st December 2016

FURTHER INFORMATION
www.Top100GraduateEmployers.com
*Register now for the latest news, campus events, work experience and graduate vacancies at **Jaguar Land Rover**.*

BOLD. BOLDER. BOLDEST.

GRADUATE & UNDERGRADUATE OPPORTUNITIES
ENGINEERING & COMMERCIAL BUSINESS AREAS

We're on a journey. A journey to redefine the benchmark for excellence. With ambitions to set pulses racing in more countries and more markets than ever before, there's never been a more exciting time to join it. The scale of our ambition is reflected by the ever-expanding breadth of our graduate programmes and undergraduate placements. From our Manufacturing and Engineering disciplines to our Commercial and Business functions, this is a place where you'll continually push the boundaries of your own potential. Where you'll develop specialist and commercial skills working alongside an industry-revered team. Where your achievements, and ours, will only go from strength to strength to strength.

Discover careers that move at **jaguarlandrovercareers.com**

The John Lewis Partnership is a multi-award winning retail business and incorporates two of the high street's most renowned brands – John Lewis and Waitrose. Combining the best of traditional and modern, it has responded to customers' needs to become a truly omni-channel business.

This commitment to innovation and outstanding customer service is part of what makes the John Lewis Partnership so different and successful. But perhaps the most unique aspect is that everyone that joins the organisation becomes a Partner. This means they own a share in the business and get to have a say in how it's run.

And key to its ongoing success are graduates. The organisation is keen to give graduates early responsibility as well as challenges that give them every opportunity to make a difference. The Partnership runs schemes that are designed to create future leaders of the business. These fast-paced and stimulating programmes offer real experiences, superb training and support, the chance to work with different individuals and to create a strong graduate community. Exposure to the most successful leaders in retail today, support from a buddy or mentor and a comprehensive development programme are also core aspects of the schemes.

A lot is expected in return. A sense of pride in ownership. The ability to make things happen. Excellent customer service skills. A commitment to personal and professional development. Openness and adaptability to change. Able to build rapport at all levels and view things from a variety of perspectives. These are qualities that the John Lewis Partnership look for (along with specific generalist or specialist skills). Graduates that bring these attributes can expect to start a unique journey with the organisation consistently voted as the nation's most loved retailer.

GRADUATE VACANCIES IN 2017

IT

RETAILING

NUMBER OF VACANCIES
30+ graduate jobs

LOCATIONS OF VACANCIES

STARTING SALARY FOR 2017
£Dependent on scheme

UNIVERSITY VISITS IN 2016-17
Please check with your university careers service for full details of local events.

MINIMUM ENTRY REQUIREMENTS
Dependent on scheme
Please see website for full details.

APPLICATION DEADLINE
Please see website for full details.

FURTHER INFORMATION
www.Top100GraduateEmployers.com
*Register now for the latest news, campus events, work experience and graduate vacancies at the **John Lewis Partnership**.*

J.P.Morgan

GRADUATE VACANCIES IN 2017

FINANCE

HUMAN RESOURCES

INVESTMENT BANKING

IT

NUMBER OF VACANCIES
No fixed quota

LOCATIONS OF VACANCIES

Vacancies also available in Europe, Asia and the USA.

STARTING SALARY FOR 2017
£Competitive

Banking is a vital part of the world's economy and everyday life. Over the last 200 years J.P. Morgan has evolved as a business to meet the ever-changing needs of some of the world's largest companies as well as many of the smaller businesses that are a cornerstone of local communities. They work tirelessly to do the right thing for their clients, shareholders and the firm every day.

J.P. Morgan's strength lies not only in the quality of its products, but also within the invaluable power of its employees. Harnessing the diversity of its people, J.P. Morgan values those with different talents, ranging from investment banking to technology, operations and human resources.

Career opportunities are available across the firm, so it pays to learn as much as possible about the industry, business areas and the roles available. Be sure to take advantage of pre-internship programmes, such as Insight Days and Spring Week, which give students a chance to get noticed early – many interns are hired directly from the Spring Week programme.

J.P. Morgan offers internship and graduate opportunities in the following areas: Finance, Global Investment Management, Global Treasury Management, Global Wealth Management, Human Resources, Investment Banking, Investor Services, Markets, Operations, Quantitative Research, Risk Management and Technology.

J.P. Morgan is looking for collaborative future leaders who have passion, creativity and exceptional interpersonal skills. Impeccable academic credentials are important, but so are achievements outside the classroom.

Working with a team committed to doing their best, earning the trust of their clients and encouraging employees to fulfil their potential. That's what it means to be part of J.P. Morgan.

UNIVERSITY VISITS IN 2016-17
BATH, CAMBRIDGE, EDINBURGH, EXETER, GLASGOW, IMPERIAL COLLEGE LONDON, LONDON SCHOOL OF ECONOMICS, OXFORD, SOUTHAMPTON, ST ANDREWS, STRATHCLYDE, UNIVERSITY COLLEGE LONDON, WARWICK
Please check with your university careers service for full details of local events.

MINIMUM ENTRY REQUIREMENTS
2.1 Degree

APPLICATION DEADLINE
27th November 2016

FURTHER INFORMATION
www.Top100GraduateEmployers.com
*Register now for the latest news, campus events, work experience and graduate vacancies at **J.P. Morgan**.*

Your career.
Your way.

Draw on all of your experiences and bring the whole you to J.P. Morgan. We'll make sure you have the training and opportunities to turn your talent into an exciting career. Wherever you want to go, and whatever you want to achieve, we'll help you get there.

If you're talented and driven to succeed, start your journey with us.

We're hosting a range of events and programs around the globe throughout the year, so we encourage you to check our careers site regularly for dates and deadlines.

Start your journey.
jpmorgan.com/careers

KPMG is one of the UK's largest providers of Audit, Tax and Advisory services. The Firm focuses on clients' big issues and opportunities by providing innovative approaches and deep expertise to deliver real results. Part of a global network, it has 12,000 people in the UK working across 22 offices.

KPMG's Audit, Tax, Advisory, Technology and Central Services programmes offer graduates the chance to work alongside some of the brightest minds, on rewarding and challenging work. It's an inspiring environment where people work with passion and purpose in a variety of diverse industries such as Media, Leisure, Financial Services and Government & Public Sector.

Delivering innovative approaches calls for diverse perspectives. So KPMG welcomes a range of personalities, skill sets and degree disciplines. Thanks to The Academy, a unique learning community created to help trainees continuously develop through workshops and networking events, the guidance and support graduates receive is as individual as they are themselves. What's more, the full-time Professional Qualification Training team is also on hand to support trainees to pass professional exams.

It's definitely stimulating work. To thrive, graduates will need resilience, curiosity and the motivation for continuous improvement. Trainees will be rewarded with the development opportunities they need to reach their full potential and a host of great benefits including secondments, preferential banking, cash towards student loan payments, and their birthday off work.

In fact, the rewards of a career with KPMG begin early with Launch Pad. An innovative, streamlined approach to the recruitment process, it allows graduates to enjoy a meaningful experience while securing a job offer earlier than ever. In short, KPMG is an award-winning employer, where graduates can learn, grow and thrive.

GRADUATE VACANCIES IN 2017

ACCOUNTANCY
CONSULTING
FINANCE
HUMAN RESOURCES
IT
PROPERTY

NUMBER OF VACANCIES
1,000 graduate jobs

LOCATIONS OF VACANCIES

STARTING SALARY FOR 2017
£Competitive
Plus 25 days holiday, pension, life assurance, accident insurance and mobile phone.

UNIVERSITY VISITS IN 2016-17
ABERDEEN, ASTON, BATH, BIRMINGHAM, BRADFORD, BRISTOL, CAMBRIDGE, CARDIFF, DURHAM, EAST ANGLIA, EDINBURGH, EXETER, GLASGOW, HULL, IMPERIAL COLLEGE LONDON, KING'S COLLEGE LONDON, LEEDS, LONDON SCHOOL OF ECONOMICS, LOUGHBOROUGH, MANCHESTER, NEWCASTLE, NOTTINGHAM, NOTTINGHAM TRENT, OXFORD, OXFORD BROOKES, QUEEN MARY LONDON, SHEFFIELD, SOUTHAMPTON, ST ANDREWS, STRATHCLYDE, SURREY, ULSTER, UNIVERSITY COLLEGE LONDON, WARWICK, YORK
Please check with your university careers service for full details of local events.

MINIMUM ENTRY REQUIREMENTS
2.1 Degree
300 UCAS points
However, it's not just academic performance KPMG is interested in. Please see website for specific programme requirements.

APPLICATION DEADLINE
Year-round recruitment
Early application advised.

FURTHER INFORMATION
www.Top100GraduateEmployers.com
Register now for the latest news, campus events, work experience and graduate vacancies at KPMG.

Curiosity loves company.

At KPMG in the UK you can work side-by-side with some of the brightest minds in business, full of innovative ideas and natural curiosity. With the opportunity to learn every day, you'll be encouraged to be yourself, focused on delivering results for our people, clients and communities. So whether your journey of discovery leads to Audit, Tax, Advisory, Technology or Central Services, we will value your contribution, and believe we can satisfy your ambition.

kpmgcareers.co.uk/graduates

Anticipate tomorrow. Deliver today.

L'ORÉAL

JASMINE,
GRADUATE,

LAUNCHES A
NEW LINE FOR
MAYBELLINE.
WE HAVE
LIFT-OFF.

Think 32 iconic international brands, selling in 130 countries. Think Ralph Lauren. Think Diesel. Think Garnier. Think The Body Shop. And now, think about the change graduates can bring, when they work for the world's number one cosmetics group. It's time to lead the change at L'Oréal.

At the forefront of a booming £10 billion industry in the UK, L'Oréal continues to invent and revolutionise. In 2015, the group registered a stunning 497 patents for newly invented products and formulae. That constant creativity, and determined exploration of every possibility, is what makes L'Oréal a global success symbol.

So, when it comes to their Management Trainee Programme, L'Oréal need more than just graduates. They need inventors, explorers, leaders and entrepreneurs. Graduates who know that when it comes to success, inspirational talent and hard work go hand in hand. Graduates who know that they should never stop exploring new ideas.

On the Management Trainee Programme, graduates work in functions across the business, gaining a sharp sense of life at L'Oréal. With three different rotations in their chosen stream (marketing, logistics, commercial and finance), they're free to develop their talent and discover new possibilities. More than that, the graduates also move through different brands – from Kiehl's to La Roche-Posay; from Armani Beauty to Maybelline – each with their own unique culture and identity to explore.

With on-the-job training and their own personal HR sponsor, graduates will progress into operational roles within as little as a year. They'll take on real responsibility, and make a palpable contribution to an international success story. From the start, they'll shape their own career and choose their own direction; leading the change with L'Oréal's outstanding brands.

GRADUATE VACANCIES IN 2017
FINANCE
LOGISTICS
MARKETING
SALES

NUMBER OF VACANCIES
28 graduate jobs

LOCATIONS OF VACANCIES

STARTING SALARY FOR 2017
£30,000

UNIVERSITY VISITS IN 2016-17
BIRMINGHAM, BRISTOL, CAMBRIDGE, CARDIFF, EXETER, IMPERIAL COLLEGE LONDON, KING'S COLLEGE LONDON, LANCASTER, LEEDS, LEICESTER, LIVERPOOL, LONDON SCHOOL OF ECONOMICS, LOUGHBOROUGH, MANCHESTER, NEWCASTLE, NOTTINGHAM, NOTTINGHAM TRENT, OXFORD, SWANSEA, UNIVERSITY COLLEGE LONDON, WARWICK, YORK
Please check with your university careers service for full details of local events.

MINIMUM ENTRY REQUIREMENTS
2.1 Degree

APPLICATION DEADLINE
31st January 2017

FURTHER INFORMATION
www.Top100GraduateEmployers.com
Register now for the latest news, campus events, work experience and graduate vacancies at L'Oréal.

GRADUATE VACANCIES IN 2017

GENERAL MANAGEMENT
LOGISTICS
PROPERTY
PURCHASING
RETAILING
SALES

NUMBER OF VACANCIES
240+ graduate jobs

LOCATIONS OF VACANCIES

STARTING SALARY FOR 2017
£36,000-£44,000

UNIVERSITY VISITS IN 2016-17
ASTON, BATH, BIRMINGHAM, BRISTOL,
CARDIFF, DURHAM, EDINBURGH, ESSEX,
EXETER, GLASGOW, IMPERIAL COLLEGE
LONDON, KING'S COLLEGE LONDON, KENT,
LANCASTER, LEEDS, LEICESTER, LONDON
SCHOOL OF ECONOMICS, MANCHESTER,
NEWCASTLE, NOTTINGHAM, NOTTINGHAM
TRENT, SHEFFIELD, SOUTHAMPTON,
STRATHCLYDE, SURREY, UNIVERSITY
COLLEGE LONDON, WARWICK, YORK
*Please check with your university careers
service for full details of local events.*

MINIMUM ENTRY REQUIREMENTS
2.1 Degree
Relevant degree required for some roles.

APPLICATION DEADLINE
Varies by function

FURTHER INFORMATION
www.Top100GraduateEmployers.com
*Register now for the latest news, campus
events, work experience and graduate
vacancies at Lidl.*

As one of the UK's retail success stories, Lidl is a phenomenon. Pioneering a do-it-different, keep-it-simple approach has helped them achieve significant international success. This is big business. With operations in 27 countries, Lidl has more than 10,000 stores and 135 retail distribution centres.

This includes more than 630 stores in the UK alone, and there's an impressive schedule of new store and warehouse openings planned for the next few years.

To achieve this level of success and customer loyalty takes a special kind of culture. It takes a special kind of person too. So Lidl has invested heavily in creating an ethos and an environment in which people can thrive.

Lidl is run as a lean business and everyone is expected to chip in and pull their weight. The more effort people make, the more they'll get back in return. In fact, nearly all of the company's senior professionals started their careers in store, successfully developing careers in Sales, Property, Supply Chain, Logistics and a wide range of Head Office positions.

Carefully structured training and development programmes take the raw potential of ambitious and eager graduates and transform them into high-performing, polished retail professionals capable of running the business.

Lidl offers impressive opportunities to travel internationally too, combined with an excellent rewards package, making this one of the most exciting opportunities on the market. In keeping with the company's simple and straightforward ethos, they look for quick-witted, problem-solving graduates with plenty of common sense.

For bright, bold graduates who aren't afraid to take decisions and lead from the front, Lidl will make the investment. Graduates can expect all the training and development support they need to take off in their career.

BIG HITTING
CAREER DEFINING
LIP SMACKING
CAREERS
FOR GRADUATES

OUTSTANDING GRADUATE PROGRAMMES

Game-changing, skill-enhancing experiences. They're waiting for you at Lidl. Whatever your interests, we've got plenty of amazing graduate opportunities that are guaranteed to equip you with everything you need to be a stand-out, best-of-the-best professional.

To top it off, all of our programmes offer amazing salaries and plenty more fantastic benefits.

Want a piece of the action?

WWW.LIDLGRADUATECAREERS.CO.UK

Linklaters

As one of the world's most prestigious law firms, Linklaters is the place where graduates can make the most of their talents. Amongst a team of exceptional lawyers, a network of international offices and through unparalleled training and development opportunities, people can live their ambition.

With the ambition to be the leading global law firm, if graduates want to make the most of their potential in commercial law, Linklaters is the place to be.

Linklaters attracts and recruits people from a range of subject disciplines and backgrounds. What they all have in common is a desire to achieve their full potential through a career in commercial law.

Linklaters helps its trainees achieve their ambitions by providing an environment in which to succeed. For non-law graduates, it starts with the Graduate Diploma in Law, giving them all the legal knowledge required to start their professional training. All graduates then come together to complete the bespoke Legal Practice Course.

Once the initial training is complete, it's time to begin working on real client matters through four six-month seats in Linklaters' global practice groups. Each seat not only builds skills and expertise in a particular area, but with ongoing training, feedback and support, it develops the professional and commercial skills that every successful lawyer needs.

As Linklaters believes in continuous learning, the unique Linklaters Law and Business School delivers the tools, knowledge and confidence for lawyers throughout their careers.

With complex and high-profile deals across a global network of 29 offices and beyond, international secondment opportunities and great rewards, Linklaters offers its trainees broad and rich experiences to springboard their careers.

GRADUATE VACANCIES IN 2017
LAW

NUMBER OF VACANCIES
110 graduate jobs
For training contracts starting in 2019.

LOCATIONS OF VACANCIES

Vacancies also available in Europe, Asia, the USA and elsewhere in the world.

STARTING SALARY FOR 2017
£43,000
Plus a bonus of up to £1,000.

UNIVERSITY VISITS IN 2016-17
BELFAST, BIRMINGHAM, BRISTOL, CAMBRIDGE, DURHAM, EDINBURGH, EXETER, GLASGOW, KING'S COLLEGE LONDON, LEEDS, LEICESTER, LONDON SCHOOL OF ECONOMICS, MANCHESTER, NOTTINGHAM, OXFORD, QUEEN MARY LONDON, SCHOOL OF AFRICAN STUDIES, ST ANDREWS, TRINITY COLLEGE DUBLIN, UNIVERSITY COLLEGE DUBLIN, UNIVERSITY COLLEGE LONDON, WARWICK, YORK
Please check with your university careers service for full details of local events.

MINIMUM ENTRY REQUIREMENTS
2.1 Degree
340 UCAS points

APPLICATION DEADLINE
Varies by function
Please see website for full details.

FURTHER INFORMATION
www.Top100GraduateEmployers.com
Register now for the latest news, campus events, work experience and graduate vacancies at Linklaters.

Linklaters

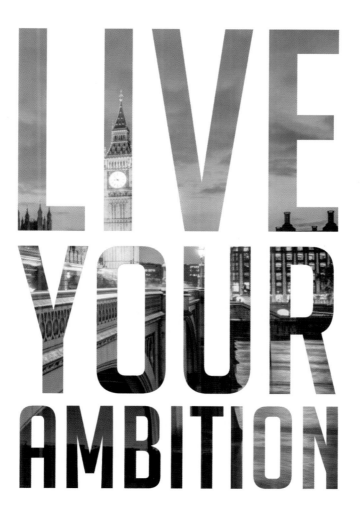

LIVE YOUR AMBITION

We are a leading global law firm. We offer training around the world in a range of practice areas, helping you find your best fit. We give you the chance to work on high-profile deals and challenging assignments so you can keep on learning and improving. And we provide the ongoing support you need to reach your full potential.

So join us, and live your ambition.

Graduate opportunities
linklaters.com/ukgrads

www.lloyds.com/graduates

facebook.com/lloyds

linkedin.com/company/lloyd's-of-london   twitter.com/LloydsofLondon

LLOYD'S

Lloyd's is the foundation of the insurance industry and the future of it. Led by expert underwriters and brokers who cover more than 200 territories across the world, the Lloyd's market develops the complex insurance needed to empower human progress.

At Lloyd's, graduates help to make new endeavours possible, from space tourism to huge, groundbreaking events. They safeguard the world against risks from cyber terrorism to climate change. Above all, they'll help strengthen the resilience of local communities and drive global economic growth.

Lloyd's 24-month graduate schemes fall into two categories: functional schemes – including HR, IT, Finance and Marketing – and the Insurance scheme.

The Insurance scheme is the first graduate programme in the industry to be accredited by the Chartered Insurance Institute. On it, graduates will complete four different placements across the corporation and the market, giving them a 360° perspective of the specialist insurance industry. Whichever route is chosen, one thing's certain: graduates will gain a wealth of experience and benefit from comprehensive training. On the Insurance Graduate Scheme, graduates will gain the internationally recognised ACII qualification, while those on the functional schemes will work towards relevant postgraduate qualifications.

And all the while, exceptional employee benefits are on offer. These include not just a pension scheme, a competitive salary and 25 days' holiday a year, but also private medical insurance and a flexible benefits package.

With Lloyd's, graduates gain not just experience, technical training and qualifications, but also valuable soft skills like leadership, project management and communication. In short, as they help to empower human progress, they will find that they progress fast too.

Lloyds Banking Group is a financial services group with over 30 million UK customers and a presence in nearly every community. The Group's main brands include Lloyds Bank, Halifax, Scottish Widows and Bank of Scotland. The Group actively supports charities and projects across the UK.

The graduate programmes at Lloyds Banking Group are as broad as the business. Opportunities range from shaping strategy to leading digital and IT innovation; from interpreting financial figures to helping high street customers and big business clients.

Lloyds Banking Group recruits a variety of individuals from a range of degree disciplines and backgrounds. It takes people as diverse as the population to help Britain prosper, but they all share the desire to make a positive impact on the customers and communities they serve.

The graduate journey provides an opportunity for individuals to discover their strengths and build new skills, as well as grow an extensive professional network. Rotational placements, mentoring, masterclasses, professional qualifications, agile working and support from experienced business leaders empower graduates to develop the key customer, consulting, managerial, commercial and innovation skills they need to advance their career.

Individuals will discover an inclusive, collaborative and open-minded culture at Lloyds Banking Group. The organisation continues to be recognised for its diversity achievements, being named in The Times Top 50 Employers for Women 2016 and as the top private sector employer for LGBT people in the 2016 Stonewall Top 100 index.

At Lloyds Banking Group, graduates will discover a professional career that matters and an exciting opportunity to shape the future of banking in the UK.

GRADUATE VACANCIES IN 2017
ACCOUNTANCY
CONSULTING
FINANCE
GENERAL MANAGEMENT
HUMAN RESOURCES
INVESTMENT BANKING
IT
LAW
SALES

NUMBER OF VACANCIES
400+ graduate jobs

LOCATIONS OF VACANCIES

STARTING SALARY FOR 2017
£28,000+
Plus a relocation allowance, flexible benefits and an annual bonus.

UNIVERSITY VISITS IN 2016-17
ASTON, BATH, BIRMINGHAM, BRISTOL, CAMBRIDGE, CARDIFF, DURHAM, EDINBURGH, EXETER, GLASGOW, IMPERIAL COLLEGE LONDON, KING'S COLLEGE LONDON, KENT, LANCASTER, LEEDS, LEICESTER, LIVERPOOL, LONDON SCHOOL OF ECONOMICS, LOUGHBOROUGH, MANCHESTER, NOTTINGHAM, OXFORD, SHEFFIELD, SOUTHAMPTON, ST ANDREWS, STRATHCLYDE, UNIVERSITY COLLEGE LONDON, WARWICK
Please check with your university careers service for full details of local events.

MINIMUM ENTRY REQUIREMENTS
2.2 Degree

APPLICATION DEADLINE
31st December 2016

FURTHER INFORMATION
www.Top100GraduateEmployers.com
*Register now for the latest news, campus events, work experience and graduate vacancies at **Lloyds Banking Group**.*

LLOYDS
BANKING
GROUP

You've learned a lot about yourself at university – the things you're interested in, good at, and passionate about. But the journey shouldn't stop there. On a Lloyds Banking Group graduate programme, you'll develop your interests, explore your strengths and expand your horizons.

Like Puja, you'll discover skills you never knew you had and opportunities you never knew existed. You'll be surprised at the variety of people who work for us – in a range of business areas and roles. Puja has experienced industry-leading training and how invigorating it is to move across teams and brands. And she's discovered her fit – easily balancing her personal passion for singing with her professional ambition to drive the banking technology that's helping Britain prosper.

What will you discover?

Discover our programmes
lloydsbankinggrouptalent.com

Discover you
discoverwhatmatters.co.uk

DISCOVER WHAT
MATTERS

"EVERY DAY I DISCOVER SOMETHING NEW"
Puja Bafna
IT Business Management

M&S

EST. 1884

MARKS & SPENCER

M&S always strives for perfection. This passion to improve and meticulous attention to detail has led them to create products that millions of people love. Not to mention the on and offline experiences that push the boundaries for the entire retail industry and perfect careers for the talented people who work for them.

For ambitious graduates, there's no better place to begin their working life. Covering everything from Software Engineering and IT to Logistics, Retail Management, Marketing and beyond, each M&S graduate programme comes packed with unique opportunities for bright people to achieve the best for themselves and the business.

As an example, for those starting in Retail Management, the path to Commercial Manager level is clearly set out and, for many, achievable in as little as 9 months. But whichever part of the business a graduate joins, the day they start is the first step on a long and rewarding career with M&S – one where they'll be in an excellent position to achieve their potential as they help one of Britain's best-loved brands do the same.

It's truly an exciting time to be at M&S. With retail moving faster than ever before, anyone joining the company now will be building the business of the future. Whether it's spotting today's trends and turning them into tomorrow's reality, refining retail channels and enhancing shopping experiences or developing products and services on offer, it's all for the taking at M&S.

For graduates with high standards, a hard work ethic and an unwavering commitment to doing the right thing, a career at the forefront of retail awaits – along with a competitive salary and a host of other great benefits.

GRADUATE VACANCIES IN 2017

FINANCE
GENERAL MANAGEMENT
HUMAN RESOURCES
IT
LOGISTICS
MARKETING
PROPERTY
PURCHASING
RESEARCH & DEVELOPMENT
RETAILING

NUMBER OF VACANCIES
200 graduate jobs

LOCATIONS OF VACANCIES

STARTING SALARY FOR 2017
£23,500-£28,000

UNIVERSITY VISITS IN 2016-17
ASTON, BIRMINGHAM, CAMBRIDGE, CARDIFF, EAST ANGLIA, EDINBURGH, KENT, LEEDS, READING, ROYAL HOLLOWAY, SHEFFIELD, SURREY, SUSSEX, UNIVERSITY COLLEGE LONDON, YORK
Please check with your university careers service for full details of local events.

MINIMUM ENTRY REQUIREMENTS
Dependent on scheme
Relevant degree required for some roles.

APPLICATION DEADLINE
Mid December 2016
Applications close earlier for some schemes – please see website for full details.

FURTHER INFORMATION
www.Top100GraduateEmployers.com
Register now for the latest news, campus events, work experience and graduate vacancies at M&S.

EST. 1884

Cook M&S   10:53

STRAWBERRY
CHEESECAKE
🕐 1h 30m

Perfect timing

Graduate careers for discerning cooks and digital connoisseurs

We're passionate about food, digital technology and innovation. So we loved creating our neat little app, 'Cook with M&S'. Offering hundreds of delicious recipes and taking consumers through every step of cooking, the app was launched for the iPhone, iPad and Android devices, before we introduced an Apple Watch version. So, if you'd enjoy pushing boundaries, setting the digital agenda and finding new ways to delight our customers, we'll give you support, learning opportunities and experience to become the perfect product of your ambition, determination and talent.

Find out how to make the most of your ambition at:

www.marksandspencergrads.com

Perfect PRODUCTS *Perfect* CAREERS

 Marks and Spencer   🐦 **@MandSTalent**

MARS

Start your own story.

Think 'work, rest and play'. Think M&M's®, Uncle Ben's®, Pedigree®, Whiskas® and Wrigley®, iconic billion-dollar brands. Think the world's third-largest food company with international operations in 370 locations. Know what makes Mars special? Think again.

Sure, Mars is one of the world's leading food companies, but it's more like a community than a corporate. Because it's still privately owned. And that means it's a place without any of the trappings of typical big business. It has a sense of humanity and a lack of vanity around leadership. It's somewhere that encourages open communication and collaboration, where people can get to grips with challenging work and take on high levels of responsibility early on.

The flat, open structure is a big plus for graduates when it comes to grabbing the opportunity to shape Mars' future. It makes for a truly creative and dynamic environment, whichever programme graduates join on. But it takes more than just freedom and responsibility to create the Mars leaders of the future. What graduates at Mars get is high levels of responsibility, a variety of possibilities and the opportunity to improve things for everyone else along the way.

Mars provides a fantastic support structure, financial sponsorship to pursue professional qualifications, extensive learning and development opportunities and personal mentoring from some of the brightest and best people in the industry. All Mars employees are called associates, and are treated as individuals, not numbers, driving their own performance and development.

In return, Mars gives its associates the autonomy to grab each and every opportunity that presents itself, and commit to improving how Mars treats its customers, communities and the planet. So that ultimately, they can make Mars mean more.

GRADUATE VACANCIES IN 2017
ENGINEERING
FINANCE
GENERAL MANAGEMENT
HUMAN RESOURCES
IT
LOGISTICS
MARKETING
PURCHASING
RESEARCH & DEVELOPMENT
SALES

NUMBER OF VACANCIES
40 graduate jobs

LOCATIONS OF VACANCIES

Vacancies also available in Europe.

STARTING SALARY FOR 2017
Up to £32,000
Plus a £2,000 joining bonus.

UNIVERSITY VISITS IN 2016-17
BATH, BIRMINGHAM, CAMBRIDGE, DURHAM, EXETER, LEEDS, NOTTINGHAM, OXFORD, WARWICK
Please check with your university careers service for full details of local events.

MINIMUM ENTRY REQUIREMENTS
2.1 Degree
300 UCAS points

APPLICATION DEADLINE
Varies by function
From 2nd December 2016.

FURTHER INFORMATION
www.Top100GraduateEmployers.com
Register now for the latest news, campus events, work experience and graduate vacancies at **Mars**.

When the heat was on, Órla had a cool idea.

We love it when demand for our products soars. But in the Middle East and Africa, demand for MALTESERS® was growing so fast that we simply couldn't keep up. Enter Órla, from our Management Development Programme. When we asked her to create a global demand plan she didn't break a sweat. Instead, she considered all the facts and successfully presented her case – for building a brand new production line on the other side of the world. It was a bold idea, but the potential returns were huge. Which left just one problem: how could we meet global demand for MALTESERS® in the meantime? Órla had an idea for that too – introducing a new superfast wrapping machine in the UK. It can wrap more than double the number of bags per minute than before, meaning we can keep our fans happy the world over. It just goes to show. Give people freedom and responsibility, and they'll go further than you ever imagined. **mars.co.uk/graduates**

MAKE IT MEAN MORE | **MARS**

McDonald's has operated in the UK since 1974 and and the business is growing consistently with its 1,250 restaurants and over 110,000 employees. It is the biggest family restaurant business in the world, serving approximately 3.7 million customers a day in the UK alone.

Training and developing people has been at the heart of the McDonald's business throughout its 41 years in the UK. Each year the company invests over £40 million in developing its people and providing opportunities for progression. Attracting, retaining and engaging the best people is key to their business.

It has a proven track record of career progression and prospective managers can create a long-term career with one of the world's most recognised and successful brands.

A graduate job at McDonald's is focused on restaurant management – it involves overseeing the performance and development of, on average, 80 employees and identifying ways in which to improve customer service, build sales and profitability. Following the training period, which can last up to six months, Trainee Managers are promoted to Assistant Managers and become part of the core restaurant management team. Successful Trainee Managers can, in future, progress to managing all aspects of a £multi million business – opportunities can then arise to progress to area management roles or secondments in support departments. Trainee Managers need to be logical thinkers, have a great attitude and be committed to delivering a great customer experience.

Working for a progressive company has its perks – including a host of benefits such as a quarterly bonus scheme, six weeks holiday allowance, meal allowance, private healthcare and access to discounts at over 800 retailers.

GRADUATE VACANCIES IN 2017
GENERAL MANAGEMENT

NUMBER OF VACANCIES
100 graduate jobs

LOCATIONS OF VACANCIES

STARTING SALARY FOR 2017
£21,500-£24,500

UNIVERSITY VISITS IN 2016-17
Please check with your university careers service for full details of local events.

APPLICATION DEADLINE
Year-round recruitment

FURTHER INFORMATION
www.Top100GraduateEmployers.com
Register now for the latest news, campus events, work experience and graduate vacancies at **McDonald's***.*

SETTING MYSELF UP FOR THE FUTURE

With McDonald's, I can.

Our Trainee Manager Programme is the first step to managing a £multi-million restaurant employing 80 staff.

After six months of training and learning the basics, our Trainee Managers are promoted to Assistant Managers – but if you've got the drive and ambition, there's no limit to how far you can go.

To find out more about working and learning with us visit

mcdonalds.co.uk/people

McKinsey&Company

GRADUATE VACANCIES IN 2017
CONSULTING

NUMBER OF VACANCIES
No fixed quota

LOCATIONS OF VACANCIES

Vacancies also available elsewhere in the world.

STARTING SALARY FOR 2017
£Competitive

UNIVERSITY VISITS IN 2016-17
BATH, BRISTOL, CAMBRIDGE, DURHAM, EDINBURGH, IMPERIAL COLLEGE LONDON, LONDON SCHOOL OF ECONOMICS, OXFORD, ST ANDREWS, TRINITY COLLEGE DUBLIN, UNIVERSITY COLLEGE DUBLIN, WARWICK
Please check with your university careers service for full details of local events.

MINIMUM ENTRY REQUIREMENTS
2.1 Degree

APPLICATION DEADLINE
27th October 2016

FURTHER INFORMATION
www.Top100GraduateEmployers.com
Register now for the latest news, campus events, work experience and graduate vacancies at McKinsey & Company.

McKinsey & Company helps world-leading clients in the public, private and third sectors to meet their biggest strategic, operational and organisational challenges. Their goal is to provide distinctive and long-lasting performance improvements – in short, it is about having an impact. Making a difference.

As a consultant in this truly global firm, graduates will have the opportunity to work with colleagues and clients from all around the world. They will come into contact with CEOs, government leaders and the foremost charitable organisations, and work together with them on their most exciting and challenging issues.

Working as part of a small team, and dedicated to one project at a time, graduates will be fully involved from the very start of their first project. No two weeks will be the same: from gathering and analysing data, to interviewing stakeholders or presenting findings to clients, the range of industries and business issues to which successful applicants have exposure will mean that they are constantly acquiring new skills and experience. Bright, motivated newcomers can expect their ideas and opinions to be encouraged and valued, right from day one.

Graduates will also enjoy world-class personal and professional development. Formal training programmes, coupled with a culture of mentoring and coaching, will provide the best possible support.

Working in consulting is challenging, but McKinsey encourages a healthy work-life balance. Successful applicants will find like-minded individuals, and a thriving range of groups, initiatives and events that bring people together.

McKinsey & Company is welcoming applications for both full time and summer internship applications.

SECURITY SERVICE
MI5

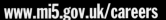

MI5 helps safeguard the UK against threats to national security including terrorism and espionage. It investigates suspect individuals and organisations to gather intelligence relating to security threats. MI5 also advises the critical national infrastructure on protective security measures, to help them reduce their vulnerability.

Graduates from a range of backgrounds join MI5 for stimulating and rewarding careers. Many graduates join the Intelligence Officer Development Programme, which is a structured 3-5 year programme designed to teach new joiners about MI5 investigations and give them the skills to run them. After completing one post of two years or two posts of one year in areas which teach aspects of investigative work, and subject to successful completion of its Foundation Investigative Training (FIT), graduates will then take up an investigative post as a fully trained Intelligence Officer. There will be opportunities to move to new roles and experience new challenges every 2-3 years.

MI5 also deals with vast amounts of data and interpreting that data is vital to its intelligence work. The Intelligence and Data Analyst Development Programme is a structured two-year programme which prepares graduates to be part of this specialist career stream. It will take new joiners from the basics through to the most advanced data analytical techniques. As they progress they will have the opportunity to work in different teams across the range of MI5's investigations using their analytical expertise to make a direct impact on keeping the country safe.

MI5 also offers a Technology Graduate Development Programme which is a structured programme that gives graduates the experience, knowledge and skills they need to be an effective technology professional in its pioneering IT function.

GRADUATE VACANCIES IN 2017
GENERAL MANAGEMENT
IT

NUMBER OF VACANCIES
150 graduate jobs

LOCATIONS OF VACANCIES

STARTING SALARY FOR 2017
£30,000+

UNIVERSITY VISITS IN 2016-17
Please check with your university careers service for full details of local events.

MINIMUM ENTRY REQUIREMENTS
2.2 Degree

APPLICATION DEADLINE
Varies by function

FURTHER INFORMATION
www.Top100GraduateEmployers.com
Register now for the latest news, campus events, work experience and graduate vacancies at MI5.

"I NEVER THOUGHT MY SKILLS COULD HELP PROTECT A NATION"

The future is in your hands.

At MI5 everyone has one thing in common — a commitment to protecting the UK from serious threats. This requires people from a variety of cultures and backgrounds with a range of skills, who can bring different perspectives to our work. Join us and you'll enjoy the chance to share your knowledge in a collaborative environment and help keep the country safe. Find out how you'll fit in at www.mi5.gov.uk/careers

To apply to MI5 you must be a born or naturalised British citizen, over 18 years old and normally have lived in the UK for nine of the last ten years. You should not discuss your application, other than with your partner or a close family member, providing that they are British. They should also be made aware of the importance of discretion.

www.morganstanley.com/campus
graduaterecruitmenteurope@morganstanley.com
linkedin.com/company/morgan-stanley [in]   twitter.com/MorganStanley [twitter]
instagram/morgan.stanley [instagram]   youtube.com/mgstnly [YouTube]

Morgan Stanley

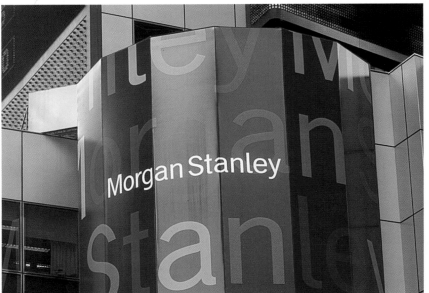

Morgan Stanley is a true global citizen, with offices around the world where talented, passionate people bring excellence and integrity to everything they do. Their vision and goals can only be achieved through hiring, training and rewarding the best people.

Morgan Stanley believe attitude is just as important as aptitude. They want to work with and develop students and graduates who show integrity and commitment to their core values, who share their commitment to providing first-class client service and who are open to innovation. They don't hold to the idea that just because something has always been done a certain way it's the best way to move forward. One result of their beliefs and management system is that new recruits are often surprised by how quickly they can advance to roles with substantial responsibility.

Morgan Stanley are proud to offer opportunities for students and graduates who are ready to grow their careers with them. There are numerous opportunities to learn and grow professionally and help put the power of capital to work. All of Morgan Stanley's programmes are designed to provide the knowledge and toolkit graduates need to develop quickly into an effective and successful professional in their chosen area. Training is not limited to the first weeks or months on the job but continues throughout a graduate's career.

Morgan Stanley believes that capital can work to benefit all. The success they envision, and then create, needs financial capital, certainly; but the foundation of this success is intellectual capital – their people are their strongest asset. The talent and points of view of diverse individuals working for them helps to build their legacy and shape their future. This is why Morgan Stanley accept applicants from all degree disciplines who demonstrate academic excellence.

GRADUATE VACANCIES IN 2017
FINANCE
INVESTMENT BANKING
IT

NUMBER OF VACANCIES
No fixed quota

LOCATIONS OF VACANCIES

STARTING SALARY FOR 2017
£Competitive
Plus benefits and a discretionary bonus.

UNIVERSITY VISITS IN 2016-17
BATH, BELFAST, BRISTOL, CAMBRIDGE, CITY, DUNDEE, DURHAM, EDINBURGH, EXETER, GLASGOW, HERIOT-WATT, IMPERIAL COLLEGE LONDON, KING'S COLLEGE LONDON, LONDON SCHOOL OF ECONOMICS, MANCHESTER, NOTTINGHAM, OXFORD, STRATHCLYDE, TRINITY COLLEGE DUBLIN, UNIVERSITY COLLEGE DUBLIN, UNIVERSITY COLLEGE LONDON, WARWICK, YORK
Please check with your university careers service for full details of local events.

MINIMUM ENTRY REQUIREMENTS
2.1 Degree

APPLICATION DEADLINE
Varies by function

FURTHER INFORMATION
www.Top100GraduateEmployers.com
*Register now for the latest news, campus events, work experience and graduate vacancies at **Morgan Stanley**.*

Morgan Stanley

Want to see the world? How about building a new one?

Anyone can tour China. How about helping create jobs there? Or helping revitalize the airline industry in Spain? Or strengthening the mobile infrastructure in Mexico? That's the kind of change we're working to create. Because we don't want to just see the world, we want to see a better one. Join us.

What Will You Create?

morganstanley.com/campus

Megan
Investment Banking Division

M M
MOTT MACDONALD

Mott MacDonald is global engineering, management, and development consultancy focused on guiding clients through many of the planet's most intricate challenges. Employees take leading roles in creating the world's highest profile infrastructure.

Active in 150 countries, Mott MacDonald's experts find opportunities in complexity, turning obstacles into elegant, sustainable solutions. By looking at scenarios from a fresh angle, employees aim to add value at every stage, for their clients, their colleagues and the lives Mott MacDonald projects touch every day.

Through practice networks Mott MacDonald's global sector leaders provide expertise, share knowledge and spread best practice for everyone to use. Mott MacDonald employees have instant access to an entire network of brilliant people.

Being employee-owned allows Mott MacDonald to choose the work taken on and focus on the issues that are important. Mott MacDonald is independent in thought and action, and therefore focus on what is genuinely right, not what is easy either for their clients or the company.

The award-winning graduate programme supports entry-level professionals in gaining experience and developing technical skills and knowledge with the support of a mentor and a dedicated learning and development team. Mott MacDonald's professional development schemes are accredited, enabling graduates to gain chartered status with their chosen institution and providing opportunities to work on some of the most exciting projects. At the start of their careers, all entry-level professionals will enrol onto the Mott MacDonald Academy, a four-year development programme that will introduce key business and commercial competencies.

GRADUATE VACANCIES IN 2017
CONSULTING
ENGINEERING
PROPERTY

NUMBER OF VACANCIES
250+ graduate jobs

LOCATIONS OF VACANCIES

STARTING SALARY FOR 2017
£24,000-£28,000

UNIVERSITY VISITS IN 2016-17
BATH, BRISTOL, CAMBRIDGE, CARDIFF, EDINBURGH, HERIOT-WATT, IMPERIAL COLLEGE LONDON, LEEDS, LOUGHBOROUGH, MANCHESTER, NEWCASTLE, NORTHUMBRIA, SHEFFIELD, SOUTHAMPTON, STRATHCLYDE, UNIVERSITY COLLEGE LONDON, WARWICK
Please check with your university careers service for full details of local events.

MINIMUM ENTRY REQUIREMENTS
2.1 Degree

APPLICATION DEADLINE
20th November 2016

FURTHER INFORMATION
www.Top100GraduateEmployers.com
Register now for the latest news, campus events, work experience and graduate vacancies at Mott MacDonald.

 networkrail.co.uk/graduates
facebook.com/networkrailgraduates

The railway is vital to Britain's future economic success. That's why Network Rail manages more engineering projects and employs more specialists than other UK organisations. The organisation's work programme for the next five years will have major benefits for the whole country.

Being a graduate at Network Rail provides succesful candidates with so much more than just a job. Graduates will have the opportunity to get involved with charitable work, take part in extra-curricular activities like team sports, attend events and, perhaps most importantly, get the chance to make new friends.

Network Rail offers two overarching routes for graduates and, after they join, they'll be able to follow any number of different career paths.

Engineering might be the perfect destination for those who love to get their hands on real projects out in the field rather than being confined to the drawing board. Graduates might find themselves using high-end technology, like the organisation's ultrasonic testing equipment, or contributing to new innovations, like battery-powered trains. And with plenty of freedom and responsibility open to them, their future will be whatever they make it. Within engineering, there are three specific schemes: Civil Engineering, Electrical & Electronic Engineering, and Mechanical Engineering.

Business Management might be the programme for those who are self-motivated, comfortable with change and keen to get stuck into a real role from the start. Back that up with plenty of drive, energy and passion, and graduates will be able to influence where the organisation goes next as well as exploring all sorts of new opportunities for their career. In Business Management, there are a number of different schemes available: Finance, General Management, Property, Human Resources, Project Management, Supply Chain and Business Technology.

GRADUATE VACANCIES IN 2017
ENGINEERING
FINANCE
GENERAL MANAGEMENT
HUMAN RESOURCES
PROPERTY

NUMBER OF VACANCIES
125-175 graduate jobs

LOCATIONS OF VACANCIES

STARTING SALARY FOR 2017
£26,500

UNIVERSITY VISITS IN 2016-17
BIRMINGHAM, BRISTOL, CARDIFF, IMPERIAL COLLEGE LONDON, LEEDS, LEICESTER, MANCHESTER, NOTTINGHAM, QUEEN MARY LONDON, SHEFFIELD, STRATHCLYDE, UNIVERSITY COLLEGE LONDON
Please check with your university careers service for full details of local events.

MINIMUM ENTRY REQUIREMENTS
2.2 Degree
Relevant degree required for some roles.

APPLICATION DEADLINE
5th December 2016

FURTHER INFORMATION
www.Top100GraduateEmployers.com
Register now for the latest news, campus events, work experience and graduate vacancies at Network Rail.

Changing the face of rail in Britain

Apply now for our graduate scheme and be part of the biggest railway upgrade since the industrial revolution.

networkrail.co.uk/graduates

Newton
The science of performance

GRADUATE VACANCIES IN 2017
CONSULTING

NUMBER OF VACANCIES
120 graduate jobs

LOCATIONS OF VACANCIES

Vacancies also available in Europe.

STARTING SALARY FOR 2017
£45,000-£50,000
Plus a sign-on bonus of £3,000.

UNIVERSITY VISITS IN 2016-17
BATH, BIRMINGHAM, BRISTOL,
CAMBRIDGE, DURHAM, EDINBURGH,
EXETER, IMPERIAL COLLEGE LONDON,
LEEDS, MANCHESTER, NOTTINGHAM,
OXFORD, SOUTHAMPTON, WARWICK
Please check with your university careers service for full details of local events.

MINIMUM ENTRY REQUIREMENTS
2.1 Degree

APPLICATION DEADLINE
Year-round recruitment
Early application advised.

FURTHER INFORMATION
www.Top100GraduateEmployers.com
*Register now for the latest news, campus events, work experience and graduate vacancies at **Newton Europe**.*

Newton brings together talented people to work with organisations that set global agendas. They don't just tell clients how to improve, they work alongside their team to make it happen, achieving real, sustainable results and the kind of change that makes a difference in the world.

When asked "Why Newton?" there are three top reasons people give: the company's 'band of brothers and sisters' culture, its 'hands on' working style and unbeatable record of producing up to 50 per cent improvement in six months without capital expenditure.

Newton is so committed to this last point, they put 100 per cent of fees at risk to deliver guaranteed results. It's a disruptive model that has led to powerful change, and numerous awards across the public and private sectors, from health and social care to defence, grocery, manufacturing, transport and utilities.

Making this type of promise and effecting this kind of change takes a team that knows how to be different. Their innovative approach to problem solving and belief that to make the most impact on a business, one must first understand it completely, sets them apart. Newton people aren't tied to the office or swamped in paperwork; they're given the means and skills to deliver real change and impact for clients and communities. They're also given the scope to accelerate their personal and professional goals, while benefitting from extensive business opportunities and career development: from grass roots to middle management, the executive team and board.

Newton is a place where initiative, creativity and versatility thrive. Colleagues are also friends who inspire and support each other in their shared goal to implement improvements that make a difference to people's lives and change the way the world works.

ARE YOU READY TO CHANGE THE WORLD?

At Newton, your life won't pass you by, nor plateau in middle gear. We'll give you the ability to deliver real societal impact.

In her first twelve months at Newton, Julia has:

- Preserved the jobs of 500 care workers
- Improved the lives of 1,500 people through better care services
- Saved the public sector over £52m

In his first three years at Newton, Tom has:

- Safeguarded 4,500 jobs
- Removed 1,500 lorries from the road per year
- Ensured that low income families can easily afford fresh fruit and veg

We put 100% of our fees at risk to deliver guaranteed results. To make this type of promise, we're different. Not just in the way we do business, but in the people we hire and how we support you to work.

TAKE YOUR CONSULTING CAREER TO THE NTH°.
FIND OUT MORE AT WWW.NEWTONEUROPE.COM/CAREERS

Newton
The science of performance

www.ngdp.org.uk

twitter.com/ngdp_LGA 　　NGDP@local.gov.uk

The ngdp is a two-year graduate development programme which gives committed graduates the opportunity and training to make a positive difference in local communities. Run by the Local Government Association, the ngdp is looking to equip the sector's next generation of high-calibre managers.

Local government is the largest and most diverse employer in the UK, with around 1.2 million staff based in nearly 400 local authorities and in excess of 500 different occupational areas. Almost 900 graduates have completed the ngdp since 2002 and gained access to rewarding careers in and beyond the sector, with many currently holding influential managerial and policy roles.

In the midst of huge changes taking place within the public sector, ngdp graduates are positioned to make a real contribution to shaping and implementing new ideas and initiatives from day one. Graduate trainees are employed by a participating council (or group of councils) for a minimum of two years, during which time they rotate between a series of placements in key areas of the council. Trainees can experience a range of roles in strategy, front-line service and support to expand their perspective of local government's many different capacities and gain a flexible, transferable skill set.

ngdp graduates also benefit from being part of a national cohort of like-minded peers. Together they will participate in a national induction event, join an established knowledge-sharing network and gain a post-graduate qualification in Leadership and Management. The learning and development programme gives graduates the chance to learn from established professionals and each other.

The ngdp has enabled graduates to build varied and rewarding careers for almost twenty years. Join now to start working in an exciting period of opportunity and change for the benefit of local communities.

GRADUATE VACANCIES IN 2017
GENERAL MANAGEMENT

NUMBER OF VACANCIES
120 graduate jobs

LOCATIONS OF VACANCIES

STARTING SALARY FOR 2017
£24,174+

UNIVERSITY VISITS IN 2016-17
ASTON, BIRMINGHAM, BRISTOL, CAMBRIDGE, CARDIFF, DURHAM, EAST ANGLIA, ESSEX, KING'S COLLEGE LONDON, LANCASTER, LEEDS, LEICESTER, LIVERPOOL, LONDON SCHOOL OF ECONOMICS, LOUGHBOROUGH, MANCHESTER, NEWCASTLE, NORTHUMBRIA, NOTTINGHAM, NOTTINGHAM TRENT, OXFORD, QUEEN MARY LONDON, UNIVERSITY COLLEGE LONDON, WARWICK, YORK
Please check with your university careers service for full details of local events.

MINIMUM ENTRY REQUIREMENTS
2.2 Degree

APPLICATION DEADLINE
11th January 2017

FURTHER INFORMATION
www.Top100GraduateEmployers.com
*Register now for the latest news, campus events, work experience and graduate vacancies at **Local Government**.*

NATIONAL GRADUATE
DEVELOPMENT PROGRAMME
FOR LOCAL GOVERNMENT

Real life. Real work. Your opportunity to **make a difference.**

Housing. Social Care. Public Health. Education.

The national graduate development programme for local government is a two year programme focussing on local government's biggest challenges. Providing work experience placements across a range of different departments and a national post graduate qualification, the scheme will provide you with unparalleled opportunities for personal and professional development.

"The ngdp offers the opportunity to deliver transformative change to local communities and to think innovatively in response to complex local problems. It has given me the developmental support to as a future leader within the public sector."

Richard Smith
London Borough of Havering Council

Start your career in local government.
Find out more at: www.ngdp.org.uk
@ngdp_LGA I #ngdp19

NHS
Leadership Academy

Graduate Management
Training Scheme

A DAY IN THEATRE
TAUGHT ME
ABOUT TEAMWORK

As Europe's largest employer with an annual budget of over £100billion, there is no other organisation on Earth quite like the NHS. And with the ability to have a positive impact on over 53 million people, the NHS Graduate Management Training Scheme really is nothing less than a life-defining experience.

It's unquestionably hard work, but this multi-award-winning, fast-track development scheme, enables graduates to become the healthcare leaders of the future.

Graduates specialise in one of five areas: Finance, General Management, Human Resources, Health Informatics, Policy and Strategy. As they grow personally and professionally they'll gain specialist skills while receiving full support from a dedicated mentor at Executive level.

The NHS provides a 20-day induction that encompasses all aspects of life in the organisation. Graduates also arrange a 'flexi-placement' which is their chance to acquire new skills and perspectives from outside the NHS setting.

Success is granted only to those who are prepared to give their heart and souls to their profession. The responsibility of the NHS demands that their future leaders have the tenacity, the focus, and the determination to deliver nothing but the best.

Because the scheme offers a fast-track route to a senior-level role, graduates will soon find themselves facing complex problems head on and tackling high-profile situations. Working for the NHS means standing up to high levels of public scrutiny and having decisions closely inspected. Graduates who want to succeed will need to be thick-skinned, resilient and able to respond to constant change.

This is a career where the hard work and unfaltering commitment of graduates not only affects the lives of others, but it will ultimately define their own.

GRADUATE VACANCIES IN 2017
ACCOUNTANCY
FINANCE
GENERAL MANAGEMENT
HUMAN RESOURCES
IT
RESEARCH & DEVELOPMENT

NUMBER OF VACANCIES
100+ graduate jobs

LOCATIONS OF VACANCIES

STARTING SALARY FOR 2017
£22,896
Plus location allowance where appropriate.

UNIVERSITY VISITS IN 2016-17
Please check with your university careers service for full details of local events.

MINIMUM ENTRY REQUIREMENTS
2.2 Degree

APPLICATION DEADLINE
December 2016

FURTHER INFORMATION
www.Top100GraduateEmployers.com
Register now for the latest news, campus events, work experience and graduate vacancies at the NHS.

I SPENT A DAY IN THE ICU

WITH A GENTLEMAN IN HIS FINAL DAYS

THE HUMANITY SHOWN TO HIS FAMILY BY THE DOCTORS AND NURSES WILL LIVE WITH ME FOREVER.

HOW MANY GRADUATE SCHEMES TOUCH YOU LIKE THIS?

The NHS Graduate Management Training Scheme is nothing less than a life defining experience. Whether you join our Finance, General Management, Human Resources, Health Informatics, or Policy and Strategy scheme, you'll receive everything you need to make a positive impact on the lives of 53 million people across England.

These aren't clinical opportunities, but this is about developing exceptional healthcare leaders. High-calibre management professionals who will lead the NHS through a profound transformation and shape our services around ever-evolving patient needs. Inspirational people who will push up standards, deliver deeper value for money and continue the drive towards a healthier nation.

nhsgraduates.co.uk

Life Defining

NHS
Leadership Academy
Graduate Management Training Scheme

NORTON ROSE FULBRIGHT

Progress with purpose

Norton Rose Fulbright is a global legal firm. It provides the world's pre-eminent corporations and financial institutions with a full business law service. The practice has more than 3,800 lawyers and legal staff based in over 50 cities across Europe, the United States, Canada, Latin America, Asia, Australia, Africa, the Middle East and Central Asia.

Recognised for its industry focus, the practice is strong across all the key sectors: financial institutions; energy; infrastructure, mining and commodities; transport; technology and innovation; and life sciences and healthcare.

Norton Rose Fulbright recruits up to 50 trainee solicitors each year. Its training contract is based on a four-seat pattern, allowing trainees to gain the widest possible exposure to different practice areas and offices around the world. Trainees have the opportunity to spend at least one of their seats on an international or client secondment, in addition to seats in Corporate, Banking and Litigation, enabling them to make the best and most informed choice of qualification.

Each year, Norton Rose Fulbright runs three vacation schemes for law and non-law applicants which are designed to provide an invaluable insight into life and work inside a global legal practice. Successful applicants will have the opportunity to participate in actual work with clients – which could involve anything from legal research to attending meetings or court. Students will also attend training sessions, breakfast briefings about Norton Rose Fulbright's practice areas and social events with current trainees, lawyers, and partners.

Norton Rose Fulbright also runs two open days for penultimate-year undergraduates, finalists and graduates, as well as a first step programme for first-year undergraduates.

GRADUATE VACANCIES IN 2017

LAW

NUMBER OF VACANCIES
Up to 50 graduate jobs
For training contracts starting in 2019.

LOCATIONS OF VACANCIES

STARTING SALARY FOR 2017
£42,000

UNIVERSITY VISITS IN 2016-17
BIRMINGHAM, BRISTOL, CAMBRIDGE, DURHAM, EXETER, IMPERIAL COLLEGE LONDON, KING'S COLLEGE LONDON, LEEDS, LONDON SCHOOL OF ECONOMICS, MANCHESTER, NEWCASTLE, NOTTINGHAM, OXFORD, QUEEN MARY LONDON, SHEFFIELD, SOUTHAMPTON, ST ANDREWS, UNIVERSITY COLLEGE LONDON, WARWICK, YORK
Please check with your university careers service for full details of local events.

MINIMUM ENTRY REQUIREMENTS
2.1 Degree

APPLICATION DEADLINE
Please see website for full details.

FURTHER INFORMATION
www.Top100GraduateEmployers.com
Register now for the latest news, campus events, work experience and graduate vacancies at Norton Rose Fulbright.

Six reasons our trainees chose Norton Rose Fulbright

. . . .

The impressive work.

"Our industry focus means that there is plenty of high quality work.
You can get involved in some huge deals here."

For me, it was the practice's ambitions.

"We're growing and ambitious, and we continue to establish ourselves
at the top of the league tables."

I knew I would go places here.

"We don't just offer secondments – we actively encourage all trainees to undertake one."

I could see this was a place I could grow.

"I wanted challenging work and a steep learning curve.
I get that here, in an environment where those around me look to help me improve."

The international focus.

"It's more than a list of offices - there is a real emphasis on working with colleagues and clients in
different jurisdictions. Pick somewhere in the world, and we've probably got an office there."

The culture felt right.

"It's collegiate, and open to individuality. There's an understanding here that people need to
feel free to explore opportunities outside of their immediate role."

. . . .

We know that choosing the right legal practice is a big decision.
So we thought we would tell you what persuaded our trainees to come here.
If you join us, we'll keep on supporting you to choose wisely throughout your career.

nortonrosefulbrightgraduates.com

NORTON ROSE FULBRIGHT

Progress with purpose

OXFAM

Oxfam is a global movement of people who won't live with poverty. For more than 70 years, they've saved and rebuilt lives in disasters, helped people build better lives, and spoken out on the issues that keep people poor. Right now they're helping people in more than 90 countries worldwide.

For the last ten years, Oxfam's voluntary internship scheme has helped provide valuable experience and skills to hundreds of people. They offer structured roles based around an individual's abilities and interests – usually for one to three days a week, for a period of three to seven months. Local travel and lunch expenses are covered to ensure no one is out of pocket while volunteering.

An Oxfam intern will have the unique advantage of joining some of the world's most passionate and inspiring people who, from campaigners to coffee farmers, are all experts in what they do. There are opportunities to work in Oxfam's UK headquarters in Oxford, in a regional office, or in one of nearly 700 shops. Interns get to put their skills to great, poverty ending use from day one. Whether that's making Oxfam's High Street presence shine as a voluntary assistant shop manager, or helping to raise vital funds as a marketing and communications assistant. Other possible roles include working in HR and recruitment to support Oxfam's staff around the world, or helping to prepare Oxfam's powerful political campaigns as a research executive.

Joining Oxfam as an intern is a great way to experience how a major international charity operates. Taking on global issues that keep people poor like inequality, discrimination against women and climate change is at the heart of everything they do. In just 15 years extreme poverty has been halved. Apply now and be part of the generation that ends it for good.

GRADUATE VACANCIES IN 2017
ACCOUNTANCY
HUMAN RESOURCES
IT
MARKETING
MEDIA
RESEARCH & DEVELOPMENT
RETAILING

NUMBER OF VACANCIES
50+ Voluntary internships

LOCATIONS OF VACANCIES

STARTING SALARY FOR 2017
£Voluntary

UNIVERSITY VISITS IN 2016-17
OXFORD, OXFORD BROOKES
Please check with your university careers service for full details of local events.

APPLICATION DEADLINE
Year-round recruitment

FURTHER INFORMATION
www.Top100GraduateEmployers.com
Register now for the latest news, campus events, work experience and graduate vacancies at Oxfam.

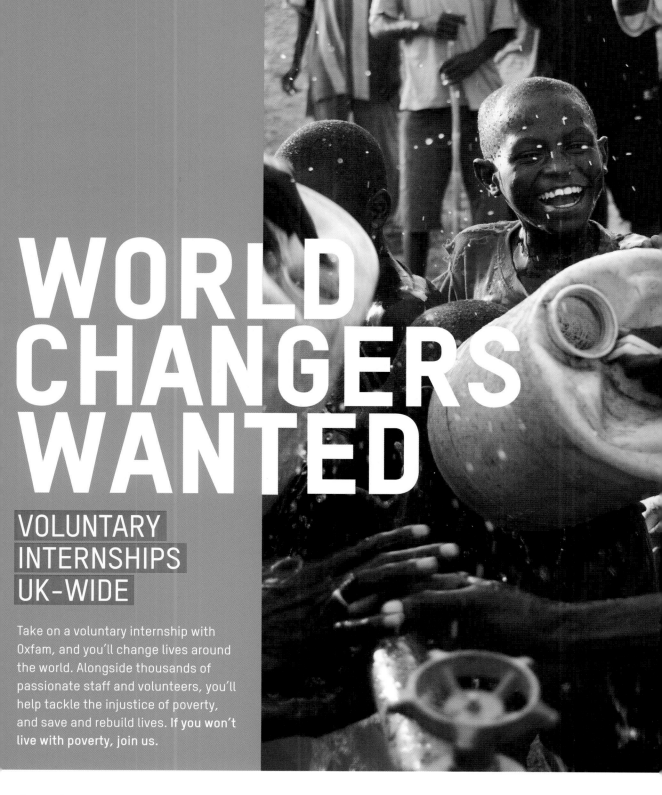

WORLD CHANGERS WANTED

VOLUNTARY INTERNSHIPS UK-WIDE

Take on a voluntary internship with Oxfam, and you'll change lives around the world. Alongside thousands of passionate staff and volunteers, you'll help tackle the injustice of poverty, and save and rebuild lives. If you won't live with poverty, join us.

Apply now at
www.oxfam.org.uk/interns

WE WON'T LIVE WITH POVERTY

Nearly five billion times a day, P&G brands touch the lives of people around the world. Whether they're shaving with a Gillette Fusion ProGlide or Venus Razor; washing their hair with Pantene or Head & Shoulders; or cleaning the dishes with Fairy Liquid.

As one of the world's largest consumer goods company, P&G has one of the strongest portfolios of trusted, globally recognised leading brands of any company in the world. The P&G community includes operations in approximately 70 countries worldwide and our employees represent over 140 nationalities.

P&G recruits the finest people in the world, because they develop talent almost exclusively from within. This means graduates won't just get their first job out of university; they are being hired into a career, with the expectation that they will grow into one of P&G's future leaders… maybe even the next CEO. New starters with P&G can expect a job with responsibility from day one and a career with a variety of challenging roles that develop and broaden their skills, together with the support of training and coaching to help them succeed.

P&G look beyond just good academic records from their applicants. They are looking for graduates who are smart, and savvy, leaders who stand out from the crowd, who are able to get things done. They want to hear about achievements at work, in clubs, societies, voluntary and community activities and to see how graduates have stretched and challenged themselves and others.

The commercial functions welcome applicants from any degree discipline. Product Supply (Manufacturing, Engineering, and Supply Network Operations) requires a technical degree. R&D requires an engineering or science degree.

GRADUATE VACANCIES IN 2017
ENGINEERING
FINANCE
HUMAN RESOURCES
IT
LOGISTICS
MARKETING
RESEARCH & DEVELOPMENT
SALES

NUMBER OF VACANCIES
100 graduate jobs

LOCATIONS OF VACANCIES

STARTING SALARY FOR 2017
£30,000

UNIVERSITY VISITS IN 2016-17
BATH, BRISTOL, CAMBRIDGE, DURHAM, EDINBURGH, EXETER, IMPERIAL COLLEGE LONDON, KING'S COLLEGE LONDON, LEEDS, LONDON SCHOOL OF ECONOMICS, LOUGHBOROUGH, MANCHESTER, NOTTINGHAM, OXFORD, SHEFFIELD, STRATHCLYDE, TRINITY COLLEGE DUBLIN, UNIVERSITY COLLEGE DUBLIN, UNIVERSITY COLLEGE LONDON, WARWICK, YORK
Please check with your university careers service for full details of local events.

MINIMUM ENTRY REQUIREMENTS
Relevant degree required for some roles.

APPLICATION DEADLINE
Varies by function

FURTHER INFORMATION
www.Top100GraduateEmployers.com
Register now for the latest news, campus events, work experience and graduate vacancies at P&G.

WHEN TOP TIER TALENT MEETS A FIRST CLASS COMPANY, A LEADER IS BORN.

YOUR POTENTIAL. IGNITE IT.

As a build-from-within Company, P&G hires individuals who we believe have the potential to become future leaders of the business.

GET TO KNOW US THROUGH AN INTERNSHIP!

We invest a lot into training and developing our people through a variety of different methods – including on-the-job training, mentoring and coaching from more experienced leaders, and formal training via our P&G Leadership Academy. Through an Internship, you will gain real-life insight into the function of your interest and our culture, as well as having the opportunity to earn a permanent entry-level manager job offer. Opportunities available in Brand Management, Sales, Finance & Accounting, HR, IT and Technical areas such as Manufacturing, Engineering, Supply Network Operations and R&D.

Learn more and apply at: UKI.PGCareers.com

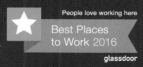

People love working here
Best Places to Work 2016
glassdoor

P&G is an equal opportunity employer.

Penguin Random House is a place for people who like to think, make and do. It is the first of a new kind of publisher – with the brand and scale to create a home for all audiences and capture people's attention with the stories, ideas and writing that matter.

Penguin Random House works with a wide range of talent – from storytellers, animators and developers to entrepreneurs, toy manufacturers and producers. This means they are more like broadcasters as they find more ways to bring stories and ideas to life.

And what career opportunities are available? Creative colleagues in editorial, marketing, publicity and design collaborate with specialist teams in Technology, Finance, Data, Digital and Sales – to name a few.

Penguin Random House value Purpose, Adventure, Openness, Trust and Heart. Whether someone is motivated by working on something new, or taking the next step in their career, the business is committed to supporting its colleagues and giving them a workplace that is somewhere they want to be – rather than have to be.

The business is comprised of eight publishing divisions as well as a successful audio publishing business. The diversity of its publishing includes blockbuster brands such as Jamie Oliver, James Patterson and Peppa Pig through to literary prize winners such as Zadie Smith, Richard Flanagan and Kate Atkinson.

Penguin Random House has three publishing sites in London: Vauxhall Bridge Road, The Strand and Ealing Broadway, distribution centres in Frating, Grantham and Rugby as well as a number of regional offices, employing over 2,000 people in the UK.

GRADUATE VACANCIES IN 2017

ACCOUNTANCY
FINANCE
HUMAN RESOURCES
IT
LOGISTICS
MARKETING
MEDIA
SALES

NUMBER OF VACANCIES
50+ graduate jobs

LOCATIONS OF VACANCIES

STARTING SALARY FOR 2017
£Competitive

UNIVERSITY VISITS IN 2016-17
Please check with your university careers service for full details of local events.

APPLICATION DEADLINE
Year-round recruitment

FURTHER INFORMATION
www.Top100GraduateEmployers.com
Register now for the latest news, campus events, work experience and graduate vacancies at Penguin Random House.

Your Story Starts Here

Finding a great story - editor, publisher, sales director, finance team. Making it look good - designer, copy writer, art director, illustrator. Making the finished book - production controller, product manager, quality controller. Getting it out there - marketing assistant, publicity manager, sales executive, social media manager.

Come and be part of the first of a new kind of publisher that captures the attention of the world through the stories, ideas and writing that matter.

Penguin
Random House
UK

POLICE:NOW
INFLUENCE FOR GENERATIONS

www.policenow.org.uk

graduates@policenow.org.uk

twitter.com/police_now   facebook.com/PoliceNow

Police Now's Graduate Leadership Programme offers outstanding graduates the opportunity to pursue a highly ambitious vision for social change. Its aim? To break the intergenerational cycle of crime in the most challenged areas by creating safe, confident communities in which people can thrive.

This two-year programme operates at pace and intensity. And the challenge is unique.

Graduates become fully warranted police officers with responsibility for an area that could be home to as many as 20,000 people. They get to know their communities – the problems, the prominent offenders and the crime hotspots within them. And right from the beginning, they are expected to use innovative ideas and tactics to tackle the toughest problems and deliver high-impact results.

The programme is challenging. But graduates are supported by mentors, coaches and line managers. Frontline training is delivered by over 40 different experts and a whole range of operational police officers. And there are opportunities to undertake prestigious three-week placements with one of Police Now's partner organisations, which give graduates exposure to the wide range of options available to them once they complete the Police Now programme.

This is a challenge that extends beyond the basic mission of the police to prevent crime and disorder. It's the chance to be a leader in society and on the policing frontline.

And as the 2017 Police Now cohort is expanding to work with 18 police forces, it means there are now more opportunities for outstanding graduates to step forward and change the story, not just today but for generations to come.

GRADUATE VACANCIES IN 2017

POLICING

NUMBER OF VACANCIES
250 graduate jobs

LOCATIONS OF VACANCIES

STARTING SALARY FOR 2017
£29,331
For London positions (regional differences apply).

UNIVERSITY VISITS IN 2016-17
BIRMINGHAM, BRISTOL, CAMBRIDGE, CARDIFF, DURHAM, EXETER, KING'S COLLEGE LONDON, LANCASTER, LEEDS, LEICESTER, LIVERPOOL, LONDON SCHOOL OF ECONOMICS, LOUGHBOROUGH, MANCHESTER, NOTTINGHAM, OXFORD, SHEFFIELD, SOUTHAMPTON, WARWICK, YORK
Please check with your university careers service for full details of local events.

MINIMUM ENTRY REQUIREMENTS
2.1 Degree
Plus a C grade in English at GCSE.

APPLICATION DEADLINE
March 2017
For a July start date.

FURTHER INFORMATION
www.Top100GraduateEmployers.com
*Register now for the latest news, campus events, work experience and graduate vacancies at **Police Now**.*

93% of older people in deprived communities feel unsafe when out after dark.

Join us.
Change the story.

National Graduate Leadership Programme

Their mums were scared to leave the house at night too. Nothing's changed. The same tough neighbourhoods, the same threatening people, the same bad feelings. This is the world as it stands. But there are ways out. Police Now is a **two-year programme** that offers the top graduates the opportunity to become Police Officers and transform communities. Not just for people today but for generations to come. The challenge is unique. The environment is high paced. And you can lead the change here **policenow.org.uk**

POLICE:NOW
INFLUENCE FOR GENERATIONS

pwc.com/uk/careers

e-recruitment.processing@uk.pwc.com ✉

twitter.com/pwc_uk_careers 🐦 facebook.com/pwccareersuk 📘

youtube.com/ careerspwc ▶ linkedin.com/company/pwc-uk 💼

The *opportunity* of a lifetime

pwc

Opportunities are at the heart of a career with PwC. Their purpose is to build trust in society, solving important problems for their clients; helping them tackle complex business challenges, improving how they work. Graduates can join Assurance, Actuarial, Consulting, Deals, Legal, Tax or Technology.

PwC's continued success, size and scale, not forgetting their extensive client base, creates an environment where undergraduates and graduates get access to the best career and work experience opportunities. They choose the best people to join them, but it might be surprising to learn they're from a wide range of backgrounds and have studied all sorts of degree subjects. With offices UK-wide, PwC are looking for graduates eager to learn, with business awareness, intellectual and cultural curiosity and the ability to build strong relationships. PwC's purpose is to identify and resolve their clients' most pressing issues, and they provide graduates with an opportunity to make a positive impact on society.

Graduates get access to the best learning and development around; learning by doing, learning from others and more formal approaches to learning. For some business areas this could mean the opportunity to work towards a professional qualification. With PwC, graduates are in the driving seat of their development, and have the support of a structured career development programme.

For undergraduates and graduates exploring work experience opportunities, or ways to help them decide where their skills, interests and career goals could best fit, they could attend a PwC career open day, or apply to a summer internship or work placement.

Join PwC. They're focused on helping graduates reach their full potential while providing a competitive salary and a personally tailored benefits package.

Take the opportunity of a lifetime.

 **Economics degree**

Our training & development is designed to help you excel in your career

Your degree is just the start

 Arts degree

 Science degree

 **History degree**

50% of our graduate intake studied non-business related subjects

 Geography degree

 pwc

pwc.com/uk/careers

 **/pwccareersuk**   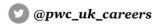 **@pwc_uk_careers**

Create value through diversity. Be yourself, be different.

My role is a dynamic one and every day is different. I really enjoy the variety and contact I have with clients.

Colette Waters
Graduate, Commercial Banking Programme

RBS is a financial services organisation focussed on its customers in the UK & Ireland. Their goal is to be the number one bank for customer service, trust and advocacy in their chosen markets. Graduate, intern and apprenticeship hiring is seen as a key way to harness the talent needed to achieve it.

Offering opportunities nationwide, RBS believes the industry's future will be determined by how well banks serve their customers, and are relying on the passion, and talent of its graduates, interns and apprentices to set new standards. To help them succeed they provide the latest in training and support, challenging them with early responsibility and a sustained career trajectory.

A wide range of graduate programmes and internships across its businesses and functions means there are a diverse range of opportunities to take advantage of. With options ranging from specialist career paths like technology or audit, to customer facing programmes in commercial or private banking, to careers in functions like HR or communications, the possibilities are impressive. And a degree in a Finance or Economics related subject isn't necessary; just talent and passion. RBS also has a commitment to diversity and inclusion which mirrors their hiring approach, with a wide range of employee support networks, and external partnerships, such as Stonewall and Opportunity Now.

Support and guidance from a strong network of managers and mentors accompanies first class formal training at every stage. Graduates and interns are encouraged to build relationships outside of work, through a variety of educational, social and charitable initiatives.

RBS is proud to be recognised as an employer of choice by Investors in Young People. Students who want to reach their full potential will find joining RBS a chance to transform their passions into an exciting, varied and dynamic career.

GRADUATE VACANCIES IN 2017
ACCOUNTANCY
FINANCE
GENERAL MANAGEMENT
HUMAN RESOURCES
INVESTMENT BANKING
IT
MARKETING
SALES

NUMBER OF VACANCIES
300+ graduate jobs

LOCATIONS OF VACANCIES

STARTING SALARY FOR 2017
£Competitive

UNIVERSITY VISITS IN 2016-17
ABERDEEN, BRISTOL, CAMBRIDGE, DURHAM, EDINBURGH, EXETER, GLASGOW, HERIOT-WATT, LEEDS, LEICESTER, LONDON SCHOOL OF ECONOMICS, MANCHESTER, NOTTINGHAM, OXFORD, SHEFFIELD, ST ANDREWS, STIRLING, STRATHCLYDE, UNIVERSITY COLLEGE LONDON, WARWICK, YORK
Please check with your university careers service for full details of local events.

MINIMUM ENTRY REQUIREMENTS
2.2 Degree

APPLICATION DEADLINE
Varies by function

FURTHER INFORMATION
www.Top100GraduateEmployers.com
Register now for the latest news, campus events, work experience and graduate vacancies at RBS.

Curious
Authentic
Great eye
At RBS, we recognise that everyone is different and everyone has different things they love to do. Our Early Careers programmes give you the opportunity to turn that passion into a fulfilling career.
We want you to have everything you need to ensure you get off to the best possible start by providing you with the tools and support to succeed with RBS.
With responsibility from the beginning and the chance to work in some great locations, you will contribute to making RBS the number one bank for customer service, trust and advocacy. We want you to bring your curiosity, commitment and enthusiasm and together, we can make a difference.
Your passion. Your potential.
Discover how your passion could shape a career.
yourpassionyourpotential.rbs.com
RBS Early Careers

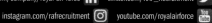

With cutting edge technology, hundreds of aircraft and more than 30,000 active personnel, the Royal Air Force (RAF) is a key part of the British Armed Forces, defending the UK and its interests, strengthening international peace and stability, as well as being a force for good in the world.

Its people lie at the heart of the RAF; they're looking for professionalism, dedication and courage to achieve the RAF's vision of being 'an agile, adaptable and capable Air Force that, person for person, is second to none, and that makes a decisive air power contribution in support of the UK Defence Mission'.

The world is a changing place and so is the Royal Air Force; it is becoming a smaller, more dynamic force able to carry out its missions. To meet the changing times and challenges, and because of the greater capability of technology, the number of people in the RAF has reduced in recent years. Recruiting people of the right quality is therefore a key part of the RAF's vision for the future.

The RAF encompasses all aspects of operations, including the use of the very latest hi-tech equipment but the centre of the RAF's vision has always been its people – and it always will be. It prides itself on attracting the highest quality recruits from all sectors of society and provides first-class training and continuing development.

Officers in the Royal Air Force are expected to lead from the front, setting standards for the men and women under their command. For graduates, there are more than twenty different career opportunities, including Aircrew, Logistics, Engineering and Personnel roles, as well as medical opportunities for qualified doctors, nurses and dentists. In return the RAF offers a competitive salary, free medical & dental, travel opportunities and world class training. It's no ordinary job.

GRADUATE VACANCIES IN 2017
ACCOUNTANCY
ENGINEERING
FINANCE
GENERAL MANAGEMENT
HUMAN RESOURCES
IT
LAW
LOGISTICS
RESEARCH & DEVELOPMENT
SALES

NUMBER OF VACANCIES
500-600 graduate jobs

LOCATIONS OF VACANCIES

STARTING SALARY FOR 2017
£30,000+

UNIVERSITY VISITS IN 2016-17
ABERDEEN, BATH, BELFAST, BIRMINGHAM, BRADFORD, BRISTOL, BRUNEL, CAMBRIDGE, CARDIFF, CITY, DUNDEE, DURHAM, EAST ANGLIA, EDINBURGH, ESSEX, EXETER, GLASGOW, HULL, KENT, LANCASTER, LEEDS, LEICESTER, LIVERPOOL, LOUGHBOROUGH, MANCHESTER, NEWCASTLE, NORTHUMBRIA, NOTTINGHAM, NOTTINGHAM TRENT, OXFORD, PLYMOUTH, READING, SHEFFIELD, SOUTHAMPTON, ST ANDREWS, STIRLING, STRATHCLYDE, SURREY, SUSSEX, SWANSEA, ULSTER, YORK
Please check with your university careers service for full details of local events.

MINIMUM ENTRY REQUIREMENTS
Relevant degree required for some roles.

APPLICATION DEADLINE
Year-round recruitment
Early application advised.

FURTHER INFORMATION
www.Top100GraduateEmployers.com
Register now for the latest news, campus events, work experience and graduate vacancies at the Royal Air Force.

ROYAL AIR FORCE
REGULAR & RESERVE

"So you think you've got what it takes to be an officer in the RAF"

There are graduate careers and then there are graduate challenges - we'd like to think we're the latter. Our officers don't just have good promotion prospects, they get competitive pay and world-class training, as well as six weeks' paid holiday a year, subsidised food and accommodation, free healthcare, and free access to our sports facilities.

As well as specialist training, you'll learn valuable leadership and management skills; you'll also have the opportunity to take part in adventurous training such as rock climbing, skiing and sailing. As you develop your career, you'll move on to face new challenges and opportunities for promotion - both in the UK and overseas.

Interested? If you think you've got what it takes to be an Officer in the RAF, take a look at the RAF Recruitment website at the roles available, what's required for entry and the 24 week Initial Officer Training Course at RAF College Cranwell. You could also be eligible for sponsorship through your sixth-form or university courses, depending on the role you're interested in. We're currently recruiting Engineers, but have opportunities in Logistics, Medical, Personnel, Intelligence and Aircrew Officer roles. Visit the Education and Funding page of the website to find out about the opportunities available.

Healthcare in action

If you've just completed a relevant medical degree, the RAF can offer you a career filled with variety and adventure, as well as first-class postgraduate and specialist training. Once you've been accepted you'll spend 13 weeks at RAF College Cranwell doing the Specialist Entrants Officer Training Course.

www.raf.mod.uk/recruitment/lifestyle-benefits/education-funding/

Throughout the course of history, a life at sea has always attracted those with a taste for travel and adventure; but there are plenty of other reasons for graduates and final-year students to consider a challenging and wide-ranging career with the Royal Navy.

The Royal Navy is, first and foremost, a fighting force. Serving alongside Britain's allies in conflicts around the world, it also vitally protects UK ports, fishing grounds and merchant ships, helping to combat international smuggling, terrorism and piracy. Increasingly, its 33,000 personnel are involved in humanitarian and relief missions; situations where their skills, discipline and resourcefulness make a real difference to people's lives.

Graduates are able to join the Royal Navy as Officers – the senior leadership and management team in the various branches, which range from Engineering, Air and Warfare to Medical, the Fleet Air Arm and Logistics. Starting salaries of at least £25,727 – rising to £30,923 in the first year – compare well with those in industry.

Those wanting to join the Royal Navy as an Engineer – either Marine, Weapon or Engineer Officer, above or below the water – could work on anything from sensitive electronics to massive gas-turbine engines and nuclear weapons. What's more, the Royal Navy can offer a secure, flexible career and the potential to extend to age 50.

The Royal Navy offers opportunities for early responsibility, career development, sport, recreation and travel which exceed any in civilian life. With its global reach and responsibilities, the Royal Navy still offers plenty of adventure and the chance to see the world, while pursuing one of the most challenging, varied and fulfilling careers available.

GRADUATE VACANCIES IN 2017
ENGINEERING
FINANCE
GENERAL MANAGEMENT
HUMAN RESOURCES
IT
LAW
LOGISTICS
RESEARCH & DEVELOPMENT

NUMBER OF VACANCIES
No fixed quota

LOCATIONS OF VACANCIES

Vacancies also available elsewhere in the world.

STARTING SALARY FOR 2017
£25,727
Plus a one-off joining bonus of £27,000 (subject to specialisation – see website for full details).

UNIVERSITY VISITS IN 2016-17
ABERYSTWYTH, BIRMINGHAM, BRISTOL, CARDIFF, EXETER, LEEDS, LIVERPOOL, LOUGHBOROUGH, NEWCASTLE, PLYMOUTH
Please check with your university careers service for full details of local events.

MINIMUM ENTRY REQUIREMENTS
Relevant degree required for some roles.

APPLICATION DEADLINE
Year-round recruitment

FURTHER INFORMATION
www.Top100GraduateEmployers.com
*Register now for the latest news, campus events, work experience and graduate vacancies at the **Royal Navy**.*

YOU MAKE A DIFFERENCE NOT MAKE UP THE NUMBERS

ROYAL NAVY OFFICER

Being an officer in the Royal Navy is a career like any other, but the circumstances and places are sometimes extraordinary. With opportunities ranging from Engineer Officer to Medical Officer, it's a responsible, challenging career that will take you further than you've been before. If you want more than just a job, join the Royal Navy and live a life without limits.

LIFE WITHOUT LIMITS
08456 07 55 55
ROYALNAVY.MOD.UK/CAREERS

www.santanderearlyincareer.co.uk

Santander is one of the largest and most successful financial groups in the world, and their ambition is to become the best bank for their customers, investors, and employees. With an eye on the future, they recognise that technology is rapidly changing how customers bank and pay on the move and they are working to be at the forefront of that change.

Motivated by strong teamwork, an innovative approach to technology, market-leading incentives packages, and a culture of support, they deliver their personal best, every day. Santander focuses on giving graduates everything they need to thrive as future leaders in their chosen areas. That means if they're genuinely passionate, and bring an enthusiasm to their role, graduates are in a great position to develop the skills, experiences and relationships that will kick-start their careers.

Graduate schemes within the business are split into the following divisions – Retail and Business Banking, Global and Corporate Banking further complemented by specialist, operational and support functions. Each is designed to give an in-depth understanding of what makes Santander tick. That could mean developing innovative products for their customers, identifying ways to improve processes for colleagues, or building relationships with high-profile clients.

Whatever the area, graduates will be making a difference from the start. This includes a Corporate Social Responsibility event for Santander's charity of the year – where the aim is to support one million people in their communities by 2020.

What's more, they'll be part of a structured training scheme which is split into four learning cycles and ends with an industry-recognised qualification (CIOBS) in their chosen area. Add this to a dedicated graduate manager for each programme during the entire scheme, as well as continuous development – there's plenty of benefits and no shortage of opportunities to grow with Santander.

GRADUATE VACANCIES IN 2017
FINANCE
GENERAL MANAGEMENT
RETAILING

NUMBER OF VACANCIES
Up to 50 graduate jobs

LOCATIONS OF VACANCIES

STARTING SALARY FOR 2017
£30,000

UNIVERSITY VISITS IN 2016-17
BIRMINGHAM, BRISTOL, IMPERIAL COLLEGE LONDON, LEICESTER, LONDON SCHOOL OF ECONOMICS, LOUGHBOROUGH, NOTTINGHAM, QUEEN MARY LONDON, SHEFFIELD, UNIVERSITY COLLEGE LONDON, WARWICK, YORK
Please check with your university careers service for full details of local events.

MINIMUM ENTRY REQUIREMENTS
2.1 Degree
280 UCAS points

APPLICATION DEADLINE
March 2017

FURTHER INFORMATION
www.Top100GraduateEmployers.com
Register now for the latest news, campus events, work experience and graduate vacancies at Santander.

Savills UK is a leading global real estate service provider listed on the London Stock Exchange. The company employs over 30,000 staff and has 700 offices and associates worldwide, providing all trainees with excellent scope for international experience as their careers develop.

Savills passionately believe their graduates are future leaders and as such make a huge investment in them. Savills graduates are given responsibility from day one, in teams who highly value their contribution, allowing them to be involved in some of the world's most high-profile property deals and developments. Graduates are surrounded by expert professionals and experienced team members from whom they learn and seek advice. Individual achievement is rewarded and Savills look for bold graduates with entrepreneurial flair.

Savills are proud to be The Times Graduate Employer of Choice for Property for the tenth year running. Great work-life balance, structured training and a dynamic working environment are amongst the factors which see Savills nominated by final year students as the preferred property employer year on year.

Savills's Graduate Programme offers the chance to gain an internationally recognised professional qualification. There are opportunities for roles within Surveying, Planning and Estate Agency, and over half of Savills Graduate Programme vacancies are for positions outside of London. The company has offices in exciting locations around the UK which work with high-profile and important clients. The diversity of Savills services means there is the flexibility to carve out a fulfilling, individual and self-tailored career path regardless of the location.

GRADUATE VACANCIES IN 2017
PROPERTY

NUMBER OF VACANCIES
170 graduate jobs

LOCATIONS OF VACANCIES

Vacancies also available in Europe.

STARTING SALARY FOR 2017
£Competitive
Plus a £1,000 signing-on bonus.

UNIVERSITY VISITS IN 2016-17
ABERDEEN, BATH, BIRMINGHAM, BRISTOL, CAMBRIDGE, CARDIFF, CITY, DURHAM, EDINBURGH, EXETER, HERIOT-WATT, LONDON SCHOOL OF ECONOMICS, MANCHESTER, NOTTINGHAM TRENT, OXFORD, OXFORD BROOKES, PLYMOUTH, READING, SHEFFIELD, SOUTHAMPTON, UNIVERSITY COLLEGE LONDON
Please check with your university careers service for full details of local events.

MINIMUM ENTRY REQUIREMENTS
Relevant degree required for some roles.

APPLICATION DEADLINE
Varies by function
Please see website for full details.

FURTHER INFORMATION
www.Top100GraduateEmployers.com
Register now for the latest news, campus events, work experience and graduate vacancies at Savills.

SHAPE **Y**OUR FUTURE

40% of our board joined us as graduates

Do you have what it takes?

Become the future of Savills

savills.com/graduate
🐦 @savillsgraduate

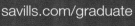

Shell is a global group of energy and petrochemicals companies. With approximately 90,000 employees in over 70 countries, their aim is to help meet the world's growing demand for energy in economically, environmentally and socially responsible ways.

Shell offers a wide range of career routes. The scale and global reach of the business means they have a huge range of technical, commercial and corporate roles across most types of Engineering, Finance, HR, IT, Contracts & Procurement, Sales & Marketing and Maritime.

The Shell Graduate Programme is open to graduates and early career professionals. Most are from Engineering, Science, Social Science or Humanities courses but, with relevant work experience, other subject areas are welcomed. The structured Graduate Programme gives graduates immediate immersion in their business with real, high levels of responsibility from day one. The Programme is typically 3 years, although this can depend on the area of the business, and graduates usually complete at least 2 assignments within this time. Throughout they receive comprehensive support from mentors, work buddies, the graduate network (Energie) and access to senior business leaders. Students apply to the Graduate Programme by completing an Assessed Internship or by applying to attend a Shell Recruitment Day.

Assessed Internships are open to penultimate year students. They are usually 12-week placements undertaken over the summer. During this time students are supported through delivery of a live project for which they have responsibility. Project topics are determined based on the student's interests and the needs of the business. Shell Internships are very sought after roles that give a fantastic insight into a fascinating business – one that has an impact on everyone.

GRADUATE VACANCIES IN 2017

ENGINEERING

FINANCE

HUMAN RESOURCES

IT

LOGISTICS

MARKETING

RESEARCH & DEVELOPMENT

NUMBER OF VACANCIES
70+ graduate jobs

LOCATIONS OF VACANCIES

STARTING SALARY FOR 2017
£32,500

UNIVERSITY VISITS IN 2016-17
ABERDEEN, CAMBRIDGE, HERIOT-WATT, IMPERIAL COLLEGE LONDON, LEEDS, LONDON SCHOOL OF ECONOMICS, MANCHESTER, OXFORD, STRATHCLYDE, UNIVERSITY COLLEGE LONDON
Please check with your university careers service for full details of local events.

APPLICATION DEADLINE
31st March 2017

FURTHER INFORMATION
www.Top100GraduateEmployers.com
Register now for the latest news, campus events, work experience and graduate vacancies at Shell.

IN SEARCH OF REMARKABLE GRADUATES

There has never been a more exciting time to work in the energy industry. With a career at Shell, you'll have a part to play in uniquely innovative projects which will provide an unbeatable experience.

www.shell.co.uk/graduates

 f in

SIEMENS
Ingenuity for life

As a global technology and engineering powerhouse, Siemens is behind a diverse range of technologies and services. They design and manufacture products and systems from rail systems and energy management, to factory automation and medical imaging technology.

Siemens is known for their engineering expertise and ingenious solutions that their customers rely on. Their people are proud of their achievements and are inspired to be the best they can be because of the impact they have on UK society.

Siemens take on tough projects that make a difference. They build infrastructure where there is none. They energise the world, help industries run smoothly and create the digital tomorrow. Siemens offers graduates the perfect opportunity to own these challenges and to build a career that is as successful and sustainable as their technologies

Located in towns and cities all over the UK, Siemens offers a diverse range of graduate and internship opportunities in Engineering and Business where the freedom is given for people to make their mark and use fresh ideas to keep the business at the forefront of innovative technology. They offer meaningful work, real responsibility, collaborative working and continuous personal development, in an organisation that is committed to innovation and making a difference.

Graduates join the company in all types of roles – from Electrical and Mechanical Engineering, to Project Management and Finance – however whatever role is undertaken, all graduates participate in the company's two-year Graduate Development Programme which is designed to give a solid foundation upon which to establish a successful career at Siemens, delivering real value to the business and making a very real difference to the world.

GRADUATE VACANCIES IN 2017

ENGINEERING
FINANCE
GENERAL MANAGEMENT
IT
PURCHASING
RESEARCH & DEVELOPMENT
SALES

NUMBER OF VACANCIES
70-80 graduate jobs

LOCATIONS OF VACANCIES

STARTING SALARY FOR 2017
£Competitive

UNIVERSITY VISITS IN 2016-17
BIRMINGHAM, CAMBRIDGE, IMPERIAL COLLEGE LONDON, LOUGHBOROUGH, MANCHESTER, NEWCASTLE, NOTTINGHAM, OXFORD, SHEFFIELD, SOUTHAMPTON, STRATHCLYDE
Please check with your university careers service for full details of local events.

MINIMUM ENTRY REQUIREMENTS
2.2 Degree

APPLICATION DEADLINE
Early January 2017

FURTHER INFORMATION
www.Top100GraduateEmployers.com
Register now for the latest news, campus events, work experience and graduate vacancies at Siemens.

sky

skystartingout.com

facebook.com/skystartingout

youtube.com/workforsky

twitter.com/skystartingout

Technology is at the heart of Sky's business. Sky in the UK and Ireland is part of Europe's leading entertainment company, which serves 21 million customers across five countries. There are plenty of opportunities available for successful applicants across Sky's award-winning teams in Technology and Business.

That's why graduates are critical to their success. As Sky grows it's looking for bright, talented graduates from any degree background to make a difference to their ever-changing business.

Whether it's working in Software Engineering, Technology or a Commercial role in areas like Finance or Marketing, graduates looking to develop their career at Sky will be part of a fast-paced business that's changing the game for the entire industry. Joining Sky at one of its state-of-the-art offices close to Central London, Leeds or Edinburgh, graduates will be right in the thick of it. Whatever their skills, wherever they join, from day one they'll be part of a network of friendly graduates that stretch right across the business. They'll work on real projects making decisions that really matter and help Sky do better than ever.

And because successful graduates play such an important role for Sky, their mentors will make sure they have everything they need to develop. This includes working on a structured and tailored plan to progress their career through plenty of development opportunities. What's more, they'll have access to great rewards such as free Sky+HD and broadband, as well as enrolment in the Sky pension plan, health insurance and a wide range of retail discounts.

So, whatever graduates are studying, there is a place for them to shine and create their own story at Sky.

GRADUATE VACANCIES IN 2017

FINANCE

IT

MARKETING

NUMBER OF VACANCIES
90+ graduate jobs

LOCATIONS OF VACANCIES

STARTING SALARY FOR 2017
£25,000-£32,000

UNIVERSITY VISITS IN 2016-17
BATH, BRISTOL, CARDIFF, DURHAM, EDINBURGH, EXETER, GLASGOW, HERIOT-WATT, KING'S COLLEGE LONDON, KENT, LANCASTER, LEEDS, LEICESTER, LIVERPOOL, LOUGHBOROUGH, MANCHESTER, NORTHUMBRIA, SOUTHAMPTON, ST ANDREWS, STRATHCLYDE, UNIVERSITY COLLEGE LONDON, WARWICK, YORK
Please check with your university careers service for full details of local events.

APPLICATION DEADLINE
Varies by function

FURTHER INFORMATION
www.Top100GraduateEmployers.com
Register now for the latest news, campus events, work experience and graduate vacancies at Sky.

Slaughter and May is one of the most prestigious law firms in the world. They advise on high-profile and often landmark international transactions. Their excellent and varied client list ranges from governments to entrepreneurs, from retailers to entertainment companies and from conglomerates to Premier League football clubs.

Slaughter and May has offices in London, Brussels, Hong Kong and Beijing and close relationships with leading independent law firms around the world.

Slaughter and May has built a reputation for delivering innovative solutions to difficult problems. This reputation has been earned because each of their multi-specialist lawyers advises on broad legal areas, combining experience gained on one type of transaction to solve problems in another. It is a full service law firm to corporate clients and has leading practitioners across a wide range of practice areas including Mergers and Acquisitions, Corporate and Commercial, Financing, Tax, Competition, Dispute Resolution, Real Estate, Pensions and Employment, Financial Regulation, Information Technology and Intellectual Property.

Their lawyers are not set billing or time targets and therefore are free to concentrate on what matters most – expertise, sound judgement, a willingness to help one another and the highest quality of client service.

During the two-year training contract, trainees turn their hand to a broad range of work, taking an active role in four, five or six groups while sharing an office with a partner or experienced associate. Most trainees spend at least two six-month seats in the firm's market leading corporate, commercial and financing groups. Subject to gaining some contentious experience, they choose how to spend the remaining time.

Among their lawyers, 32 nationalities and over 84 different universities are represented.

GRADUATE VACANCIES IN 2017

LAW

NUMBER OF VACANCIES
80 graduate jobs
For training contracts starting in 2019.

LOCATIONS OF VACANCIES

STARTING SALARY FOR 2017
£43,000

UNIVERSITY VISITS IN 2016-17
ABERDEEN, BIRMINGHAM, BRISTOL, CAMBRIDGE, DURHAM, EDINBURGH, EXETER, GLASGOW, KING'S COLLEGE LONDON, LEEDS, LONDON SCHOOL OF ECONOMICS, MANCHESTER, NEWCASTLE, NOTTINGHAM, OXFORD, SHEFFIELD, ST ANDREWS, TRINITY COLLEGE DUBLIN, UNIVERSITY COLLEGE DUBLIN, UNIVERSITY COLLEGE LONDON, WARWICK, YORK
Please check with your university careers service for full details of local events.

MINIMUM ENTRY REQUIREMENTS
2.1 Degree

APPLICATION DEADLINE
Please see website for full details.

FURTHER INFORMATION
www.Top100GraduateEmployers.com
*Register now for the latest news, campus events, work experience and graduate vacancies at **Slaughter and May**.*

SLAUGHTER AND MAY

A world of difference

Laws, international markets, global institutions… all changing every day. So how do we, as an international law firm, create the agility of mind that enables us to guide some of the world's most influential organisations into the future?

By allowing bright people the freedom to grow. By training lawyers in a way that develops a closer understanding of clients through working on a wider range of transactions. By fostering an ethos of knowledge sharing, support and mutual development by promoting from within and leaving the clocks outside when it comes to billing. To learn more about how our key differences not only make a world of difference to our clients, but also to our lawyers and their careers, visit

slaughterandmay.com/careers

80
training contracts

250+
workshops
and schemes

Lawyers from
84
universities

graduate_recruitment@standardlife.com

twitter.com/SLcareers_   facebook.com/StandardLifeCareers

youtube.com/StandardLifeplc   linkedin.com/company/standard-life

Standard Life | **Standard Life Investments**

Standard Life is an investment company, with over 190 years' experience of helping people manage their money. It employs around 6,500 people, and supports clients and customers across 46 countries. For graduates and interns, there are real challenges, real responsibilities, and a genuine career path.

Based in Edinburgh, Standard Life supports around 4.5 million customers and clients worldwide. It administers over £307 billion of assets, with Standard Life Investments managing £253 billion of these. The business also supports around 25 million more clients through partnerships in India and China.

Whether it's by helping people save for their future, investing responsibly, or supporting the communities in which it operates, Standard Life strives to make a positive long-term impact. To do this, it relies on talented people, with diverse skills and perspectives, working collaboratively and playing to their strengths.

Graduates and interns have a big part to play in this. In return there's a first-class programme, with great benefits, and the foundations to start an exciting career.

It's a two-year programme, offering challenging rotational placements across Standard Life and Standard Life Investments. There are opportunities in accountancy, actuarial, client relations, human resources, investments, legal, marketing, business operations and technology.

There's also a supportive environment in which to work. Graduates have opportunities to learn from senior leaders from the very start – as well as a personal development programme to complement their on-the-job learning. For those studying towards professional qualifications, there's support along the way. And there's the benefit of belonging to a big community of graduates and interns – with various social and professional networks to join too.

All figures as at 31 December 2015.

GRADUATE VACANCIES IN 2017
ACCOUNTANCY
FINANCE
GENERAL MANAGEMENT
HUMAN RESOURCES
IT
LAW
MARKETING

NUMBER OF VACANCIES
50 graduate jobs

LOCATIONS OF VACANCIES

STARTING SALARY FOR 2017
£Competitive
Plus a performance-related bonus.

UNIVERSITY VISITS IN 2016-17
ABERDEEN, DUNDEE, DURHAM, EDINBURGH, GLASGOW, HERIOT-WATT, IMPERIAL COLLEGE LONDON, LONDON SCHOOL OF ECONOMICS, MANCHESTER, NEWCASTLE, OXFORD BROOKES, READING, ST ANDREWS, STIRLING, STRATHCLYDE, WARWICK
Please check with your university careers service for full details of local events.

MINIMUM ENTRY REQUIREMENTS
2.1 Degree

APPLICATION DEADLINE
Varies by function
Please see website for full details.

FURTHER INFORMATION
www.Top100GraduateEmployers.com
*Register now for the latest news, campus events, work experience and graduate vacancies at **Standard Life**.*

We offer a first-class programme for graduates and interns. Big challenges, real responsibilities, and a great support network. If you're starting on your career path - and your ambition matches ours - we'll help you create a clear route to follow.

From great potential

to making an impact

TeachFirst

GRADUATE VACANCIES IN 2017

ALL SECTORS

NUMBER OF VACANCIES
1,750 graduate jobs

LOCATIONS OF VACANCIES

STARTING SALARY FOR 2017
£Competitive

UNIVERSITY VISITS IN 2016-17
ABERYSTWYTH, ASTON, BANGOR, BATH, BIRMINGHAM, BRISTOL, BRUNEL, CAMBRIDGE, CARDIFF, DURHAM, EAST ANGLIA, EDINBURGH, ESSEX, EXETER, GLASGOW, HULL, IMPERIAL COLLEGE LONDON, KING'S COLLEGE LONDON, KENT, LANCASTER, LEEDS, LEICESTER, LIVERPOOL, LONDON SCHOOL OF ECONOMICS, LOUGHBOROUGH, MANCHESTER, NEWCASTLE, NORTHUMBRIA, NOTTINGHAM, NOTTINGHAM TRENT, OXFORD, OXFORD BROOKES, QUEEN MARY LONDON, READING, ROYAL HOLLOWAY, SCHOOL OF AFRICAN STUDIES, SHEFFIELD, SOUTHAMPTON, ST ANDREWS, SURREY, SUSSEX, SWANSEA, UNIVERSITY COLLEGE LONDON, WARWICK, YORK
Please check with your university careers service for full details of local events.

MINIMUM ENTRY REQUIREMENTS
2.1 Degree
300 UCAS points

APPLICATION DEADLINE
Year-round recruitment
Early application advised.

FURTHER INFORMATION
www.Top100GraduateEmployers.com
Register now for the latest news, campus events, work experience and graduate vacancies at Teach First.

Teach First are looking for graduates who want a real challenge – one where they can use their intelligence and personality to help solve one of the country's biggest problems – educational inequality. Apply now for a unique and career-defining opportunity.

The link between how well children do at school and how much their families earn is stronger in the UK than almost anywhere in the developed world. Teach First are part of a movement that's changing this.

They believe that inspirational teaching and leadership are vital to helping every child succeed, regardless of their background. Teach First support graduates to become influential leaders through their Leadership Development Programme (LDP) in schools across England and Wales.

Informed by 14 years of development, their world-class programme combines global best practice in leadership development and teacher training. During the programme participants gain a fully-funded Postgraduate Diploma, worth double the credits of a PGCE, to become a qualified teacher. Covering both education and leadership, they then have the option to top the qualification up to a Master's degree. The LDP gives graduates the key skills and personal qualities needed to develop into an effective leader – someone who can make a real impact. Those who can inspire in the classroom will bring resilience, efficiency and imagination to any environment, no matter where their career takes them.

Over 10,000 people have joined the Teach First LDP so far. Many have remained in the classroom and many others are working in leadership roles across all sectors of the economy. What they all have in common is a belief that every child should have equal opportunities in education and in life, and the knowledge they are contributing towards this goal.

TeachFirst

Gain the skills you need, wherever your career takes you.

☑ **Communication**
☑ **Problem solving**
☑ **Resilience**
☑ **Leadership**

Join our Leadership Development Programme and help end educational inequality.

teachfirst.org.uk/recruitment

Hannah Cusworth
HR Analyst, Goldman Sachs
Taught: English

Tesco's people are its biggest asset – with over half a million employees across the world. Its success as the largest retailer in the UK is shaped by the vision and ideas of the people who work there, who have the ability to turn these ideas into fantastic shopping experiences for customers.

Tesco puts the customer at the heart of everything it does – always working to provide a better shopping experience, whether through a seamless online journey or reducing queuing time within stores. Tesco is looking for talented individuals who share a passion for great service: collaborators with the energy and enthusiasm to manage and deliver large-scale projects; problem solvers who can work under pressure and maintain their attention to detail; and organisers who can communicate at different levels and thrive when working in teams. In return, Tesco provides plenty of learning and support along the way – with mentors and buddies for every graduate, and a renowned training academy.

Tesco is proud of its early career programmes and the training provided. The company firmly believes the most rewarding way for graduates to learn is through the responsibility of real-life business situations, where they can apply their knowledge, be entrepreneurial and make things happen. No two days are the same at Tesco, and the wide range of programmes on offer can set graduates on a career path for life.

People who imagine working at Tesco often think of working in store. That's certainly true for those that choose the Store Graduate Programme. But with around 20 graduate programmes across the business, including Finance, General Merchandise, Technology and Product Quality, there are many other exciting areas outside the store.

GRADUATE VACANCIES IN 2017

ENGINEERING
FINANCE
GENERAL MANAGEMENT
HUMAN RESOURCES
IT
LOGISTICS
MARKETING
PROPERTY
PURCHASING
RETAILING

NUMBER OF VACANCIES
150-200 graduate jobs

LOCATIONS OF VACANCIES

STARTING SALARY FOR 2017
£24,000-£32,000

UNIVERSITY VISITS IN 2016-17
BATH, BIRMINGHAM, CAMBRIDGE, DURHAM, EAST ANGLIA, LEEDS, MANCHESTER, NEWCASTLE, NOTTINGHAM, SHEFFIELD, SOUTHAMPTON, WARWICK
Please check with your university careers service for full details of local events.

MINIMUM ENTRY REQUIREMENTS
2.1 Degree
300-320 UCAS points
Relevant degree required for some roles. No UCAS requirement for Store Graduate Programme.

APPLICATION DEADLINE
31st January 2017
Applications will be dealt with on a first-come-first-served basis.

FURTHER INFORMATION
www.Top100GraduateEmployers.com
Register now for the latest news, campus events, work experience and graduate vacancies at Tesco.

Will Etherington, Commercial Strategy & Operations Graduate

"The opportunity to develop and progress in Tesco was the deciding factor for me."

"I've been given the freedom to explore the business, get involved in high profile pieces of work and find out what I can do to deliver an amazing customer experience.

The support I've had from the Early Careers team has also been great. They really invest time and energy into helping you further your career."

Tesco Graduate Careers
Too many great programmes to fit in store

www.tesco-earlycareers.com

TRANSPORT FOR LONDON
EVERY JOURNEY MATTERS

With a population of over 8.6 million and more than 17 million visitors every year, London is a city that's always on the move. Transport for London (TfL) is responsible for looking after the intricate planning and everyday operation of the Capital's transport system.

TfL's people make sure that millions of residents, workers and visitors arrive safely at their destinations, day in, day out. Every journey matters to them. Join them on one of their graduate schemes and, as well as enjoying some exciting career opportunities, the work of successful applicants could also have a direct influence on the future of London and the people who live, work and visit there.

Improving and expanding London's transport network is central to driving economic growth, jobs and housing in the city. And the work that TfL does has a direct impact on the lives of millions of people every single day.

Their remit is broad. It includes everything from the Tube, London Overground, Docklands Light Railway, TfL Rail, London Trams, London River Services, Dial-a-Ride, Victoria Coach Station and Emirates Air Line, to Santander Cycles and of course, their iconic red double-decker buses. But there's a lot more to it than that.

TfL also regulate taxis and the private hire trade, run the Congestion Charging scheme, manage the city's 580km red route road network and operate every one of the Capital's 6,200 traffic signals.

They're pioneers in integrated ticketing and in providing information to help people move around London. Oyster is the world's most popular smartcard, and contactless payment is making travel even more convenient. Real-time travel information is provided by them and through third parties, who use their data to power apps and other services.

GRADUATE VACANCIES IN 2017

ACCOUNTANCY
ENGINEERING
FINANCE
GENERAL MANAGEMENT
IT
PROPERTY
PURCHASING

NUMBER OF VACANCIES
150 graduate jobs

LOCATIONS OF VACANCIES

STARTING SALARY FOR 2017
£Competitive

UNIVERSITY VISITS IN 2016-17
ASTON, BATH, BIRMINGHAM, BRISTOL, CAMBRIDGE, CARDIFF, DURHAM, EDINBURGH, EXETER, GLASGOW, IMPERIAL COLLEGE LONDON, KING'S COLLEGE LONDON, KENT, LEEDS, LEICESTER, LONDON SCHOOL OF ECONOMICS, LOUGHBOROUGH, MANCHESTER, NEWCASTLE, NOTTINGHAM, NOTTINGHAM TRENT, OXFORD, OXFORD BROOKES, QUEEN MARY LONDON, ROYAL HOLLOWAY, SOUTHAMPTON, STRATHCLYDE, SURREY, UNIVERSITY COLLEGE LONDON, WARWICK
Please check with your university careers service for full details of local events.

MINIMUM ENTRY REQUIREMENTS
Dependent on scheme
Please see website for full details.

APPLICATION DEADLINE
Varies by function

FURTHER INFORMATION
www.Top100GraduateEmployers.com
Register now for the latest news, campus events, work experience and graduate vacancies at Transport for London.

Shape the future of London – become a TfL graduate

We want to be as diverse as the city we represent and welcome applications from everyone regardless of disability, faith, sexual orientation, ethnicity, age or gender.

Take a wider look at tfl.gov.uk/graduates

MAYOR OF LONDON

TRANSPORT FOR LONDON
EVERY JOURNEY MATTERS

GRADUATE VACANCIES IN 2017

HUMAN RESOURCES

INVESTMENT BANKING

IT

MARKETING

SALES

NUMBER OF VACANCIES
300 graduate jobs

LOCATIONS OF VACANCIES

Vacancies also available in Europe, the USA and Asia.

STARTING SALARY FOR 2017
£Competitive

UNIVERSITY VISITS IN 2016-17
BATH, BIRMINGHAM, BRISTOL, CAMBRIDGE, DURHAM, EXETER, IMPERIAL COLLEGE LONDON, LONDON SCHOOL OF ECONOMICS, MANCHESTER, NOTTINGHAM, OXFORD, SURREY, UNIVERSITY COLLEGE LONDON, WARWICK

Please check with your university careers service for full details of local events.

MINIMUM ENTRY REQUIREMENTS
2.1 Degree
300 UCAS points

APPLICATION DEADLINE
Varies by function

FURTHER INFORMATION
www.Top100GraduateEmployers.com

Register now for the latest news, campus events, work experience and graduate vacancies at UBS.

UBS employees are experts in wealth management, investment banking, asset management, private retail banking in Switzerland, and in all the support functions it requires to make a large financial services firm like UBS run smoothly. They serve corporations, private and institutional clients worldwide.

There are 60,000 employees at UBS working in 900 offices in more than 50 countries in all the major global financial centers.

UBS's diverse workforce spans four generations and is from 135 countries – and the average length of employment is nine years. UBS offers its people a supportive, challenging and diverse working environment and invests time and resources in its people and their careers.

And it's not just UBS that says so. Universum and Euromoney (and others) have consistently voted UBS as one of the most attractive employers – internationally and in Switzerland. Why? Because UBS values passion, commitment and excellence, and rewards performance. Succeeding at UBS means respecting, understanding and trusting, but also challenging and being challenged by colleagues.

Interested in Wealth Management, Investment Banking, Asset Management or Retail & Corporate Banking? Or how about IT, Legal, Compliance, Risk, Operations, HR or Marketing? At UBS, a world awaits. UBS offers talented individuals a wide range of programmes; from first year Insights or Horizons, through to Summer Internships, Industrial Placements and Graduate Opportunities.

Don't have an economics or business degree? Don't worry – there's a position for everyone at UBS to inspire and challenge those who have drive and creativity.

Grow with us

Let's shape the future together.

We don't just look at what you're studying. (Really we don't.) We care about your attitude. And it doesn't matter if you like things fast-moving or measured. You like reading people or plotting charts. Deliberating or deciding. Or some of all of those things. It doesn't matter if you don't know yet. We can help you find out.

ubs.com/graduates

www.unilever.co.uk/careers-jobs/graduates

enquiry@unilevergraduates.com ✉
twitter.com/UnileverGradsUK 🐦 facebook.com/UnileverCareersUKandIRE f
youtube.com/user/TheUnileverUFLP ▶️ linkedin.com/company/unilever in

Unilever, a leading consumer goods company, makes some of the world's best-loved brands: Dove, Knorr, Magnum, Lynx, Sure, Tresemmé and Hellmann's to name a few. Two billion consumers use their products every day. Unilever products are sold in 190 countries and they employ 168,000 people globally.

Around the world, Unilever products help people look good, feel good and get more out of life. What's Unilever's challenge? To double the size of its business, while reducing its environmental impact and increasing its social impact. Unilever is looking for talented graduates who have the will and the drive to help Unilever achieve this ambition.

The Unilever Future Leaders Programme (UFLP) helps fast track talent to senior management quickly. Graduates can apply to one of the following areas – Supply Chain Management, Customer Management (Sales), HR Management, Marketing, Business & Technology Management, Research & Development, Research & Development Packaging and Financial Management. Whichever area they join, graduates will make a big business impact.

The three year, world-class development programme is packed with variety and challenge, collaborating with both local and international teams. Graduates will have real responsibility from day one, an opportunity of becoming a manager after two years, and a great support network to see them develop and attain their future professional goals. Unilever will support them in achieving Chartered status and qualifications such as CIMA, IMechE, IChemE, IEE, APICS, ICS, and CIPD.

With such a great ambition lie exciting challenges for the company and its brands, and a fantastic opportunity for graduates to have a great head start in their career, make a real difference to Unilever's business and the wider world.

GRADUATE VACANCIES IN 2017

ENGINEERING
FINANCE
HUMAN RESOURCES
IT
LOGISTICS
MARKETING
RESEARCH & DEVELOPMENT
SALES

NUMBER OF VACANCIES
50 graduate jobs

LOCATIONS OF VACANCIES

Vacancies also available in Europe.

STARTING SALARY FOR 2017
£30,000+

UNIVERSITY VISITS IN 2016-17
ASTON, BATH, BIRMINGHAM, CAMBRIDGE, DURHAM, EXETER, IMPERIAL COLLEGE LONDON, KING'S COLLEGE LONDON, LANCASTER, LEEDS, LIVERPOOL, LOUGHBOROUGH, MANCHESTER, NEWCASTLE, OXFORD, STRATHCLYDE, TRINITY COLLEGE DUBLIN, UNIVERSITY COLLEGE DUBLIN, UNIVERSITY COLLEGE LONDON, WARWICK
Please check with your university careers service for full details of local events.

MINIMUM ENTRY REQUIREMENTS
2.1 Degree

APPLICATION DEADLINE
Year-round recruitment
Early application advised.

FURTHER INFORMATION
www.Top100GraduateEmployers.com
Register now for the latest news, campus events, work experience and graduate vacancies at Unilever.

help@virginmediagraduates.co.uk

linkedin.com/company/virgin-media   twitter.com/VirginMediaJobs

instagram.com/VMGradsAndInterns   youtube.com/VirginMediaCareers

GRADUATE VACANCIES IN 2017

ACCOUNTANCY
ENGINEERING
FINANCE
GENERAL MANAGEMENT
HUMAN RESOURCES
MARKETING
SALES

NUMBER OF VACANCIES
50+ graduate jobs

LOCATIONS OF VACANCIES

Virgin Media is part of Liberty Global plc, the world's largest international cable company. Together, Virgin Media and Liberty Global serve millions of customers across 30 countries, helping to connect people and enabling them to experience the digital world's endless possibilities.

Since the invention of the internet, digital technology has had an increasing impact on the way people live. But it's not just technology that interests Virgin Media. What matters is how technology can be used to improve lives and prospects. From TV and mobile to home phone and their famously fast broadband services, Virgin Media is constantly opening up new possibilities – helping to make people's lives easier, fuller, and even more fun. And Virgin Media is looking for graduates to help them.

Virgin Media are after the future leaders and experts who'll help them stay ahead of the game. In return, their graduates will be put right in the thick of things – dialling up their strengths, stretching and challenging the norms, and broadening their knowledge of the business and the industry beyond. Virgin Media make good things happen for graduates.

Plus, whether a candidate sees their future in finance, engineering or any of the other amazing schemes on offer, every Virgin Media graduate will gain the knowledge, skills and experience they need to supercharge a brilliant career. That's because everything is achievable in the Virgin Media family. On Virgin Media's graduate scheme, it's possible to grab new opportunities, get involved in something big – and growing – and quickly learn the Virgin Media way through exposure, education and experience.

So, why not join Virgin Media in one of the most exciting and superfast businesses on the planet – and help to make good things happen.

STARTING SALARY FOR 2017
£29,000
Plus a £2,000 welcome bonus, a performance-related bonus and other benefits.

UNIVERSITY VISITS IN 2016-17
ASTON, BATH, BIRMINGHAM, DURHAM, IMPERIAL COLLEGE LONDON, LEEDS, LOUGHBOROUGH, MANCHESTER, NOTTINGHAM, READING, SHEFFIELD, SOUTHAMPTON, UNIVERSITY COLLEGE LONDON, WARWICK
Please check with your university careers service for full details of local events.

MINIMUM ENTRY REQUIREMENTS
2.1 Degree
Relevant degree required for some roles.

APPLICATION DEADLINE
Varies by function

FURTHER INFORMATION
www.Top100GraduateEmployers.com
*Register now for the latest news, campus events, work experience and graduate vacancies at **Virgin Media**.*

Virgin Media is growing. Grow with us.

Through Project Lightning, Virgin Media is extending its unrivalled network to reach 4,000,000 more homes and businesses in the UK. By 2020, we aim to serve almost 10 million customers in the UK and Ireland.

Lightning is the country's biggest ever network expansion plan – and we'll be calling on all our talent to pull it off. As part of our graduate programme, you could play a key role in helping us connect more customers with everything and everyone they love.

Find out more about our graduate programmes at **virginmedia.com/tt100**

www.wellcome.ac.uk/graduates

n.hannan@wellcome.ac.uk

twitter.com/wellcometrust   facebook.com/WellcomeTrust

youtube.com/wellcometrust   linkedin.com/company/wellcome-trust

Wellcome exists to improve health for everyone by helping great ideas to thrive. Wellcome is a global charitable foundation, both politically and financially independent. It supports scientists and researchers, takes on big problems, fuels imaginations and sparks debate.

Wellcome is looking for recent graduates that want to make a difference in global health. Its two-year graduate development programme allows graduates to try out four different jobs for six months at a time. This could involve helping to develop funding schemes, researching investment opportunities or identifying new ways to engage the public with Wellcome's work. No matter which rotations graduates choose, they'll be a valued member of the team, with support from mentors, line managers and peers, on-the-job and formal training opportunities, real responsibilities, and the knowledge that they're contributing to Wellcome's overall purpose.

Wellcome is well known for funding scientific and medical research, but it's not just looking for scientists – it's open to candidates from any background. It's previously recruited scientists who want to use their degrees without working in a lab, an engineering graduate who found a passion for communications, and an art history graduate who first discovered Wellcome through Wellcome Collection, its free cultural space that explores connections between medicine, life and art.

Wellcome is looking for graduates who enjoy a challenge, are passionate about improving health and want to collaborate with people across the organisation while developing their skills. By taking on a new role every six months, graduates will develop confidence and resilience and learn skills they can take anywhere.

GRADUATE VACANCIES IN 2017

FINANCE
GENERAL MANAGEMENT
HUMAN RESOURCES
INVESTMENT BANKING
IT
LAW
MARKETING
MEDIA

NUMBER OF VACANCIES
10-12 graduate jobs

LOCATIONS OF VACANCIES

STARTING SALARY FOR 2017
£26,000+

UNIVERSITY VISITS IN 2016-17
BATH, BIRMINGHAM, BRISTOL, BRUNEL, CAMBRIDGE, CARDIFF, CITY, DURHAM, EAST ANGLIA, EDINBURGH, EXETER, IMPERIAL COLLEGE LONDON, KING'S COLLEGE LONDON, KENT, LANCASTER, LEEDS, LEICESTER, LONDON SCHOOL OF ECONOMICS, MANCHESTER, QUEEN MARY LONDON, ROYAL HOLLOWAY, SCHOOL OF AFRICAN STUDIES, SHEFFIELD, SOUTHAMPTON, SURREY, SUSSEX, UNIVERSITY COLLEGE LONDON, WARWICK, YORK
Please check with your university careers service for full details of local events.

MINIMUM ENTRY REQUIREMENTS
2.2 Degree

APPLICATION DEADLINE
Varies by function

FURTHER INFORMATION
www.Top100GraduateEmployers.com
Register now for the latest news, campus events, work experience and graduate vacancies at Wellcome.

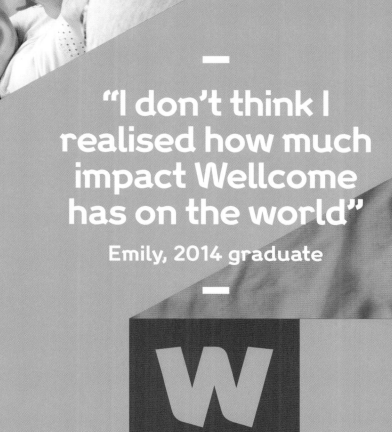

"I don't think I realised how much impact Wellcome has on the world"

Emily, 2014 graduate

Credit: *Jo Metson Scott*

WPP

GRADUATE VACANCIES IN 2017

MARKETING

MEDIA

NUMBER OF VACANCIES
1-10 graduate jobs

LOCATIONS OF VACANCIES

Vacancies also available in Europe, Asia, the USA and elsewhere in the world.

STARTING SALARY FOR 2017
£Competitive

UNIVERSITY VISITS IN 2016-17
BRISTOL, CAMBRIDGE, DURHAM, IMPERIAL COLLEGE LONDON, KING'S COLLEGE LONDON, LONDON SCHOOL OF ECONOMICS, OXFORD, QUEEN MARY LONDON, UNIVERSITY COLLEGE LONDON
Please check with your university careers service for full details of local events.

MINIMUM ENTRY REQUIREMENTS
2.1 Degree

APPLICATION DEADLINE
10th November 2016

FURTHER INFORMATION
www.Top100GraduateEmployers.com
Register now for the latest news, campus events, work experience and graduate vacancies at WPP.

WPP is the world's largest communications services group – including Advertising; Media Investment Management; Data Investment Management; Public Relations & Public Affairs; Branding & Identity; Healthcare Communications; Direct, Digital, Promotion & Relationship Marketing and Specialist Communications.

WPP has more than 160 companies setting industry standards and working with many of the world's leading brands, creating communications ideas that help to build business for their clients. Between them, WPP's companies work with 352 of the Fortune Global 500; all of the Dow Jones 30 and 77 of the NASDAQ 100. WPP employs over 190,000 people (including associates) in over 3,000 offices in 112 countries.

WPP Fellowships develop high-calibre management talent with unique experience across a range of marketing disciplines. Over three years, Fellows work in three different WPP operating companies, each representing a different marketing communications discipline and geography. Fellows are likely to work in a client management or planning role, although some work on the creative side of an agency. Each rotation is chosen on the basis of the individual's interests and the Group's needs.

Fellowships will be awarded to applicants who are intellectually curious and motivated by the prospect of delivering high-quality communications services to their clients. WPP wants people who are committed to marketing communications, take a rigorous and creative approach to problem-solving and will function well in a flexible, loosely structured work environment. WPP is offering several three-year Fellowships, with competitive remuneration and excellent long term career prospects with WPP. Many former Fellows now occupy senior management positions in WPP companies.

WPP
The Fellowship 2017

Ambidextrous brains required

WPP is the world leader in marketing communications, with more than 160 companies setting industry standards in Advertising; Media Investment Management; Data Investment Management; Public Relations & Public Affairs; Branding & Identity; Healthcare Communications; Direct, Digital, Promotion & Relationship Marketing; and Specialist Communications.

We are manufacturers of communications ideas that help to build business for our clients, through creating and developing relationships with the people who buy and use their products and services. We do this through a demanding combination of hard work and flair; logic and intuition; left brain and right brain thinking.

The Fellowship was started, 21 years ago, to create future generations of leaders for our companies. Fellows tend to be intellectually curious people who are motivated by the challenges of marketing communications and by the prospect of working at the confluence of art and business. They spend three years on the Program: in each year they work in a different WPP company, in a different marketing communications discipline and, usually, on a different continent.

Long-term prospects within a WPP company are excellent, with many former Fellows now occupying senior management positions.

Deadline for entry:
10 November 2016

Visit our website and apply online at
www.wpp.com

For further information contact:

Harriet Miller, WPP
T: +44 (0)20 7408 2204
E-mail: harriet.miller@wpp.com

Useful Information